LITTLE HOME HISTORIES IN OUR EARLY HOMES

Belmont County Ohio

M. Marie Bundy

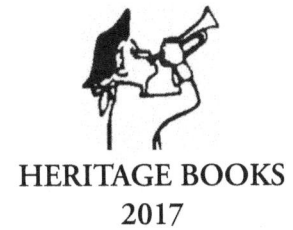

HERITAGE BOOKS
2017

HERITAGE BOOKS
AN IMPRINT OF HERITAGE BOOKS, INC.

Books, CDs, and more—Worldwide

For our listing of thousands of titles see our website
at
www.HeritageBooks.com

Published 2017 by
HERITAGE BOOKS, INC.
Publishing Division
5810 Ruatan Street
Berwyn Heights, Md. 20740

Copyright © 2017 M. Marie Bundy

All rights reserved. No part of this book may be reproduced or transmitted in any form or by any means, electronic or mechanical, including photocopying, recording or by any information storage and retrieval system without written permission from the author, except for the inclusion of brief quotations in a review.

International Standard Book Number
Paperbound: 978-0-7884-5796-8

Little Home Histories in Our Early Homes – Belmont County, Ohio

Foreword

This book was first published in 1943 by my father's first cousin, Beulah Patten McDonald, and her husband. It contains first-hand accounts and information passed down in families about life in the early 1800's through the turn of the century in this section of southeastern Ohio.

Most of the families were Quakers who migrated here, seeking a land free from the evils of slavery. The easternmost part of Ohio was the entry to the Northwest Territory which had banned slave ownership. Before land ownership could occur, this section of Ohio was surveyed into the Seven Ranges which were divided into townships and the townships into sections. These divisions are still in place today and I have used this system in some cases to identify locations. Where possible, I have used the current number and street address to identify location of property.

The book is being reprinted from the original with some minor changes and additions for clarification. The order of the articles is the same as the original book with two changes. William Henry Stanton's article was moved to the front of the book because he urged the production of this book to follow "Our Ancestors the Stantons", which he authored. Also the article on John H. Edgerton was moved to follow the Kidnapped Doudna Tradition, because it contains a different version of that same story. For clarification, the person's name has been substituted for a pronoun used in some of the articles. The attempt has been made to not correct the grammar or spelling of the original articles, however, dates and the spelling of names have been checked for accuracy.

Additions to the articles are italicized. Pictures have been included where available. The attempt has been made to provide accurate identification of the location of the places talked about in these articles.

This book has held a special interest to me because many persons in the book are either directly or indirectly related to me. For example, Jesse and Asenath Patterson Bailey, "Black Bill" Bundy, and James Steer III, were my great-great-grandparents.

The original writers in this book are preserving a forgotten part of our local history which this book can recapture for today's readers and readers in years to come.

M. Marie Bundy

Little Home Histories in Our Early Homes
Belmont Guernsey Counties, OH

Foreword	by Marie Bundy	i
Table of Contents		iii
Introduction	by Beulah & Robert McDonald	v
An Old Residence (Jesse Bailey)	by Anna Bailey Patten	1
William Henry Stanton	by Paul & Anna Marie Holloway	3
Jesse and Asenath Patterson Bailey	by Anna Bailey Patten	7
Joel Bailey	by Eliza Foster Leeds	11
Lindley Patterson and Elizabeth Stanton Bailey	by Sarah J. Bailey	13
Early Times in Barnesville, Ohio	by Elma D. Bailey	19
The Bundy Ancestors	by Dillwyn C. Bundy	23
Anna Stanton Bundy	by Beulah Patten McDonald	27
The Chalkley Bundy Home	by Anna Mary Bailey	29
Flax-Wool-Soap Making	by Dillwyn C. & Elizabeth Bundy	33
John Bundy Homestead	by Lloyd Bailey	35
William "Black Bill" Bundy	by Bernita Bundy	37
The Clay Pike	by Dr. D.O. Shepherd	39
The Francis Davis House	by Joseph E. Stanton	41
Joseph F. Doudna	by Alice Doudna Smith	43
Anecdote of Joseph F. Doudna	by Wilford T. Hall	44
The Kidnapped Doudna Tradition	by Joseph H. Doudna	45
John H. Edgerton	by Ella Coventry Galloway	47
Historical Data Concerning the Joel & Rebecca Doudna Family	by Lucinda Bundy Hanson	49
The Birthplace of Joseph W. Doudna	by Beulah M. Doudna	53
Joseph W. Doudna	by Elma D. & Mary J. Doudna	55
The Home of Sara Doudna	by Ella L. Galloway	61
My Pioneer Grandmother: Anna Hall Edgerton	by Anna Walton	65
Edgerton History	by James Walton	69
Aaron Frame, 1815 – 1896	by Sara (Bundy, Holloway) Cooper	71
Some Friends Meetings in Belmont & Guernsey Co., OH	by W.V. Webster	75
Friends Boarding School "Olney"	by Sarah Pickett Walton	79
Some Historical Sketches of Friends at the Ridge	by Elma Doudna Bailey	81
Otho French Home History	by Anna Bailey Patten	83
The Gibbons Family	by Edward V. Gibbons	85
William Green	by Anna M. Hoge & William G. Steer	87
The James Steer Home	by Anna M. Hoge & William G. Steer	89
John Hall	by Elvira Hall	93
The Thomas Hall Home	by Elma C. Hall	95
Anecdotes of School Days of Wilford T. Hall	by Harold L. Holloway, Jr.	97

Elijah Hanson	*by Mary S. Smith*	99
David Ball	*by Elizabeth Burgess*	101
The Thomas Hobson Home	*by Elizabeth Burgess*	103
Benjamin Hoyle	*by Laura J. Hoyle*	105
Dr. Carolus Judkins	*by Dr. D.O. Shepherd*	109
Some History of Wool, Flax, Nettles in Leatherwood Valley	*by Debora Webster Dearing*	111
Historical Reminiscences of Joseph Edgerton Family	*by Sarah Maxwell*	115
Anecdotes Concerning Charles Livezey	*by Elizabeth Smith Livezey*	119
Memory Lane	*by Isaac Hall*	121
The Patterson History	*by Elizabeth J. Hartley*	123
Joseph Patterson	*by Elma Doudna Bailey*	127
Bob Peters	*by Anna Bailey Patten*	129
Edward Pickett	*by William G. Steer*	131
William Pickett	*by William G. Steer*	133
The Plummer Farm	*by Laura Hoyle*	135
Centennial	*by Elizabeth Hartley*	139
Jonathan T. & Abigail Steer Schofield	*by Anna M. Hoge & William G. Steer*	141
Anecdotes of No. 1 and No. 2 Schools	*by Dorothy L. Holloway*	143
Copy of a Letter to Margaret Bailey	*by Mary J. Doudna*	144
Anecdotes of Anna Doudna Sears and Henry Doudna	*by William H. Sears*	147
Home of Benjamin and Esther Sears	*by William H. Sears*	149
Home of Peter Sears	*by William H. Sears*	151
A House Built About 1810	*by Willis W. Webster*	154
The Smith Homestead & Smith Stories	*by Robert H. Smith*	157
The Old Log House of Eli Stanton	*by Emma C. (Stanton) Webster*	159
Eli Stanton's Sorghum Mill	*by Harold Holloway Jr. & Sr.*	161
Eli Stanton Family Anecdote	*by Helen Hall Holloway*	162
James Stanton	*by Dorothy L and Harold L. Holloway*	163
Wedding Certificate of James Stanton and Rachel Scholfield	*by James J. Winder*	164
The James Stanton Home	*by Dorothy L. and Harold L. Holloway*	167
Anecdotes Written by William G. Steer	*by William G. Steer*	171
Camm and Elizabeth Thomas	*by Sara Cooper and Lura Frame*	179
Samuel Walton	*by James Walton*	181
Thomas Webster, Sr.	*by Edward Hall*	183
John Webster, Jr.	*by Mary L. Webster*	185
Homes of Thomas Webster, Sr.	*by Thomas Webster*	189
Dr. Ephraim Williams	*by Robert H. Smith*	193
Richard Williams	*by Elma Doudna Bailey*	195
Wolf Den Story	*by Kenneth Lloyd Doudna*	197
Few Facts Concerning the Edmund Fowler Family & Home	*by Elizabeth Burgess*	199

"The Little Home Histories in our Early Homes, Belmont County, Ohio"

INTRODUCTION

During the summer of 1941, William Henry Stanton of Ridley Park, Pennsylvania, in his eighty-first year, expressed his wish while visiting his numerous friends and relatives of Stillwater Quarterly Meeting, east of Barnesville, Ohio, that some history be written of the development of this section of Belmont County which started in the early 1800's.

As he talked of "old Homesteads" and the primitive ways of living with these people, he became deeply interested in this thought of writing about their experiences of earlier years and the stories they had heard from their parents and grandparents and early settlers.

To make this "Little Home History" possible, we are indebted to those who have so faithfully written to him with their stories and past experiences and hope that the coming generation shall enjoy reading it and benefit from the stories related herein by their ancestors and friends.

Robert D. McDonald
Beulah Patten McDonald
Aldan, Pennsylvania

AN OLD RESIDENCE

An event occurred in Warren Township, Belmont County, in the winter of 1806-1807 which presents the privations of the pioneer in so strong a light that we are constrained to present it to our readers.

Jesse Bailey, a Quaker, from the State of North Carolina, arrived in the township late in the Fall of that year. He had not time to build a cabin before the hard winter would set in. So looking about for some place in which to winter, he found, situated on the lands now owned by Jesse Judkins, in section 27 *(Warren Township)*, a rock, the upper ledge of which projected out beyond its fellows from fifteen to twenty feet. He immediately determined to turn it to his advantage.

Splitting out some puncheons he placed them upright, inclosing a space even with the edge of the out-cropping rock. In one corner, the rocks were so formed as to make the part of a natural chimney. Topping this out with four puncheons like a funnel, and daubing its sides with clay mud, formed a fine outlet for the smoke. In this structure he and his family passed the winter.

Timid deer, frightened, bounded away from its ungainly front by day. At night wolves howled around his humble mansion. Bears came and clawed at the door, and wild cats on the limbs of adjacent trees screamed at the unwelcome intrusion. But Bailey, secure within, lived through the winter in comparative comfort.

(Extract from <u>Belmont – Jefferson County History 1880)</u>
Written by Anna Bailey Patten, Tacoma, Ohio
Baileys Mills is said to be named for this man. We are not able to trace any connection with our branch of the Baileys'.

(Note: A puncheon is lumber cut out of a log and roughly dressed with an axe or adz.)

WILLIAM HENRY STANTON
1860 - 1943

William Henry Stanton, son of Eli and Mary P. (Bundy) Stanton was born August 2, 1860, nine months before the outbreak of the war between the States. The sixty-year old log house in which he was born was located about two miles east of Barnesville, Ohio city limits. As one goes down "Sandy Ridge" toward Captina Creek they may arrive at the site of this log house by turning down the first road to the left after passing "Pigeon Point". The present road passes over the exact location of the log house at a point about two hundred feet west of Eli Stanton's second house (built in 1867 and now 1942 owned by Ross Bailey).
(Currently on a lane running off Sandy Ridge Rd., address 61245 Sandy Ridge Rd.)

The older folks now know him as "Cousin Will". To the younger folks he is either "Uncle Will" or "Uncle Billy". His business associates respectfully address him, Mr. Stanton. Many others know him as the author of <u>Our Ancestors the Stantons</u> – that treasure chest of family history. Now in his eighty first year his ambition has been to record the early history of some of the notable old homes in the Barnesville vicinity. Up until the writing of this little book, the early history of these homes has existed only in the minds of men who either heard it from their fathers and grandfathers or who are old enough to remember some of this from their childhood. It had been Uncle Billy's desire that this information should be recorded before it is lost to the coming generations. He has had another, and perhaps, even more important purpose in mind; that of arousing the interest of the younger generation in the history of their families and their community. It has been a subject close to the heart since he was a young man. It is natural that he should want to keep alive this interest.

His boyhood included attendance at the Friends Primary School located on the Stillwater Meeting House grounds. In January 1876 the Barnesville Friends Boarding school opened its doors to students and he had the distinction of attending the first term. This term lasted from January until spring and he attended the succeeding summer and winter terms. The summer of 1887 he spent on his father's farm. In November of the same year, after the corn had been husked, he went to work in Joseph Kennard's blacksmith shop, located at "Pigeon Point" beside the school house (now torn away). He spent fourteen weeks there learning general blacksmithing (except shoeing).

By previous arrangement he left Joseph Kennard's employ to work as an apprentice to Charles Kugler, proprietor of the Belmont Machine Works situated on south Chestnut Street in Barnesville. His letter of recommendation from Joseph Kennard reads in part as follows "I considered him a natural mechanic not requiring the attention and instruction in my line of business that the average apprentice demands." He began in March 1878 and worked in the Iron and Wood Departments for about two and one half years. His first job was shaping the wooden prongs for a revolving horse hay rake. His day's work included getting up at five o'clock in the morning, starting the fire under the boiler, oiling line shafting and loose pulleys, returning to his boarding house for breakfast, and back to the shop by seven o'clock. The day closed at six pm with an hour out for lunch, except on Saturdays when the day closed at five o'clock.

Every Saturday after quitting time he walked the three miles from the shop to his home to be with his family over Sunday. While working at Charles Kugler's he boarded first with Amasa Frame, then with his employer, Charles Kugler, and finally with Tabitha (Stanton) Davis. To this day he recalls, pleasantly, the excellent lunches that Amasa Frame's wife put up for him in a half gallon pail.

In the summer of 1880 while making a pattern, he cut his hand seriously. Doctor Ely sat him in the shade of a tree outside his drugstore and sewed up his hand with a needle and string.

While recovering from this injury he made arrangements to work for James W. Queen and Company, "Makers of Mathematical, Optical, and Philosophical Instruments" in Philadelphia, Pennsylvania. He made the journey from Barnesville on the B&O railroad, arrived in Philadelphia the sixth of September 1880. Here, as an instrument maker, he found precision work to fully test his ability. He made the first Toepler Holtz machine (static electricity induction machine) in the United States for the electrical industry then in its infancy. He also made for Professor George F. Barker, of the University of Pennsylvania, the first secondary battery made in this country. He worked late several nights at the shop in order to complete the batteries in time for Professor Barker to use them to illustrate a lecture. He rose quickly to assistant foreman and took the place of Schubert, the foreman, when he made a trip to his homeland Germany. While working at Queen he attended night school at the Franklin Institute where he studied mechanical drawing. He realized his need for more schooling and the opportunity presented itself when Professor John B. DeMotte of the DePauw University, his Mathematics Professor, suggested that he study at a technical school. Accordingly, he entered Rose Polytechnical Institute at Terre Haute, Indiana, in the Fall of 1889. He had hardly become accustomed to his new environment when the Philadelphia Quartz Company offered him a position as manager of their Anderson, Indiana plant which was just being built. He accepted, and after a big Thanksgiving dinner, left Terra Haute for Philadelphia.

He began working for the Philadelphia Quartz Company on December 1, 1889 and spent a short period learning the business in Philadelphia before he left for Indiana to assume active management of the Anderson plant. He met Louise Smith in Anderson and married her in 1898 after a courtship in the best "bicycle-built-for-two" fashion of the day.

Under his capable management the plant prospered and the company's business expanded until they were induced to build a plant at Chester, Pennsylvania in 1904. He had an active hand in planning and building of this plant and became a member of the Executive Board in the same year. In 1907 he was appointed President of the Brenan Sand Mining Company, a subsidiary of the Philadelphia Quartz Company. He and Aunt Louise lived in Maryland in 1907 and 1908 while he supervised the mining of the quartz sand which was shipped by boat to the Chester plant located on the Delaware river in Pennsylvania. In 1909 he returned to Anderson to reassume the management of the Anderson Plant. The company's now rapidly expanding business warranted the building of another plant. They selected Buffalo, New York, as a site and he went there with his wife in 1910 to supervise the construction of this plant. In 1913 he was made General Manager of all the Company's plants; a position which made it necessary for him to live near the executive offices located in Philadelphia, Pennsylvania.

Accordingly, he moved to Ridley Park and in 1913 built the attractive stone house in which he now lives. He was made a Vice-President of the company in 1919 and retired the same year after thirty years of active service.

At the present time he has served the company for twenty-three years in an advisory capacity. When he retired from the company they presented him with a barometer. In 1939 a company dinner was given in his honor to celebrate his completion of fifty years of service with the company at which time he was presented with a watch with his name engraved on the case. His record of service with the Philadelphia Quartz Company is an inspiration to any young man with ambition. His attitude toward the company is shown by the manner in which he referred to it; he never said he was working "for" the Quartz Company, but rather that he was working "with" them.

When Uncle Will was leaving Rose Polytechnical Institute to go with the Quartz Company, his Mathematics Professor, C.A. Waldo, said to him. "Now Stanton when you get out, don't just read a little here and there. Have a hobby. Take up one line of reading or study and follow the subject until you feel you are through with it; then take up another." He not only remembered this excellent advice, he followed it. He had been interested in and has made a study of nearly twenty different subjects. A few of the more important are Landscape, Gardening, Weather, Astronomy, Family History and Wood Turning.

His interest in Landscape gardening is evident to anyone who has visited the Stanton's in Ridley Park, and has seen the pleasant appearance of the grounds.

While in Anderson, Indiana, he was made President of the Maplewood Cemetery Association and he supervised the landscaping of the Maplewood Cemetery. He wrote a series of articles in 1905 for the <u>Anderson Daily Bulletin</u> on the planting and caring of trees. A park in Anderson, Stanton Park, bears his name. He had the United States weather forecasting station in Anderson and the weather forecasts were signaled to the farmers in the vicinity by means of a large steam whistle. This steam whistle was located at the plant and was blown every day at noon. It is reported that this whistle was once heard for a distance of twenty-nine miles.

The barometer given him by the Philadelphia Quartz Company when he retired was in recognition of his interest in weather forecasting.

In 1901 he made a five-inch telescope with which he saw the snow on the mountain peaks of the planet Mars, at a time when Mars was nearest the earth. He made all the parts for this telescope except the lenses. He, himself says it is the finest piece of work he ever did. One of the most difficult jobs an instrument maker meets is that of making a rack and pinion. The rack and pinion on his telescope is an example of his ability as an instrument maker and he has reason to pride himself in this piece of work. A letter of recommendation written by Professor

John B. DeMotte and dated August 28, 1899, bears testimony to his ability thus . . . "As a maker of fine instruments, I doubt if he has a superior in America."

The articles he has made while working at his wood turning hobby number more than three thousand and are made from fifty different kinds of wood. He has made lamps, candlesticks, salad bowls, fruit bowls, napkin rings, bracelets, beads, buttons, and many other articles, nearly all of which he has given away to friends and relatives. His work has been exhibited in schools of Philadelphia and New Jersey, and attracted so much attention that in 1939 The Philadelphia Evening Bulletin carried a write up on his turning hobby.

While visiting Barnesville, Ohio in 1940 he recognized, in the shop of William H. Sears, the movable slide rest on which he had served his apprenticeship in the shop of Charles Kugler. He had previously found in Philadelphia the instrument maker's precision lathe on which he worked while with Queen and Company, from 1882 to 1884. This is the one he bought and has used for his wood turning.

In addition to his extensive travels throughout the United States, he has traveled through South America and has made a trip to Hawaii. Wherever his business has called him, Aunt Louise has gone with him to make a home for him. She is an active church worker, being particularly interested in missionary work, and she has made many friends where ever she has lived.

Anyone who has engaged in a conversation with Uncle Will is impressed by his seemingly limitless knowledge, yet on several occasions he has been heard to remark "How little we know." Also one cannot help but be impressed by his extraordinarily keen memory and his capacity for detail. To give an example. Many years after he had left the Barnesville community he remembered that as a small boy of five or six he sat in the Stillwater Meeting house beside an octagon shaped column on which was cut the outline of the hull of a boat. He knew when the present Meeting House was built, the wooden columns from the inside of the old Meeting House were used for the south edge of the women's porch and out of curiosity he determined to look for the boat shaped cut on the next trip to Barnesville. At first he did not find it and was disappointed to think he had been wrong, but after careful searching he found it. Anyone wishing to see this boat shaped cut may find it on the first column from the west end about two feet up from the floor, and on the side of the octagon wheel that faces northwest. He has known the struggle to gain a foothold at the bottom of the ladder of success and he has helped many through this struggle.

If you happen to be discouraged and were telling him your troubles in a "Oh, what's the use" mood, he would probably cheer you up with these words, "A dead fish floats downstream – it takes a live one to swim up."

A review of Uncle Will's life to date, his kindness, his thoughtfulness, his ambitions, and his accomplishments is an inspiration to those of us who are young and who have only started down the long path of usefulness to mankind.

Written by Paul and Anna Marie Holloway, Germantown, Philadelphia, PA

JESSE AND ASENATH PATTERSON BAILEY

Jesse Bailey was born 1-1-1815. He was the third son of Jesse Bailey Sr. and Phariba, his wife, and married Asenath Patterson, who was born 7-4-1820, daughter of Silas and Rachel Patterson, who came from Deep River, North Carolina in 1808. Silas' parents came from England. His mother, Elizabeth Patterson was a minister in the Society of Friends and traveled extensively in that service. At one time she rode horse-back from Belmont County to North Carolina.

Jesse and Asenath were married in 1837 at Stillwater Meeting House and went to housekeeping in a very primitive way in Somerset Township near the present Union Church. *(Somerset Twp. Section 6)* The house had no glass for windows and they used oiled paper. They lived here six months when Jesse's mother, Phariba, died. Then they went to his father, Jesse Bailey Sr. home to keep house for him, on the farm now owned by Ross Bailey, a grandson of Jesse and Asenath. They lived in the hewn log house built by Jesse Sr. pictured and described on page 215 of the book Our Ancestors the Stantons. *(Warren Twp. SE Section 3)* They lived here ten years. Here Silas, Sarah, and John were born. *(This cabin later owned by Eli Stanton.)*

From this home they moved to Asenath's mother's farm on Long Run. *(On Long Run Creek, Goshen Twp. Sect. 32).* They lived in this house while building a two story frame house close by. Part of the old log house still stands. Here on this farm Lindley, later called L.P., Allen, Rachel and Mary were born. The latter two died in infancy and Sarah in her twenty-first year.

By the new house they dug a well, drew the water by windlass and wooden bucket. This well was only ten feet deep but has never been known to go dry. It now has an iron pump and produces an abundance of good water.

As a child I used to stay at Grandfather's a good deal. My mother was not very strong and often sick, and as I was too young to help at home, Grandmother would take me to her home. I loved to stay there with them. I well remember the spring-house just on the other side of the house from the well. I can see yet the trough through which the water flowed from the spring above. This trough was filled with stone crocks of milk and cream. Here, Grandmother churned and made the rolls of good butter, part of which she exchanged for groceries in Barnesville.

There was no cellar under the house but just a little beyond the spring-house was a cave built in the side of the hill where they kept their fruits and vegetables.

Each room of the house down stairs had an open fireplace and how cozy on a long winter evening to sit beside the open fire. Long years after this we lived in this home and here our son was born. In the old kitchen there was a large wood fireplace with a crane on which to hang the large iron and brass kettles. And the big kettles of apple-butter Grandmother used to make there, stirring it with a long apple-butter stirrer until it was thick and so well cooked it kept without sealing. It was put in large stone jars and a cover of muslin tied on. No glass fruit jars in those days.

Just a little ways down the lane, a large creek "Long Run," crossed the road and how I used to love to wade in that creek, sometimes I would fall down and get wet but that didn't seem to worry me. They had to drive across this creek to get out to the public road and sometimes when the creek was high they would have a little trouble.

Just a little way above this home, on the "Goshen Road," there stood in the edge of the woods a little school house and here my father, L.P. Bailey, and his brothers and sister went to school. *(Goshen Road, now gone, ran between 61705 Sandy Ridge Road and Long Run Road, Goshen Twp. 186.)* Father used to show us children where the school house stood and tell us of his first day in school. He had never been used to sitting still and it wasn't easy for him. In the afternoon of his first day he commenced rolling his slate pencil on his desk saying, "rolly, rolly," unconscious that he was disturbing others until the teacher spoke gently to him. After he was through school here he attended Boarding School at Mount Pleasant, Ohio and when through there taught in the same little school where he rolled his pencil.

Just about a quarter of a mile below the home, on the same farm, stood a little house just where the road turned off the Goshen Road, crossed the creek and turned up the hill to the Sandy Ridge Road about a half mile further up the hill. In this little house, with the big outside stone chimney, each of Jesse and Asenath's four sons, when he married, took his wife there and made it their home until they located elsewhere. This was called the "weaning house." *(Located on Goshen Twp. 183 near the intersection with Long Run Rd, Twp. 186.)*

The Long Run home of grandfather's was two and one half miles from Stillwater Meeting *(by way of Goshen Rd.)* The road, as all roads were in those days, was bad during much of the year but Jesse and Asenath were always in their accustomed seats at Meeting twice a week unless prevented by sickness. Asenath Bailey was one of the most remarkable women belonging to Stillwater Meeting. She was a recommended minister of that Meeting. She had very little education, as schools were not close to her home and her father dying when the children were very young, her mother was not able to give the children much schooling. But when she would rise to speak in Meeting, her strong voice and earnest pleadings attracted the attention of all her listeners and made them feel that the voice of God was speaking through her to them. She visited other Meetings and often went to prisons to speak to the convicts. Once, while on a religious visit to Iowa, she felt a call to speak to the prisoners in the State Penitentiary at Animosa, Iowa, and I have been told by one who accompanied her that she spoke so earnestly, pleading with them to lead better lives, she held the attention of all the prisoners and there was scarcely a dry eye when she finished her sermon.

As Jesse and Asenath grew too old for the duties of a farm, their youngest son Allen and family moved to this home from the "weaning house" and the farm is still owned by his family. Jesse and Asenath moved to a home on the Sandy Ridge Road about a quarter of a mile from the Stillwater Meeting House. There they spent many happy years. With their horse and the old carriage they went to Meeting and visited their children and friends. Active in the Meeting and loved by all who knew them.

Asenath's crippled sister Elizabeth and their niece "Lib" Patterson lived with them in this home. "Lib" was faithful in caring for them in their declining years. Jesse died in 1898 and Asenath in 1905 and they were laid to rest side by side at Stillwater Cemetery.

Written by Anna Bailey Patten, daughter of L.P. and Elizabeth S. Bailey and granddaughter of Jesse and Asenath Bailey.

Bailey land in Goshen Township, Belmont County

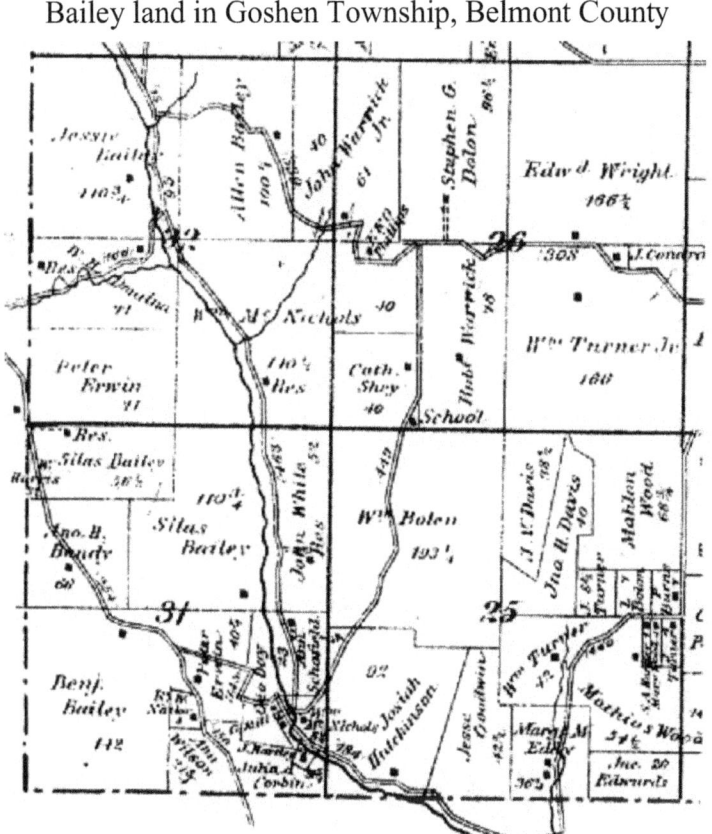

JOEL BAILEY
1823 - 1876

Joel Bailey was the son of Edmund and Margaret Bailey. He married Ruthanna Patterson in April 4th, 1844 and they lived south of Barnesville, Ohio. They were members of Somerset Monthly Meeting, but soon moved to a home three miles east of Barnesville, at the place now known as "Quiet Side," the home of Henry and Eliza Leeds, on the Sandy Ridge Road. *(60561 Sandy Ridge Rd.)*

Their membership was transferred to Stillwater Monthly Meeting.

The house, a two-story frame building was built a portion at a time on the site of the present dwelling. A kitchen was added later which was moved from the place now occupied by William H. Sears. A well, about thirty-five feet deep was dug near the house. This is still in use.

The Baileys had five children. After his wife's death in November 29th, 1856, Joel married Lydia Holloway and they had two children.

An incident during the early infancy of one of the children is still vivid in William Sear's memory. It was about 1859, when he was but a young boy, that he and his mother were calling on Lydia, who was ill in bed. While there, a severe hail storm wrought such havoc that the west windows were broken. Precipitating wind, rain, and hailstones. Esther Sears picked up the tiny babe and ran to the closet and held it inside, protecting it in the half open doorway as the closet was too small to admit her.

In the following summer, a late freeze caused much damage. The "June Frost" destroyed corn that was knee high and all the wheat, clover, garden vegetables and flowers.

Joel's blacksmith shop, which was located on the main road, was just south of the house. Here he was mostly occupied. His brother assisting in the caring for the needs of farmers and neighbors. The shop has long since been torn down.

On the terrace in back of the house, stood the old sorghum mill which was often running night as well as day. When a lad, William Sears remembers hauling the cane from a distant hill with two yoke of oxen and bringing it to Joel's mill.

Joel Bailey and his family travelled the two miles to Stillwater Meeting twice a week, driving his horses over the poor roads.

He passed away at his home in 1876.

Written by: Eliza Foster Leeds, Barnesville, Ohio (not a relative)

LINDLEY PATTERSON AND ELIZABETH (STANTON) BAILEY

There was an unusual stir of excitement at the Stillwater Meeting the twenty-sixth day of July in the year of our Lord eighteen hundred and seventy-one. Lindley Patterson Bailey and Elizabeth Stanton had announced their intention to wed thirty days previously and on that day they were married.

Elizabeth, the youngest daughter of Joseph and Mary *(Hodgin)* Stanton, was born on a farm a short distance northwest of Tacoma, Ohio, on December 24, 1846. *(Located on Warren Twp. 177 between Mt. Olivet Rd. and SR 800.)* Lindley Patterson, who was the third son of Jesse and Asenath Bailey, was born on March 8, 1850.

Elizabeth's birthplace near Stillwater Creek (off SR 800 on road to Mt. Olivet)

The charming Elizabeth Stanton was the same young girl, who not so many years before had attended the Mount Pleasant Boarding School. In those days the rules of boarding school life were very strict. There was no social relationships between boys and girls, except under strict supervision. One day Elizabeth and one of her girlfriends were out in the yard, and seeing some boys on the roof, stopped to see what they were doing. But by a strange trick of fate a watchful teacher saw this "misdemeanor" and their registers were marked, for "looking at the boys."

In this stalwart, attractive looking young man was a youthful orator, who many times had mounted a stump, and with the birds and animals of his father's farm for an audience, had delivered an oration which caused much stir among the animal life.

After leaving school, Elizabeth Stanton was invited to attend the wedding of Lindy Bundy and Ruanna Frame and to be a "waiter" with Lindley P. Bailey, almost a stranger to her at the time. From the friendship formed at this wedding came the seed of a youthful romance which blossomed into full glory on July 26, 1871 and remained in all its loveliness for almost sixty long years.

The happy couple lived for a while in "the weaning house" – a little log cabin on his father's farm. From this home they went to an adjoining farm, where Lindley worked during the summer and taught school during the winter. While living here, they advanced another step on the ladder of life, for on July 18, 1872 they became the proud parents of a red and wrinkled baby boy, their eldest son, Edwin Macy Bailey. The year after the birth of their first child they bought a farm near Tacoma of one hundred sixteen acres, which proved to be a heavy burden during the financial panic of 1873.

Lindley and Elizabeth lived on this farm for six years, during which time Lindley continued the combination of farming and teaching. While here three more children came to bless the home: Oscar Joseph, December 5, 1874; Anna, August 16, 1876; Clara, June 25, 1878.

Elizabeth had a natural inclination for cows. She made high class butter, commanding a premium price in the village. Lindley did not share this liking for dairy cows, preferring beef cattle and sheep, but finally acknowledged that Elizabeth's cows brought in better returns than some of the other farm interests. James Edgerton, a few years before, had imported from Rhode Island three registered Jersey cattle, said to be the first ever shipped across the Allegheny Mountains. Elizabeth desired to own some of these Jerseys, so she persuaded Lindley to trade a threshing machine which he was running somewhat against her wishes, for a Jersey bull, a cow and a heifer calf. At last Lindley became interested in dairying and more particular in Jersey cows. The children of this family feel that they are justified in calling their mother the sponsor of the Jersey cow interest in Ohio.

In the Fall of 1877, Lindley, always interested in raising fine crops, took special care in one wheat field, and the next year he had a fine field of grain. This turned out to be fortunate for him. The county was looking for a tract of land on which to build a children's home and to have additional space for raising various products. Lindley sold his farm to the county, partly because of the fine impression which his wheat field made. It is doubtful if he ever could have paid off the debt on the place and the selling of it was good luck for him. The family remained there until 1880. The brick for the building of the Children's Home were made on the farm and Elizabeth boarded the men who made the brick. (*The Belmont County Children's Home was located on SR 147 in Tacoma*)

BELMONT COUNTY CHILDREN'S HOME.

One day while still in their third home, Lindley went to get some coal and Edwin came to meet him on his return. The little boy got up on the load of coal to ride the rest of the way home, but going over a bad spot in the road, he fell off. The rear wheel went over his chest, but good fortune was with them for Edwin was not injured.

In 1880 the family rented a farm near Speidel, Ohio and lived there for six years. While in this home the two youngest boys were born: Alva Caleb, April 26, 1880; and Jesse Stanton, April 15, 1884.

The log house in which they lived was surrounded by big walnut trees and the water which they used came from a spring nearby. They had no cellar under their house so they built a cave in which they kept their fruit and vegetables. On this farm there was a small log stable but as Lindley became more and more interested in the dairy business, they built a larger cattle barn on the hill just above the house.

The six years they spent on this farm were years of happiness, mingled with sadness but always busy years. Six hearty children had to be fed, clothed and sent to school. The nearest school was over a mile away. *(Located on Rogers Rd, Goshen Twp.187 SE Sect. 34.)*

The boys can well remember attending No. 8, Speidel school, where it was the custom to put the teacher out at least once a term. One day the larger boys, who were enrolled in the school, locked the teacher out while he was ringing the bell. Instead of becoming angry, the teacher asked the little boys and girls to go skating with him. That act won the favor of the whole school and he was soon let back in.

Very often when the children were coming home from school they would walk up the railroad tracks to the station at Speidel. Just beyond the station was a deep cut in the hill. One evening Oscar walked home with some friends, and leaving them, he walked down through the cut towards the station. An old lady, who lived nearby saw him just before he went out of sight. A train was coming, but wasn't near enough for a little boy who was skipping and running along to hear. The station master ran out and called to him and the old lady ran out on the hill waving her apron. This attracted his attention and seeing his danger he threw himself to the side and was off of the tracks before the train went whizzing by.

To go from this story to the one of Alva and Clara sliding down the side of the cave on this place seems ridiculous, but so is life; the common place with a touch here and there of the unusual. The children were not allowed to slide down the side of the cave but Alva and Clara thought it too great a temptation and took the chance. When Elizabeth saw them, she came after them with a stick and they ran, as children will. They crawled into a hole which went under the house but their mother was not discouraged by this and called sister Anna and told her to go after them. Anna couldn't refuse and go after them she did. Then – POOR CHILDREN – Well you couldn't blame them for running.

It doesn't seem that Anna profited too much from this experience for she and Oscar were likewise tempted beyond their power to resist. One day they decided they wanted some apples to eat. The apples were still green but nevertheless they went to the orchard and climbed the tree. In place of picking a few and eating them, they shook the tree vigorously and enjoyed seeing the apples fall to the ground. Things might have turned out all right, but their father coming from the barn saw the performance and their only reward was being whipped by their father, while their big brother Ed laughed at them from his hiding place behind the chicken house.

There is a pathetic story told about Oscar. His mother and father had gone away from home, taking Edwin and Anna with them and Oscar was left to be the man at the house. This didn't quite suit Oscar's liking so he went to seek work elsewhere. At that time there were some tenants on the farm who raised tobacco. One of them, Aaron Bishop, needed a hired hand. Oscar, although just a little tyke, asked for the job. Aaron assured him laughingly that he would be glad to have him and would pay a dollar a day. Oscar was very serious about it all. He went home and told Ella Butcher, the hired girl, that he had a job and asked her to pack some clean clothes for him. Then he went to Carl McIlvane, the store keeper in Speidel, and talked, man to man, about his job and Carl gave him an account book and a pencil with which he might keep an accurate account of his time. The next morning, Oscar trudged to work, but he was soon told it was all a joke. The hill seemed awfully long as a little boy trudged back home, swallowing his tears of disappointment and grief; the first great tragedy of his life.

At another time during the six years on the farm near Speidel, Mag McKnight worked for the family. For some reason or other she got mad and quit. They owed her twelve or fifteen dollars in wages and Lindley wrote a check for this amount. But no, she must have cash that she could count with her own hands, so Lindley went to town and got ten dollars in pennies and the rest in nickels and dimes. He gave her the money and let her count it to her satisfaction.

Many, many things of interest come to the mind of the members of this family as they think over those days of their youth. For instance, they all remember with somewhat a thrill, the torch light procession which was held in Speidel for James G. Blane and John D. Logan who were running for president and vice president respectively.

In this home at Speidel there was a large fireplace and one time as Lindley was putting in a big back log he slipped and broke his leg. At another time the children all had the measles. While Susan Wharton was working for Elizabeth, her daughter Bird, took the measles. Susan would either have to stay home or bring Bird with her when she came to work. Elizabeth told her to bring the girl, so that all the children would have the measles and that one childhood disease would be done with. She did and all six of the Bailey children were sick with the measles at the same time.

It was while the family lived on this farm that Elizabeth had a very serious illness. For a few days her condition was critical, but she had a mission yet unfulfilled and was spared to her family. Dr. Kemp, the family physician, attended her.

After her recovery she nursed Oscar through a case of typhoid fever and often went to other homes to offer her services as a practical nurse. A boy, who lived close to them, was shot in the hand. The wound became seriously infected and amputation of two fingers was necessary. Elizabeth assisted the doctor in this operation and for several weeks afterward, she would go every day to change the dressing on his hand.

During this time the Jersey cow had become the leading breed of dairy cows in Belmont County and even in Ohio. Lindley seeing this demand made a trip to Massachusetts for a car load of Jerseys. The demand seemed to increase and Lindley realizing this, made other trips to New England and brought back some prize cattle. It was then that they began to ship their cream to Bellaire.

All these Jerseys meant extra work. The Bailey children were taught to work as well as play and they all remember the days spent there with pleasure.

As we have said these years were busy years but never too busy to think of some of the bigger things in life. Elizabeth and Lindley always had a keen interest in the affairs of their community. The school and the church as well as the home, held a high place in their lives. They were never too busy or the cares of the home were never so great but that they found time to go to the

Friends Meeting of which they were life-long members. They looked forward to these days as times in which they gained strength for the tasks that followed through the week.

There are many things which this account leaves untold, but perhaps it gives to one a glimmering into the life of two grand people and their children up until the year when they moved to the John Bundy Farm.

    Written by: Sarah J. Bailey (Daughter of Oscar J. Bailey and Granddaughter of Lindley and Elizabeth S. Bailey)

L.P. Bailey, Alva Bailey, Edwin Bailey, Clara Bailey (Bundy), Oscar Bailey
Seated, Anna Bailey (Patten), Jesse Bailey and Elizabeth Stanton Bailey

EARLY TIMES IN BARNESVILLE, OHIO

The following was written by Jonathan Bundy, an old time resident of Barnesville, Ohio. It was printed in the Enterprise of 3rd month 13th, 1884. Descendants of Mr. Bundy have furnished us with a copy of the paper in which it was published, and believing it will be of interest to many of the readers of today, we again print it.

(Taken from the Enterprise *(reprinted)* 3rd month 16th, 1911.)

-----Editor Enterprise; Some months ago there was a notice in your paper to the effect that I had passed through the place where Barnesville is now situated, at an earlier date than anyone else now living near there. Since then I have been repeatedly asked to write out some account of those early days, for publication, as variety is sometimes pleasant and useful, it may not be amiss to compare the present flourishing condition of this town and vicinity with the difficulties and hardships with which the earlier settlers had to contend, though I am aware it must be a very crude article which my aged hand can produce.

As my father's family were the little company of pioneers who passed through Barnesville in 1805, and settled one mile west, I remember well the beginning of the town, and many incidents occurring among ourselves and neighbors, and when I enter the Barnesville of today with its turnpike, railroads, telegraphs, gaslights, glassworks, with its large mills and magnificent houses, with schools and lawyers, doctors and preachers, with its banks and stores and pleasant homes, a vision rises up before me of the broken wilderness, where we hastily threw up our log cabins without aid of carpenter or mason.

Our fireplaces were made of sticks and clay, our floors of puncheon, our door shutters of clapboard pinned to wooden hinges, and never a nail or screw or pane of glass in the whole structure. We had an unbroken forest to subdue before we could raise our provisions, and the first object was to obtain something to live on, while felling the great trees and clearing away the underbrush and rubbish so that the land could be tilled. For no matter what a man had at his old home, he could not get it here because there were no roads.

This provision was furnished in a great measure by killing or capturing the wild animals with which the woods abounded. Powder and lead were high priced, so the smaller game was mostly taken by stratagem. To catch the wild turkey, we built a pen about ten feet square and three or four feet high and covered with rails. A little ditch as dug in the ground terminating on the inside near the center of the pen and covered near the wall. The bait was then placed so as to be seen from the outside but only reached by going in the ditch. When they have entered, helped themselves and wished to escape, they walk round and round trying every crack, and even over the cover of the ditch, but never think of getting down into it and go out as they came in.

A good fat bear was our first choice, but they were hard to find and take so the deer furnished the greater part of our meat. We also saved for food, every quail, squirrel and bird we could trap or capture in any way, for when the gun had to be resorted to, in order to obtain meat, it took a good hand from his work of preparing new fields, and land had to be cleared and corn raised before we could have hogs or cattle and when we did get hogs, it was hard to keep them, for the bears were very fond of fresh pork. We let them run in the woods in the daytime, but they came to their beds at night, and we were obliged to keep one or two old ones with long tusks to fight off the bears from the smaller ones.

I well remember a very exciting circumstance of my boyhood. Mother had gone from home for a visit of three or four days. I stayed at grandfathers and father also worked there, going home mornings and evenings to feed. One night he found his hogs all out and gone. He began calling them but soon saw a large bear between himself and the house which he observed was mad, having been whipped by the hogs, and coming towards him with his bristles raised, all ready for a fight. Father made all the show he could, hoping to scare him but to no purpose. He could not get his gun, which was in the house, so he turned and ran a short distance thinking the bear would not come farther than the fence, but when he looked he beheld Bruin in full chase and gaining on him rapidly. He then, as I have heard him say, let out every link he had in reserve and ran for dear life, but the bear gained on him until he could hear him at every bound closer and closer behind him. When he came to the fence, and laying his hands on the top bar and leaped over, he heard Bruin light on the fence the moment he touched the ground. It was then uphill to the house and as a bear cannot run up hill well, father gained on him and rushing in took down grandfather's gun and went back to meet him, but grandfather saw the bear run round the house and disappear in the woods while father was inside. He came back that night, however, and took two pet pigs whose bed was under the wagon at the end of the house, eating one and leaving the other dead. The next day they put the dead pig in the end of a hollow log nearby, and set two guns in position so that he could not get the pig without pulling the strings attached to the triggers and thus firing upon himself. The two bullets did their work that night, and the next morning he was dressed and made us a good supply of meat.

    Many bears were taken in this way. Often we would hear the hogs rallying, as we called it, and go to see what disturbed them. If it proved to be a bear, we would generally find a dead pig, for he would quickly kill one by biting it through just between the shoulders, and then leave it till the big hogs were quiet, then he would go and eat it, or get shot as in this instance. But it required great care to go near those angry and frightened hogs for they were but half domesticated breed and quite dangerous.

    Two of our neighbors went out for a hunt one morning, taking their dogs with them. They had not gone far before coming onto a lot of these half wild hogs. The dogs ran for their masters, and the men seeing their danger, betook themselves each to his tree. The dogs played round and round the tree keeping out of the way of the hogs but would not leave their masters, thus keeping them in their trees until the hogs went to their beds at night.

    The wolves also would often take our young stock, if not well protected. Hearing a stir among his hogs one night, father slipped quietly out to take observations. Soon a wolf appeared at the door of the hog house and the large hogs rushed after it. In a moment it dodged back, picked up a pig and ran off with it before the large hogs returned. Evidently it had laid a plan and carried it out successfully. Thus it was the cunning of man contriving against the cunning of wild animals for protection of his stock. The wolves would howl around our cabin almost every night and sometimes during the day and the dogs would sit in the yard and bark at them, but let a panther scream out his peculiar wail imitating, some fancied, the cry of a woman, and every dog would run under the house trembling and growling.

    The wild cats and the catamounts were very plentiful and sometimes quite impudent. One of our neighbors having cut some trees down one day, after trimming up the tops, thought the brush and green leaves made so inviting a bed that he lay down upon them to rest a little and fell asleep. He was rudely awakened by a wild cat springing upon him, evidently aiming to get hold of his throat, but he with much difficulty turned him under, crushed and mastered him receiving many deep scratches in the process.

    Benja Parker, who lived near us, hearing a stir among his hogs one dark night, seized a chunk of fire and rushed out, shouting to scare away the intruders. As the bear was black, he did not see him until so close that the bear raised his paw and with one stroke, struck the fire from his hand, leaving him in the darkness, in very uncongenial company. In a moment he turned and fled for life, leaving his hogs to fight for their lives.

Our pathway east ran a little north of where the main cross street now is, *(Main and Chestnut Sts.)* and near the cross used to be a muddy place which was a favorite wallowing place for the bears, for they resort to such places the same as hogs do. Father once saw a bear coming down a large tree which stood for many years after the land was cleared, about where the Frasier tavern now stands. He supposed he had been up there hunting bees, as they are great lovers of honey and would often gnaw great places in the tree to get at it. My grandfather was quite a bee man and often found large swarms of wild bees. When he cut the trees down to get the honey, he would save the bees also, if he could, and hive them in an old-fashioned bee gum made of a cut in a hollow log.

Once when he went to look after a hive of this kind he found that a bear had thrown it down, and he supposed, run his head so far in that he could not withdraw it, and so, dragged off the hive leaving a great track wherever he went. Grandfather, thinking he was sure of that bear, followed on the trail until he came to the hive fast between two trees which had held it fast while Bruin pulled out his head.

Thus in toil and privation, adventure and excitement, the days of our early life sped on, and when I began to write of them, such a throng of memories come crowding up for utterance, that I know not where to close.

Nearly all of the first settlers of Barnesville are silent in death and soon none will be left to tell the story of its wild beginning, yet of all who have been instrumental in bringing about its present flourishing condition, those early pioneers, who broke the first road through the forest and lived in danger and hardship, had the hardest part to bear. The young girls of Barnesville, who flit gracefully about their dainty stoves never think how their great-grandmothers cooked and roasted and baked with only an open fireplace, and the young men who drive their fast horses swiftly along the smooth streets, do not reflect that the very necessities of their ancestors, as salt and *(gun)* powder, were packed laboriously over mountains, through underbrush and fallen logs, and come to us at a very high price. The hand of progress has swept away all trace of the wilderness that was, and it is well, for in its place we behold a fertile and productive country, contributing to the growth and enterprise of a happy and industrious people.

Jonathan Bundy Anecdotes

When uncle Jonathan Bundy was 19 years old, he was splitting rails out of a log from a large chestnut tree. He split 90 rails to the cut. He was working at the foot of the second hill from my great-grandfather Doudna's house. Great-grandfather came riding along on horseback with his daughter Achsah, who was 12 years old, on their way to town (Barnesville), and they stopped to talk to Jonathan a little bit and while they were talking, Aunt Achsah peeped out from behind her father at him, and he thought then she was to be his future wife.

It so happened, for they were married near the last of the 4th month, 1824, and lived here in our neighborhood until the 25th of 10th month, 1830. They got a certificate of removal to Deerfield Monthly Meeting, Morgan County, Ohio.

They had three children at that time, and six altogether. Later they moved to Iowa, and since I can remember, when he came back to Yearly Meeting and to visit, he would come to our house to visit and we children just loved to hear him and our grandmother, Asenath Doudna, father's mother, tell stories of the olden times such as he told in the above article.

One night when he was at our house there was an owl bothering some of our chickens that were roosting up in the cedar tree at the south end of the house. He was sleeping in the parlor bedroom and the tree was nearby. Along about five o'clock in the morning, he heard it fall. He then came out and told our folks about it and said if they would get it right away and cut its head off it would be all right to eat. He would take walks out in the fields to gather the plant called Life Everlasting and we children would go with him and help him get it and hear him tell pioneer stories.

                                                              Written by: Elma D. Bailey, Barnesville, Ohio

THE BUNDY ANCESTORS

In the late 1700's five brothers came from England. One of them settled in Louden County, Virginia and the other four in Wayne County, North Carolina.

One of these became dissatisfied and went to central New York where there are still folks of the Bundy name and such given names as Hezekiah, John and William. The earliest record is of Dempsey and Mary, his wife, who both died in North Carolina. Their estate was settled by Wm. Bundy who married Sarah Overman in 1803 near the southern edge of the state. Sarah Overman was not able to write her name on the marriage certificate, but she was energetic and skilled in caring for her family.

After his mother's death, William Bundy brought his wife and small children to a squatters permit in Section 16 in Somerset Township in Belmont County, Ohio. *(1806)* He with Joseph Cox and John Coyler, paid the wagoner $250 to bring their goods here from North Carolina.

William Bundy also entered a quarter section in Section 27, Warren Township and bought 26 acres in Section 13, Somerset Township. On this 26 acres he built a weather-boarded log house and painted it red. It was known as the red house farm. The house was moved away in 1965.

Thomas Marshall, a land speculator from Baltimore, entered a half of section 4 in Warren Township under a patent signed by President James Madison. In his travels, Thomas Marshall saw the red house and was so taken with it and its surroundings that he traded his 320 acres of unimproved forest for this 26 acres with the red house. *(Actually he purchased the whole section, 640 acres, and traded half of it to William Bundy.)*

William Bundy started at once to make a home on the new purchase. *(This was located on the north side of SR 147.)* He took his oldest son Ezekiel and his daughter Mary, to cook for them and help with the work. They stayed at night while he went back to his wife and younger children. At first they had only a homespun blanket to cover the opening for the door, so Mary would sit and sew or knit most of the night to keep a bright fire so that the wolves would not come into the house. The log house had two rooms, one of which was used for spinning and weaving.

In 1822, William Bundy contracted with a brick-maker for bricks to build a large house. *(This was located at 37545 Barnesville Bethesda Rd. – SR 147)* The written contract provided the terms and methods of payment. Clay for the brick was dug from the cellar and ground in a wooden mixer operated by a horse walking round and round in a circle. After mixing, the clay was molded into bricks and laid one in a place to dry. Then the brick-maker hoped earnestly for sunny days till the bricks were dried enough to cover up around and over furnaces which were fired with wood till the brick-maker deemed them hard enough to put in the wall. Also in the same year, a contract was made with Elias Williams to dress and lay the stone range work for the foundation and for the chimney and sills and caps for the windows. This work was to be done in a workmanlike manner in the warm season of the year. William Bundy was to pay $50.00 and 200 pounds of swingled flax. The written contract shows the delivery of flax.

BRICK RESIDENCE BUILT BY WILLIAM BUNDY IN 1824
Later the home of his son Ezekiel.

The carpenter and joiner work was done by Giles Brooks. For pay, he was to receive board and lodging and a deed for the east half of Section 27 in Warren Township, where William Bundy had formerly lived and made improvements. The new house was built with the view of keeping drovers, and as they were sometimes a rough set, there was a brick wall partition with no doors dividing the upstairs.

In order to get white lime for the plastering, teams were sent to haul mussel shells from the Ohio river. When these were burned in a kiln and sorted from among the ashes, they yielded a very hard white surface which is smooth and hard after 120 years. As William Bundy was picking shells from the ashes, a neighbor George McNichols came along and joined him in the work while they "visited". However, George soon got tired and raised up with the remark "Mr. Bundy, you are stronger in the faith than I would be." William replied "Thee is as strong in the faith as I am, but thee is too lazy to work for it". It so happened that William Bundy did not live long enough to enjoy the fine house he had built. He and his wife rode away one morning to attend Quarterly Meeting of Friends in Morgan County and to visit their oldest daughter who married William French and lived near Chesterhill, Ohio. As they started away, mother stooped down and told the little boy to be a good boy till mother gets back. His father said "I cannot say till I get back."

While they were visiting at Mary French's, he was taken suddenly ill and died and was buried at Elliott's Cross Roads. Sarah Bundy came home alone leading her husband's horse and took up the work of making a home for her children. She was also active in aiding escaped slaves on their way to Canada and freedom.

On one occasion they had a whole family hidden away in the hay mow for more than a week. It was son William's job to take their meals to them and to help entertain the children till they could be sent on their way. With such a mother, it was no wonder the children grew up to be abolitionist, and son William, known as Black Bill, in later years became a successful conductor on the underground railroad, but such was the respect for him, that with a price on his head for helping the negroes, he was never in the toils of the law.

On one occasion he was passing the Ebenezer Baptist Church *(a little west of Bethesda)* just as a protracted meeting broke up on a moonlight night and the road was full of church goers but none of them betrayed him.

In 1843 Thomas Marshall sold 108 acres adjoining the William Bundy farm to Thomas Schofield. *(In 1841 Thomas sold it to William II, who built his house and barn here.)* He *(William)* dug a deep well, planted an orchard of fruit trees and built a two story house on a rising knoll, 200 yards from the highway. *(37520 Barnesville-Bethesda Rd.)* Not long afterward, Schofield sold to Dempsey Bundy *(William's brother, a parcel east of William's property)*. Of this transaction, we do not have as clear records as those left by William Bundy. Before many years, Dempsey decided he wanted to live nearer the road and entered into a contract to have the brick made on the premises to build a large 8 room two story house. The building was plain and substantial and still stands, a monument to the work of those early days. *(37850 Barnesville-Bethesda Rd.)*

He *(Dempsey)* built a large barn in 1869 and again it happened as in the case of his father, William Bundy, he did not live long enough to enjoy the new home, but died in 1877. The farm has passed to strangers but is kept in excellent repair.

Written by: Dillwyn C. Bundy, Tacoma, Ohio – son of William II.

ANNA STANTON BUNDY
1837 - 1917
Taken from the Stanton Book *(Our Ancestors the Stantons)*

Anna Stanton Bundy, daughter of Joseph and Mary Stanton, was born at the old Stanton home a few miles north of Barnesville, Ohio, on Stillwater Creek, Eighth Month, eighth, 1837. On the thirtieth day of Third Month, 1859 she was married to Nathan Bundy, son of Ezekiel and Mary Bundy.

Anna Stanton Bundy was educated at the Friends School near Stillwater Meeting House and at Mt. Pleasant Boarding School, Ohio. *(Mt. Pleasant, Ohio)* It is said by those who knew her in her girlhood days that she was of an unusually gay and happy temperament, enjoying to the fullest the innocent pleasures of life. Anna Stanton Bundy and Nathan Bundy lived for a short time on Sandy Ridge in what was probably the first house built by Henry Doudna for his home. *(Located in the NE quarter of Section 2, Warren Twp.)* At the death of his mother they moved to the old home. Here the following children were born to them: Joseph S. (1-19-1860), Caleb L. (12-12-1862), Mary M. (7-7-1864); and some years later, while living in Barnesville, Ohio, Clara Elma (11-7-1871). Clara died when she was but eighteen months old. *(Their Barnesville home was located across from the library and beside the Senior Center on E. Main St.)*

In 1865, Nathan Bundy and his cousin, Chalkley Dawson, put down a coal shaft which they operated for a few years. About 1870, Nathan purchased a men's tailoring store, and not long after, his health began to fail. He decided to go to Oregon in the Fall of 1873, thinking the climate might be of benefit to one with lung trouble. It turned out to be only a temporary relief.

While he was in Oregon, Anna and her family lived with her brother Eli Stanton, who did so much for them at that time. Many happy hours were spent there. Nathan returned home in the spring, but his health continued to fail and he passed quietly away in the late summer of 1874, at the age of thirty-seven.

Once again, Anna had her children to take care of and they went to live with her sister Elizabeth Stanton Bailey. They lived with them all that winter and in the spring purchased a little home near them and close to Tacoma *(railroad)* Station. The children went to District School #2, and each in turn taught there for a short time. *(Tacoma school was located on the east side of the first curve on Bailey Road.)* They attended Barnesville School and Lebanon, Ohio Normal School.

Anna Stanton Bundy's friends were numerous and her relatives very dear to her. "To love and to be loved is the greatest happiness of existence" was especially true to her. She had a great gift of humor.

Not being a good sleeper, she complained of lying awake many hours in the night and would get sleepy early in the evening. One evening after trying in vain to keep awake, she suddenly arose from her chair and said, "I'll go to bed, I know I can keep awake there." She was a great lover of flowers and spent many happy hours in the flower garden.

Possibly her greatest sorrow was the passing away of her only grandson, Clifford B. Colpitts, on Ninth Month, fifth, 1911, at the age of 21. After his death, she began to decline. She had heart trouble, and although she had been in poor health for two years, she did not become worse until within two weeks of her death, which occurred Tenth Month, fifth, 1917 at the age of eighty.

Written by: Beulah Patten McDonald, Aldan, PA.

Picture – Left to right – Mary Bundy Colpitts, Joseph S. Bundy, Caleb L. Bundy and Anna Stanton Bundy. Joseph died 12/20/1885 and Caleb died 11/28/1890, both having succumb to Typhoid Fever. Mary married John Colpitts of Barnesville and they had one son, Clifford B., who died 9/5/1911. Mary passed away in the 1950's.

THE CHALKLEY BUNDY HOME
1823 - 1866

The old home of Chalkley and Sarah Doudna Bundy was built by Robert Hodgin, Sarah's uncle.

The following story of my grandfather Bundy's old homestead has been related to me, a little at a time, by my father, Nathan Bundy, now in his 94th year. He enjoys going back through memory's lane and giving me a history of his early home and life. It is remarkable how much he remembers after so many years.

The main part of the house was of brick construction, two stories high, with a lean-to frame addition, four or five steps lower, used as the kitchen.

Telling me of the lean-to kitchen reminded father of an incident that happened when he was a very small boy. One night, grandfather heard a noise in the kitchen. The doors were left open in the summer time for ventilation. Going to the top of the steps leading to the kitchen he saw a crazy man, one Stoke Newman, standing in the middle of the kitchen with an axe over his shoulder. In the olden days there were no institutions for the feeble-minded, and such persons were taken care of by their relatives as best they could. Grandfather just stood still and looked at Stoke, saying not a word. Presently, Stoke turned on his heel and walked quietly out of the kitchen door. Later it was discovered that he had taken the axe from great-grandfather Doudna's wood shed.

The downstairs of the brick part, consisting of one large room and two bedrooms, was about eight feet in height. There were three bedrooms and a hallway upstairs. There were two open fireplaces upstairs and one in the living room downstairs. In the kitchen was a fireplace that would hold a big back log set on andirons. Father says they studied their lessons in the evening in front of this big fireplace, reaching out occasionally, as did Abraham Lincoln, kicking the logs to make them burn brighter so they could read.

Here he told me about a young colored slave boy from the south who had come to live with them. His name was George Matthews and he could not read or write, although he was 18 years old. He went to the colored school and studied his lessons with brothers, Lin and Joe, by the light of the logs. They were all reading the first reader, but when school was out he was way ahead of the other two boys. George lived with them until he married a girl from No. 1 school district. *(No. 1 school in Warren Township was located in the far southeast corner of Section 8 on Pigeon Point Rd.)*

The cooking was done over a wood stove. Grandfather had a circular saw run by horsepower for cutting the wood. The logs were cut about a foot and a half long, then split. The splitting of the wood for the cook stove was the first job given the colored boy when he came to live with grandfather.

The windows in the whole house were rather small, consisting of twelve small lights, six above and six below. Under the brick part of the house was the cellar with its dirt floor and another big fireplace. The butchering work was all done in the cellar by this open fire. Lizzie Peterson, a colored woman, who helped grandmother, took care of the butchering work. Apples, potatoes, etc. were stored in the basement for winter use.

The water supply was from a spring over which was built a two room, dressed stone spring house. In the first room was the spring and in the second a stone trough into which the water ran from the spring. The milk was kept in this trough in open crocks. At the barn, which was built by grandfather, was a dug well. In this well was an old log pump built by Jeptha Blower's father. He bored the log out by hand and put in the pump part.

There was no sugar camp on the farm but they would tap the big sugar maple down by the spring house and made maple syrup over an open fire in the yard.

Grandfather raised sorghum and made molasses, black as tar, in an open kettle. Sometimes the barrel of sorghum would turn to sugar.

They raised sheep but sold wool except what Sarah would use in making socks for her family.

After Grandmother's death, Grandfather married Deborah Hanson Bundy. *(Deborah first married Caleb Bundy, a nephew of Chalkley, and Caleb died nine months later leaving Deborah pregnant with her only child, Mary.)* Grandmother Debbie used to weave carpets. When Grandmother Debbie came into the family, her own daughter, Mary Caleb, and Aunt Mary were little girls together. They used to call them the "twins."

DEBORAH H. B. STANTON

Grandmother Sarah hired Sally Van Law to make suits and clothing for them. They bought most of the material right there in Barnesville, however, during the Civil War some material was gotten from Wheeling. The suits were made from corduroy and had no lining, making them of little value as far as warmth was concerned. Father says Sally used to make the boys' suits so they wouldn't outgrow them in a hurry and his were often big enough for two or three more his size. The suits were worn out before the boys could grow into them.

Grandfather always kept a dog or dogs for the children. One little dog was a great coon dog. Several of their dogs were killed by the coons who would lead them to a creek and then drown them, but this little fellow was too smart for them and always got his coon.

Great-grandfather John Doudna had a dog named Ranger who would follow him every place he went. At the time of his funeral, Ranger went right along in the carriage, and stood at the edge of the grave while they lowered the casket.

The dogs were used a great deal in fox hunts.

Uncle John Bundy had one of the first McCormick Reapers. Grandfather used a sickle to cut wheat and a grubber for thrashing.

The apples were taken to George Tatem's cider mill *(located in Tacoma at 62160 Tacoma Rd.)* to be made into cider. There was always such a throng there, that one time Grandfather thought he would be a little smarter than the other farmers, so they took a load of apples and went to the press in the middle of the night, only to find another load already there ahead of him.

On June 19th, 1859 there was a severe frost that killed all the wheat in that area.

This is just a small insight into the home life of my grandfather and grandmother and in spite of the hard work and the lack of all the modern conveniences that we deem it impossible to get along without, they were a simple, honest, peace-loving, home-loving folk, and we might do well to pattern our lives a little more after the fashion of theirs.

The following is an exact copy of the records in the Chalkley Bundy family Bible.
Births:
> Chalkley Bundy, son of William Bundy and Sarah, his wife, was born 24th of 2nd month, 1823.

Sarah Doudna, daughter of Joel Doudna and Rebecca, his wife, was born the 16th of 9th month, 1824.

Lindley Bundy, son of Chalkley Bundy and Sarah, his wife, was born the 28th of 1st month, 1845.

Joel L. Bundy, son of Chalkley Bundy and Sarah, his wife, was born the 22nd of 10th month, 1846.

Nathan W. Bundy, son of Chalkley Bundy and Sarah, his wife, was born the 11th of 6th month, 1848.

Lucinda Bundy, daughter of Chalkley Bundy and Sarah, his wife, was born the 11th of 9th month, 1850.

Rebecca D. Bundy, daughter of Chalkley Bundy and Sarah, his wife, was born the 11th of 12th month, 1853.

Emma Bundy, daughter of Chalkley Bundy and Sarah, his wife, was born the 8th of 12th month, 1856.

Mary Elizabeth Bundy, daughter of Chalkley Bundy and Sarah, his wife, was born the 23rd of 5th month, 1860.

Chalkley Bundy, son of Chalkley Bundy and Sarah, his wife, was born the 5th of 6th month, 1862.

Mary Caleb Bundy, daughter of Caleb Bundy and Deborah H., his wife, was born the 3rd of 2nd month, 1860.

Deaths:

Sarah Bundy, Consort of Chalkley Bundy, departed this life 8th month 1st, 1862. Age 37 years, 10 months and 15 days.

Chalkley Bundy departed this life 12th month 1st, 1866. Age 43 years, 9 months and 7 days.

Chalkley Bundy, son of Chalkley Bundy and Sarah, his wife, departed this life 9th month 28th, 1862. Age 3 months and 23 days.

Emma Bundy, daughter of Chalkley Bundy and Sarah, his wife, departed this life 8th month, 25th, 1863. Age 6 years, 7 months and 17 days.

Joel Bundy, son of Chalkley Bundy and Sarah, his wife, departed this life the 31st of 3rd month, 1873. Age 26 years, 5 months and 9 days.

Written by: Anna Mary Bailey, daughter of Nathan W. Bundy and Grandaughter of Chalkley Bundy

CHALKLEY AND SARAH (DOUDNA) BUNDY

– Anecdote –
FLAX – WOOL – SOAP MAKING

Every farm grew flax and almost every home had its spinning wheel and many had looms set not only for weaving carpets, but for making woolen cloth, called "Linsey Woolsy." The boy who had a "Linsey Woolsey Wampus" had something to be proud of.

Lye for soap making was a part of each family's outfit. It was made by pouring water over wood ashes and collecting the liquid to be boiled down to the right consistency. Various methods were used. A common one was to set a bottomless wooden barrel on a wooden slab with four legs. The front ones being short so the lye could run into an iron or stone container by means of a groove in the slab around the barrel and to the lower side. Ashes were placed in the barrel and water poured on from time to time until the required amount was made.

One small boy mistook a saucer of lye for a saucer of molasses being cooled for taffy, and drank some with the result of having no tonsils to be removed in later years.

Ezekiel Bundy brought the first grain separator to the township. It was made by Hoyle Brothers at Smithfield and was kept in operation most of the winter. A colored man, Jim Peterson, got his arm mangled so that Ezekiel Bundy kept him and his family as pensioners. In later years, the colored man's son spoke of it as the good old times. They did not have money to spend but when flour, cornmeal and meat were needed, these things came from Ezekiel Bundy's storehouse. Each Fall he would take them to the store and outfit them with good warm clothing and good stout shoes.

Before the grain separator came into use, the grubber, which was a cylinder mounted on a frame and operated by horsepower, was used to separate the grain from the straw. Men kept the straw pitched to one side and grain and chaff on the other. The old Robert Smith barn had a floor laid of strips and when the horses tramped the grain out of the straw, it would drop to the floor below ready for the mill. *(This farm was where the Walton Home now stands, east of Barnesville on Roosevelt Rd.)*

The first reaper in the neighborhood was owned by Ezekiel Bundy. The driver rode the saddle horse and the operator sat on a stool with a wooden rake to push the grain onto the platform and bunches were pushed off to be bound by hand. Later a second man stood on the platform and bound the sheaves before they were thrown off.

The first grain drill was left in the shed for years because the farmers said it took more work to get the ground in order to use the drill than it did to sow the grain by hand.

Written by: Dillwyn C. and Elizabeth Bundy, Tacoma, Ohio

JOHN BUNDY HOMESTEAD

JOHN BUNDY
1813-1898

The old John Bundy home, now occupied by Alva Bailey, was built in 1825 by Isaac Stubbs on a part of the original land entered by Joseph Stubbs about the year 1804. The clay for the bricks was dug on the farm, molded and burned there. John Bundy bought the farm from Isaac Stubbs and built a frame kitchen to the south of the original brick kitchen with porches to the west and east. The house was originally strengthened with iron rods running through it which are still in evidence. Lindley P. Bailey remodeled the house, building a frame extension to the west end of the brick in the 1890's. A frame kitchen has been added to the south east corner in the last few years.

The large barn is a building of great interest. It was built in 1854 by John Bundy, one of the most progressive farmers of this section. He was noted for his good equipment. The master carpenter on the barn was Isaiah Fields who rode each day in mid-winter from Morristown, a distance of approximately eight miles, to supervise the building. Due to the exposure he developed pneumonia. Two full days were needed to raise the barn with all neighbors help, most barns taking only one day. The barn is sixty feet by seventy feet and the long timbers are hand hewn and fastened together by wooden pegs. The timber for the barn was probably cut on the farm. The hinges for the doors were forged at Slabtown by Mason Thomas for one hundred dollars. Some of the hinges are still in use. John Bundy filled the barn only once and the mowing scythe and hand rake were the tools used for harvest. Wooden forks were made from white oak pieces split at the end into four prongs. Lem Bailey has one of the old barley forks as a relic. The barn was the first to be equipped with a horse hayfork.

John Bundy owned the farm until 1888 when Lindley P. Bailey bought it. With some remodeling of the old barn and the building of a new dairy barn in 1909, the farm has become one of the leading dairy farms in the country.

Written by: Lloyd Bailey, Tacoma, Ohio

WILLIAM "BLACK BILL" BUNDY
1819 - 1905

William "Black Bill" Bundy was born in 1819, the eighth child of a family of eleven. His parents were William and Sarah Overman Bundy who came over the mountains from Wayne County, North Carolina in a cart and settled in this section of Belmont County.

He was five years old when the "brick house" was built. The children loved to run up and down the inclined runways used by the masons in constructing the (then) unusual house which is located on the Barnesville-Bethesda Road a mile west of Speidel and is familiarly known as the "Alden Lee Place." *(This house was located at what is now 37545 Barnesville-Bethesda Rd. on SR 147.)*

At the age of nine, his father died and he grew to manhood under the guidance and care of his pioneer mother. She taught him to hate the institution of slavery, and later he took an active part in the discussions of the leading questions of the day. The foremost of these was the abolition of slavery and he naturally became a conductor on the Underground Railroad. It was his duty to take the passengers from the next man south and conduct them as far north as possible and get back by daybreak. The aged slaves and children rode in the wagon and the rest marched behind. It was because of this experience that he became known as "Black Bill", although he was quite dark complected, the name suited him.

When he reached the age of 24, he married Prudence Wood. She died eighteen months later and left an infant son. About the time of his marriage, "Black Bill" built a story and a half house across the road from his father's famous brick house. It consisted of two ground floor rooms and two rooms upstairs. He had a windlass well, outside Dutch oven, and an outside cave to accommodate the housewife. This is quite different for the conveniences of today. '

Three years later "Black Bill" married Asenath Doudna and to them nine children were born. In 1860 a lean-to kitchen was built on to the house and in 1868-69 the final addition was made by Samuel Williams. It is still standing today as it was finished in 1869. *(This house has had the exterior bricked over and is located at 37520 Barnesville-Bethesda Rd. SR 147.)*

In the early days, one toiled for the necessities of life. Soft soap was made by leaching wood ashes, cloth was made by spinning their own flax, and carpets were made of woven rags. They had a maple sugar camp and also raised cane for molasses. They progressed from the sickle to the combine, from the tramping out of grain to threshing machine, in their generation.

There was an interesting reason for enlarging the farm house to such proportions in 1868. "Black Bill" was very much interested in the "Drove Road" and its purpose. This road is only a tradition now, but it existed for a very good reason. When the National Road was built *(US 40)*, it was surfaced with hand crushed stones which were too sharp and rough to drive the herds of sheep, cattle, mules and horses on from the middle west to the east coast, and so the "Drove Road" was built. It entered Belmont County at Putney Ridge, winding east through Barnesville, passing on south of Bethesda and Belmont to the Ohio River at the mouth of Grave Creek where the cattle could ford across.

"Black Bill" would give these drovers and their herds accommodations for the night as they passed through. As many as 5000 head of sheep or 1000 head of cattle would be cared for in a few days. At one time, four drovers brought 149 mules and four horses through. The mules were herded into the mule lot and the neighbor boys were hired to watch them while the drovers rested and slept. One night they played "hookey" and it took all the next day to round them up again.

Always interested in public advancement and in the forefront of action, he was elected to represent Belmont County in the Ohio State Legislature in 1875, although he was a Republican in a Democratic county.

His wife, Asenath, died in 1888, after 42 years of happy family life. His son Clark Bundy and wife Rachel Crew Bundy, were living on the west coast at this time and asked him to come and live with them. "Black Bill" said "No, it is hard to transplant an old tree."

In 1891 he sold his large farm to Allen Bailey and it is still known by that title. He built a new house which is now owned by the Belmont County Children's Home, but is better known as the Wilfred T. Hall Farm. He lived there until his death in 1905 at which time he was in his 86th year. *(That house, now gone, was on the same side of SR 147 but a little further west.)*

William Bundy opened his farm home to every orphaned or aged relative that he had and sheltered close to 20 at some time in his life. Of his nine children, only Dillwyn C. Bundy of Tacoma, Ohio is living. He is my grandfather and it is from him that I gained the facts for this history.

Written by: Bernita Bundy, great-granddaughter of William "Black Bill" Bundy

THE CLAY PIKE

This road was surveyed by the State through Belmont County and other counties. It paralleled the National Road and entered the county from the west, near Barnesville and extended through Tacoma, the site of Bethesda, Jacobsburg, and crossed the river at the flats of Graves Creek, which was on the West Virginia side.

It was used chiefly as a drove road after the National Road was macadamized or stoned. The hard road was very damaging to the animals hoofs so the clay pike was used during the 1830's, for driving all kinds of stock, but cattle predominated. A number of farmers made a business of feeding and caring for these droves. The drover would start in central or southern Ohio and plan to fatten the stock by the time he reached the eastern market with his droves.

After the railroad was completed, this road soon became just an ordinary country road.
Written by: Dr. D. O. Shepherd, Barnesville, Ohio

[Tracing this "Clay Pike" or "Drover's Road" through Belmont County begins where it entered the county on Pultney Ridge Rd. west of Barnesville. The road entered Barnesville on West Main Street. Thomas C. Parker had a farm that served Drovers on the western outskirts of Barnesville. The road traveled through Barnesville, leaving the town on SR 147, traveling through Tacoma. Otho French's home in Tacoma (62158 Tacoma Rd.) was a Drover's stop, as was the Plummer house (SR 147 and Dusty Lane). The road continued on SR 147 through Speidel and turned south on Twp. Road 190 east of Speidel. There it went past the Joshua Gregg farm, "Woodside", which was a known Drover stop and had a store for the drovers. The road continued on Twp. 190 and then Twp. 200 until it connected up with SR 147 below Belmont. From there it followed SR 147 through Centerville, passing by the James Kinney Farm (44680 Belmont-Centerville Rd.), known to have been a Drovers stop. At Jacobsburg it turned southeast onto Twp. 239, making the slow descent following Pipe Creek to the river near Dilles Bottom. This was across from the flats of Graves Creek on the West Virginia side and apparently a good place for crossing. When the river was down, the cattle could ford across and otherwise they crossed on rafts.

The original road would have varied in some places, but this route comes the closest to following the original route on today's roads.]

Added by: Marie Bundy, Tacoma, OH

THE FRANCIS DAVIS HOUSE

When I was a very small boy, my grandfather and grandmother, Francis and Mary Davis, decided to build a larger and more modern house so that they might be better prepared to entertain visiting Friends, especially at Yearly Meeting time.

They made a deal with my father (William Stanton) and moved their house over on to his land near his greenhouses, and built a new home on the site of their old one. *(The old house is located at 62085 Tacoma Rd. and the new house is at 62420 Tacoma Rd.)*

The new house, which was two and one half stories high, rectangular in shape, with a one story ell in the rear, made an unusual appearance with its four large red brick chimneys and a lookout on top of the roof.

From this lookout, one had a broad view of the surrounding neighborhood. The house itself being located on top of one of the highest hills in Belmont County and exactly on the watershed between the Ohio and Muskingum rivers. In fact, the rain which fell on one part of the roof drained off to the Ohio and from the other part to the Muskingum River.

This new house was considered quite modern and up to date, having gas lights and running water. It also had a few features which show that the idea of entertaining was considered when the plans were being drawn. One was the twin parlors separated by folding doors, which when open, threw the two into one. Another was the third story which was finished in one huge room for men and boys while the four large bedrooms on the second floor took care of the women and girls.

The large dining room was, no doubt, of interest to many of their guests, for as I remember, grandfather was a generous provider and grandmother was a good cook.

Written by: Joseph E. Stanton, son of William Stanton, grandson of Francis Davis, Westtown, Pennsylvania.

JOSEPH F. DOUDNA
1824-1914

Near the Sandy Ridge Road, about two miles east of Barnesville, Ohio (near what is locally called Pigeon Point) my grandfather, Joseph F. Doudna and his wife Belinda Hobson, my grandmother, lived.

The house, a large two story frame stands today, very little changed I am told, from what it was when grandfather bought it from the builder, Joel Dawson.

Joseph F. Doudna (born 12/18/1824) died 12th month 11th, 1914. He was the son of Hosea and Mary Farmer Doudna. Grandfather and grandmother (John and Sarah Knowis Doudna) came from Edgecomb Co. North Carolina in 1804. The oldest child of Joseph F. and Belinda Doudna, was my father, Josiah W. Doudna.

My aunt, Ruth S. Hibbs, was the youngest, and only child now living. She recalls that the house was bought early in the Spring of 1861 and that my father was sent over to plow several fields, before the family moved. She had scarlet fever at the time and they were unable to move until she had recovered. There were two other children, Mary H. (Hoyle) and Edwin F. Doudna.

The house had five rooms and large halls on each floor. There were open fireplaces on both floors, and a large coal cook stove in the kitchen. There was a nice cellar under the house. The windows were numerous, of small panes of glass. The well was a dug one, from which water was drawn by windlass and rope.

Among other farm implements, grandfather had a grain cradle and mower.

My Aunt Ruthie, as we called her, remembers hearing her mother speak of the now famous "June Frost." *(Occurred June 1859.)* Her mother had been up all night, to sit up with a sick neighbor, and on her return home in the morning, she found flower and vegetable gardens stiff with frost.

The first recollections I have of my grandparents were when they had moved from this house to a smaller one on Sandy Ridge. The children all being married had left the home for homes of their own. The slat backed rocker that grandmother sat in, is the piece of furniture I remember best of all. (It is similar to the Stanton rockers shown on page 144, <u>Our Ancestors the Stantons</u>. This rocker had a soft green pad on the back and a soft cushion to match, made with a deep ruffle around it, falling to the rocker and slashed at the corners so that it swayed as she rocked. My aim was to sit in this chair when she vacated it.

I remember how the flies were kept off our food as we sat at a long table at thrashing time. Someone had to stand and wave to and fro over our heads, a long, lightweight pole, to which long bright colored paper streamers were attached.

Grandfather raised strawberries, and we were always delighted to help ourselves from the patch.

I have a hammer my father gave me once and told me to keep it, as he said, "Grandfather Doudna used to use it to make brooms."

Outside the white picket fence which encircled the yard of this cottage home, stood a large horse block, or "up-on-block" as we called it. As it was three steps up from the ground, it made a splendid place to mount or dismount from the back of our old sorrel "Bob", or when we came to visit, by buggy or surrey, it was equally useful. Grandfather was always very fond of horses and took this same "Bob" to care for, years later, when we moved to town.

This is the house where grandmother died. Hers was the first funeral I can remember.

Joseph F. Doudna later married Ann Eliza Wilson, and they moved to Pasadena, California, where she died. Grandfather died at the home of my parents in Barnesville, Ohio.

Written by: Alice Doudna Smith, Barnesville, OH

Anecdote of Joseph F. Doudna

Joseph Doudna was a man of great energy and a very good cradler. One time while he was living in the Dawson house, he went over to James Edgerton on the Ridge to cradle wheat. An expert cradler was to be there and a contest had been arranged between them. Joseph decided to take Belinda, his wife, along to visit for the day. When they arrived, the expert had already started. Joseph watched a while, then said "I see he doesn't have my stroke." He started in after him and soon caught up, cradled around him and left him in a patch of uncradled wheat. As Joseph related, "He drew his cradle on me in a threatening manner."

Written by: Wilford T. Hall, related to Alice Doudna Smith, Barnesville, Ohio

Knowels and Knowis

There seems to be a difference of opinion as to the spelling of the name of one of the ancestors of the Doudna's. Knowels and Knowis being used by the different branches of the Doudna family.

The name is given as Knowis in the early birth records of Stillwater Meeting, while Knowels is handed down from the other early history. However, as far as we can learn, Knowels and Knowis apply to the same family.

"KIDNAPPED DOUDNA" TRADITION

Different versions of the same tradition are quite common. Therefore, it seems desirable that when the facts are no longer known, except by tradition, we should not dismiss or ignore either, but a record should be kept of both because either one might be true. There could be confused understanding in later years when both a kidnapping and an attempted kidnapping, so similarly described, are believed to have occurred.

A KIDNAPPING INCIDENT (John Doudna I – 1769 – 1820)

Many years ago, while at the wharf of England, a little boy who had accompanied his father with a load of vegetables to trade with the sailors was induced to go aboard a ship, which furnished ample amusement for him until sometime after the ship had left the shore. But as soon as the boy realized his situation, he burst into an agonizing fit of tears which was kept up until he cried himself to sleep.

The next morning he awoke to find himself very lonesome without his parents, but ere long forgetting his troubles, he became helpful as a sailor boy, and quickly learned to climb to the top of the ship's mast, also learned the meaning of the words the sailors used.

He would often ask his master where his parents were, but would be put off by a promise that he would some day tell him. All that the little fellow could remember was that his name was John Doudna, and that his father's name was Henry and his mother's was Elizabeth.

John grew rapidly and soon became a trusty sailor, but as a sailor's life is a very rough one, no attention was given to education except in the line of managing a ship and learning all they can about storms which influence sailors lives very much. John Doudna was kept by the same sea captain for twenty years, and in all that time, never once heard from home. The captain had not yet told him where his home was. He had reached his 26th year, when it was noticed one day that a great storm was arising. It proved to be a great ocean windstorm which finally wrecked the ship. But providentially, our ancestor, John Doudna, with two others of the crew got astride some boards which served as a raft and succeeded in reaching a very small island on which they took refuge.

As soon as the storm abated, they began to realize their situation. They were on a small island in the great Atlantic, with nothing to sustain life except a little rain water they found in the chinks of a rock which was on the island. They waited patiently to meet their fate with some hopes, however, that the morrow would bring them good tidings in the form of another ship. But alas! Their hopes were in vain.

The morning dawned, but no ship came into view. They now began to long for something to appease their hunger, but their longing for this was also in vain. The second and third days came and still no tidings, and now it became apparent that they must starve to death if relief did not come.

They were tempted to throw themselves into the sea, to shun such a death, but they waited on with higher hopes for deliverance growing weaker, without food or shelter, for eight days. But on the eighth day one of them sighted a ship, but being too weak to stand up, they in turn raised a hand or waved a hat to the ship. Soon they observed the ship had changed its course and was coming toward them.

They were taken on board and were only allowed one teaspoon each of broth without any salt in it. This began to bring back their appetites again and they almost went crazy with hunger. At the end of two hours they were given two teaspoonsful each and at the expiration of every two hours the quantity increased until their severe hunger was satisfied, and in three or four days the ship reached port, and John Doudna was landed in North Carolina without a cent of money in the world.

According to a vow he had made, never to sail on the ocean again if he ever reached land, he started out to find a place to work for his board, until he learned how to manage farming implements. He had not proceeded far, until he met a girl on her way to school by the name of Sarah Knowis. This was the first girl he had met in this strange land and her kind words and sympathies made a deep impression on John, not soon to be forgotten. She directed him to her father's house, and after working there less than two years, John Doudna and Sarah Knowis were united in marriage, John being 28 and she being 14 years of age. John took his young wife and settled in Edgecomb County, North Carolina, there to spend his time in peace and happiness.

But in the year 1804, he with his wife and most of their children, migrated to Belmont County, Ohio. Here he remained the rest of his days and in all probability helped to build the first meetinghouse that was ever erected in Warren Township for the public worship, near where Stillwater meetinghouse now stands.

His wife survived him several years, being over 80 years of age at the time of her death. At which time there were 450 people who called her mother, grandmother or great-grandmother. The above account was taken mostly from an article written by J.H. Edgerton, a great grandson of the "Kidnapped Boy" and a descendent of John's daughter, Zilpha, who married John Edgerton.

In connection with this, an article written by my father, Joseph W. Doudna (another great-grandson) says "Our great-grandfather settled about one and a quarter miles east of the Stillwater meetinghouse, on the farm that afterwards became the home of his son Hosea, who lived there until his death in 1888, aged 95 years, and about 80 years after the death of John, his father." His oldest son, Henry, settled on a farm farther down Sandy Ridge, on or near the home of William H. Sears, where he built a barn before the days of cut nails. The roof was put on with wooden pins instead of weighting it down with poles, log cabin fashion.

John Doudna, the second son, settled on a farm in the Chestnut Ridge neighborhood, near two miles south of Barnesville. He was the father of William, John, Jr., Isaac and Elisha, (and grandfather of the writer) where he lived until his death in 1863 at the age of 90. Another son, Knowis, settled at Leatherwood where he raised a large family, which with his oldest sister Mary's family composed the most of the Friends settlement there. (Mary married Isaac Hall and was the one of whom my mother Rosetta Hall Doudna was a descendent.)

Another son, James, died in boyhood before they left North Carolina, also a little girl, Peggy (Margaret), between eight and nine years of age. Joel, the youngest son, remained within the limits of the Society at Stillwater Anna and Elizabeth, two other daughters, both married and lived at Stillwater, while Asenath settled within the limits of Ridge and Zilpha married John Edgerton and removed to Morgan County, Ohio where she lived until her death in 1858 at age 62 years. (Zilpha was the grandmother of J.H. Edgerton, the writer of the early part of this history.) We have never understood that any of these 450 descendants could ever trace their ancestry farther back than the particulars given in the foregoing account.

Written by: Joseph H. Doudna, Barnesville, Ohio – Son of Joseph W. Doudna and 4th generation of the "Kidnapped Boy".

JOHN H. EDGERTON
(With another version of the "Kidnapped Boy" story.)

John H. Edgerton of Morgan County, Ohio was a great-grandson of the first John Doudna. His grandparents were John and Zilpha Doudna Edgerton who removed in 1835 to Deerfield Friends Monthly Meeting, Morgan County, Ohio from Somerset Monthly Meeting, south of Barnesville, Ohio, where John H. Edgerton's father, John Edgerton (son of John and Zilpha) was born 5/19/1829. Zilpha Doudna Edgerton died in 1858 and John Edgerton Sr. in 1869.

Zilpha was third from the youngest child of the first John Doudna's family of fourteen children, being eight years old when the Doudna family came to Ohio from North Carolina in 1804.

The historical sketch written by John H. Edgerton, concerning John Doudna's early life appears to be almost the only account of that early period which has been preserved in writing. There is, however, in another branch of Doudna descendants – descendants of another and older child, Knowis Doudna - a quite different tradition relating to the way in which John Doudna was stolen.

It is, that the boy who was afterwards known as John Doudna was with his parents on a vessel bound for America, when yellow fever broke out and both parents died and were buried at sea, and then it is believed the boy was kept a captive on the vessel again at sea.

By the former account this boy is said to have been only six years old when stolen, and while kidnapping boys and young men to be trained as sailors was a common practice in earlier times, it would seem to be an exceptional case for a boy of six to have been deliberately kidnapped for that purpose at a wharf in England. Generally, the victims of such "body snatching," as it was called then, were older, at least ten or twelve.

The oldest son and child of John Doudna was Henry and the following tradition relating to him suggests that possibly in the course of time, the earlier tradition (if different from that account) might have been mostly forgotten and so became confused with the circumstances connected with an attempted kidnapping in North Carolina of Henry Doudna, when he was about ten or twelve years old.

Henry was with his father, John Doudna, who was selling provisions for a vessel preparing to sail from a North Carolina port, and when his father was about to leave and turned to look for Henry, he was nowhere in sight. Instantly recalling his own experience and the way he was hidden on a ship long before, John Doudna lost no time in going aboard and was just in time to see Henry's head disappearing down the Hatchway.

This tradition was well remembered by both Joseph W. Doudna and Anna Livezey Hall, from their early years, and later likewise has been by other descendants of John Doudna II, the second son and second child of that first Doudna family, who must have been about ten years old when this incident occurred.

When the first Doudna family reunion was held at Stillwater Meeting grounds, 8-5-1932, there were present, fourteen great-grandchildren whose ages ranged along with those of the older ones present. At this reunion, one of the great-grandsons, Jesse B. Doudna, made known to several who were present, that his father, Knowis Doudna, Jr. passed on to him the very different tradition, before mentioned, that John Doudna I was with his parents on a vessel bound for America when yellow fever broke out, and both parents died and were buried at sea, and it was then and in that way that this ancestor was separated from his parents and kindred.

Jesse B. Doudna said further, that he must have been at least twelve years old when his father talked with him about these matters. Also said that he never once heard of the other story, that John Doudna was kidnapped at some seaport in England until he read the sketch by John H. Edgerton when it was published in the *Barnesville Enterprise* in 1908.

Jesse B. Doudna attended several of the Doudna-Hall reunions after that and at one held in 1936, he made a talk to the company assembled on this same subject and repeated these statements besides mentioning, also, the tradition that John Doudna was in service at the siege and battle of Quebec, and was one of the company that scaled "the heights of Abraham," and this too his father had told him in his boyhood.

This later tradition is referred to in the biographical sketch of Hosea Doudna, in the History of Belmont and Jefferson Counties, by Caldwell, published in 1880, and no doubt Hosea himself was the historian's authority for what he stated.

The same tradition also was mentioned in the obituary notice, in the local papers, at the time of Hosea Doudna's death, 7-3-1888, at the age of ninety-five years. Hosea Doudna had a family Bible which is said to have contained, besides birth records of his brothers and sisters, some account of his father's early life and some facts relating to his mother's people, but inquiries in recent years have disclosed no knowledge of its whereabouts.

Anna Livezey Hall remembered seeing this Bible many years ago, in the home of Hosea's son, Joseph F. Doudna.

Written by: Ella Coventry Galloway, whose mother was a sister of Joseph W. Doudna.

HISTORICAL DATA CONCERNING JOEL AND REBECCA DOUDNA AND FAMILY
OLD BRICK HOUSE,
built in 1811 by William Hodgin

This old brick house is believed to have been the first brick house built in Warren Township, Belmont County, Ohio. The date 1811 was cut in one of the black walnut joists over the second story at the top of the stairway. It was torn down in 1901.

This was located on the road now running past the Grange Hall just outside of Barnesville, Ohio. *(Twp. Rd. 122)* We would cross the creek, go up the hill, on the level for a little, then up another rise. There was an old double hollow walnut tree where an old blacksnake lived. In the hollow just before this rise the old brick house stood.

Before this was built, my grandmother's parents lived in a log house. After the oldest child, Ezekiel, was married and the others were older, grandmother's father Hodgin built this brick house. There was a loft over the kitchen. The only way to get to it was by a ladder off the porch. The kitchen was a lean-to. In the kitchen in the corner by the fireplace, there was a cook stove. There was a large fireplace in the living room.

Joel and Rebecca lived in this house until the board house at the top of the last above mentioned rise was built. My mother was born in this house. Joel and Rebecca's daughter Sarah and her husband Chalkley Bundy set up housekeeping in the old brick. These are my father and mother.

It has been said that Joel Doudna was known as "The Good Joel Doudna." He would loan to his neighbors and friends the things he needed for himself.

Rebecca E. Doudna Bundy, before she was married, lived with us a great deal and helped mother. She was making apple butter. It was in large kettles over the fire. There was a long stirrer which was a very long square stick. At right angles there was a stick that went down into the kettle. This enabled us to stir the butter while we were sitting down. My little sister was standing with her back to the fire, and Rebecca cautioned her to go away or the hot butter might pop onto her. She went away. I then went there, not thinking, and some hot butter splashed out onto my neck. Then Rebecca said she had not spoken to me because she thought I knew better. (I was about 10 years old.)

My mother died here in August, 1862.

SPRING

My father, Chalkley Bundy, built a milk house by and partly over the spring. I can remember when it was dug out square around it. Bill Starky came to break the stones for the house. *(These would end up large rectangular square stones.)* This was done by hand with a hammer as I remember it. After breaking the stone, he would smooth it the same way. The house was high enough to walk into. There were three steps from the spring down into the milk house. Two large pieces of stone were hollowed out to make troughs on the inside on two sides. The spring water ran through these troughs. I used two gallon crocks covered with large, clean boards and would set these filled crocks in the trough to cool the milk. Each day I would skim the previous day's milk and put the cream in the cream crock. After this had soured, I would churn it into butter. The temperature of the cream had a great deal to do with the quality of the butter. At the door of the milk house and around the side of the spring, was built up with the stones. When the weather was good, I would churn here.

We would very often sit on the long, wide board that ran in front of the spring to amuse ourselves with our reflection in the water. One day sister Rebecca and I were bending over to drink from the spring. She tumbled in head first. The spring must have been three or four feet deep. I pulled her out by the heels and she was all right.

Above the spring on a little hill was a maple tree. We always had a play house under it. In the springtime, Father would tap it by boring a hole in it. Then he would insert a little trough and hang a bucket on it. The sap would drip into the bucket, and we would then boil it down into sugar. From sassafras roots, tea would be made. The maple sugar sweetened it and it was good. Under the maple trees there was a fireplace which we used for washing. Large kettles hung by chains over the fire. There were five beech trees around the spring. My father was very fond of the nuts, and we children would gather them in the fall and he would reward us by paying us a penny for a given number.

TOBACCO HOUSE, TOBACCO GROWING, AND DOG HOUSE

Father's tobacco was always considered as among the very best in the neighborhood. When the tobacco was ripe, they would bring it to the tobacco house on sleds drawn by horses. They would then unhitch the horses, leave the filled sled, and hitch them to an empty sled to take back to the field. The stringers (the persons tying the tobacco) would put the tobacco on a table about three feet long and two feet wide. They had a stick about four feet long, twine, and a long needle. After tying one end of the twine to the stick and threading the needle with the other end, they would thread the needle and twine through the stem of the tobacco. Then it was pushed up as far as possible. When the sticks were full, they were tied in horizontal pieces on top and between posts which were in long rows, placed grape arbor fashion. These horizontal pieces were placed just far enough apart to leave the yard sticks to hang free. The first filled

A TOBACCO HOUSE

sticks would be tied at the top of the house. It was great fun to play hide between the full rows of strung tobacco. In the middle of the dirt floor, a "flue" was built. This ran the full length of the house and was covered over the top. It was made of stone and bricks. At the end they pushed in long logs. This kept burning for two or three days.

Close to the tobacco house was built a little shack of logs. It was equipped with straw and old quilts. The one's attending the fire in the tobacco house would sleep there. This was called the "Dog House." At first, father himself would tend it, not trusting the boys. Afterwards the boys would do it. The neighbor boys would come in, and they would have watermelon. They told how they would catch chickens, kill, clean, and cook and eat them there.

Gypsum weed grew on the place. The stem sometimes was as big as my wrist. The tobacco blower, a kind of butterfly, laid its eggs on this weed. The worms hatched from these eggs ate the tobacco leaves. Father would give us pennies for catching these large, ugly worms. They could be caught best about sundown.

LOG BARN

This was built on the hill to the north of the house. The part next to the house had the stables with enough room for ten or twelve horses. On the other side there was a sawed board floor. Feed and hay were kept there. The hay mow was only of logs close enough together to hold the hay. Here the chickens would make their nest. By my time, the logs were pretty shaky.

NEW BARN

In the fall of the year that father died, he was gathering timber for a new barn. On December third, 1866, he died. The boys got the barn started as early as spring as the weather would permit. When the first floor was laid, all the young folks had a party there. I suppose it was on a Sunday because they would be working through the week. They built it during the summer and it was ready to put hay into it at harvest. The lower part was high enough to drive a carriage under and that is where they kept it. A bridge went across the upper part under which they drove the carriage. Aaron Frame, chief carpenter, said when it was finished that "it was the biggest barn and highest in the county".

CHANGE BY PURCHASE

The purchaser of this place tore down the old brick house. He used the old bricks to build a new house on the side of the old log barn.

NEW SAWED BOARD HOUSE

This was located on the hill to the south of the old brick house. *(Just past 36430 Co. Rd. 122.)* Grandfather Joel Doudna built this house of sawed boards. They piled the boards one on top of each other to make the walls. The partitions were made the same way. Inside it was plastered. There were five rooms. On the outside, the boards were not even, they allowed for a toe-hold. From the porch we would climb up that wall by using these cracks. There were fireplaces in the sitting room and in the room where grandmother and grandfather slept.

When Uncle John Doudna's wife died, he was left with several small children, including little Walter who was only a few weeks old. Aunt Eunice told John that if he could get along with the older children, she would take the baby to grandfather's and take care of him there. She was not in very good health. She arrived at grandfather's house one night about nine o'clock. She had come from Chesterfield *(in Morgan County)* on hack, boat and train to Goshen *Township*. She slept in the room next to grandmother's. Grandmother heard her in the night and after inquiry found out that she was up fixing the baby's bottle. The next morning, she did not arise when the others did, so they thought she was tired from her travel. After a while, someone went in her room and found her dead.

MEDICATION APPLIED TO A CRUSHED THUMB

During thrashing, my right thumb was crushed. My father made splints for it, and put them around the thumb joint. Then he put sugar and camphor on it and wrapped it. This was not changed, as I remember, unless it was to put on a clean outside wrapper. I was about ten years old. The joint was left deformed, but entirely useable.

JUNE FROST

As I remember this, it was in the first part of June, it killed all the corn except a few stalks that were growing under trees. It must have been as high as my head. Not enough being left for father to gather, we children would take our wagons and wheelbarrows and gather the ears of corn which grew to maturity on the stalks under the trees.

We had some "greening" apple trees. These apples were very much in demand in Barnesville for apple butter. These apples were killed. We also had a row of "never fail" apples which we generally did not use or pay any attention to except to let the hogs eat them. The year of this frost, the "never fail" apples were the only ones that were not killed. We took very good care of these apples from this time on.

Written by: Lucinda Bundy Hanson, Richmond, VA, Feb. 12, 1942 – daughter of Chalkley and Sarah Doudna Bundy. *(She was 91 when she wrote this.)*

THE BIRTH PLACE OF JOSEPH W. DOUDNA

A part of the house in which the writer is now living, has been called home for more than one hundred years. Originally there were but two rooms, one built directly above the other. The rooms were seventeen feet square. The joists under the floor were small logs hewn on the upper side. The joists overhead were of small logs hewn on the upper and lower side, and were spaced near three feet apart. These are still faithfully serving their purpose.

Sometime between the years 1804 and 1841, this two-roomed house was built on the same location where the home of Kenneth Lloyd Doudna now stands. *(59864 Hall-Boston Rd.)* This land was originally purchased from President Thomas Jefferson by John Doudna, Jr. in 1804. It was here during the winter of 1841 that Joseph W. Doudna was born to John Doudna, III and his wife Asenath. They continued to make this their home for some years.

A short time before the death of Joseph's father, which occurred in 1848, neighbors slid the house down the hill a few rods nearer the spring so that water could be more easily carried. A few years later, a large house was built on the same location from whence the smaller one was moved. Later the two-room house was again moved to its present location, now the home of John A. Doudna, son of Joseph W. Doudna, and a lean-to kitchen was added. *(59760 Hall-Boston Rd.)*

Here in the year 1876, twin daughters, Mary and Sara, were born to Joseph W. and Rosetta H. Doudna, in the same room in which their father was born, thirty-five years before.

The lean-to kitchen has long disappeared. But the two original rooms still stand with the addition of six new ones, making for us today, a comfortable eight room house instead of two. I like to think of the busy hands and loving hearts who long ago worked so diligently to establish their little home midst the great trees of the forest.

Written by: Beulah M. Doudna, Great-great-granddaughter of John Doudna, Jr.

JOSEPH W. DOUDNA
(picture of Joseph W. holding a distaff with flax preparatory to spinning)

Having been requested to write about our father Joseph W. Doudna, who was a great-grandson of the kidnapped John Doudna and his wife Sarah Knowis Doudna. John and Sarah's second son John, who married Miriam Hall, daughter of Isaac and Ann White Hall, was Joseph W. Doudna's grandmother and grandfather. John and Miriam had three children when they moved from North Carolina to Belmont County, Ohio, in 1804. Nearly two miles south of where Barnesville is now located, they came and settled here four years before the town was laid out. Here John and Miriam's son John III, was born 6th month 24th, 1808. John III married Asenath Garretson on 10th month 8th, 1840. Asenath was granddaughter of Robert Williams. Robert's oldest son was Richard Williams, who married Sara Stanton. Richard's mother was Elizabeth Dearman, who died in 1773 in London, England. Robert Williams was from Ruthin, North Wales.

Robert and Elizabeth D. Williams came from Wales to North Carolina on their honeymoon which took nearly three months, and brought with them Anna Shoebridge, a friend of Elizabeth's. She wanted her to come along for company. They arrived just before the Revolutionary War and settled in Beaufort, Carteret County, North Carolina.

Robert established trading stores at Newberne and also at Beaufort, N.C, besides owning hundreds of acres of land. Robert and Anna S. Williams' daughter, Elizabeth, who was born 4th month 28th, 1778, married Joseph Garretson, who was born 11th month 29th, 1782, a son of William and Mary Garretson. They came from Pennsylvania and moved to Ohio about the year 1800 and settled at Concord, Belmont County, Ohio.

Joseph and Elizabeth were married at Concord, 4th month 26th, 1804 and in 1811, they moved to Barnesville, Ohio, where they lived about a year, and then settled on a farm near one and a half miles south of town. He died there on 4th month 13th, 1855.

It has been said, from accounts we have of Joseph Garretson, that he was a man of great ability and was regarded as one of the best teachers in this part of the state. He spent much of his time teaching school.

It was their oldest child, Asenath Garretson, who was married to John Doudna III, 10th month 8th, 1840. She also taught school and learned the tailor trade and did spinning, knitting and weaving goods for clothes, blankets, coverlets, and carpets. We remembered she had a loom which our father made, with which we used to see her weave when we were children. She also used a twisting wheel, reel, spinning wheel and warping mill. We children used to like to see her use all of these so well and took lots of rides on the warping mill, which we enjoyed very much.

I now have the twisting wheel, spinning wheel and reel that she used to use. Father fixed an attachment on the reel that would click at every hundred rounds, so that she did not have to keep account of the rounds in getting out the warp for carpet.

John and Asenath Garretson Doudna were the parents of four children, Joseph W., Ann, Jesse I. and Sara. The oldest was our father, who was born 100 years ago this winter, 12th month 26th, 1841, on the farm that was left to him by his father, which was a portion of the original land from Thomas Jefferson to John Doudna II. Here

THE REEL

father lived all of his life (over 91 years), except a little while in 1875, the year he and mother were married, while he was helping to build the Boarding School building and barn. That summer Joseph W. and his wife lived at Stillwater near Tacoma on the Francis Davis place *(62420 Tacoma Rd.)* so he could be near his work. They lived there until late fall or early winter and then moved to the home were John A. Doudna now lives, for a short time. They then moved back to the home farm on which he was born and where he lived until his death on 1st month 21st, 1933.

Joseph's father, John Doudna III, died 4th month 3rd, 1848, leaving his mother and four small children. Joseph was a little past six years old. He and his mother and brothers and sisters got along as best they could with the help of relatives at times and neighbors and hiring, until the children grew up. When they were little, they would go quite a distance, some three miles on horseback to the mill. One would ride and hold the grist on, while the other would walk, and open the gates, as the one on the horse could not very well get off to do it and hold the grist on.

One time when they were going to the mill, Joseph W. was on the horse with grinding and they had to pass a school house, and Uncle Jesse Doudna, who was walking, had a little red jacket on, and the school boys took after him and called him a red fox. My, but he did run. He was so badly scared they ran after him for a long way, clear to Aquilla Crews, and Aquilla came out and stopped them, then went and told the teacher about what they had done. The teacher told the boys that if they ever did that again he would whip them even if it was the last day of school. The teacher was Elam Bailey.

When father (Joseph W.) was a small boy, after his father's death, he went with his mother to the pasture by the big woods to look after the sheep, and found that they had gotten out. A snow had fallen, the kind that sticks heavy to the branches of the trees, which made it harder for them to see. She had to go into the woods to look for them and she left him by the bars (of the fence), and told him to stand there until she came back. After a while she got turned around and did not know which way to come back to him. She called to find out where he was, and when he answered it sounded in such a different direction from where she thought she left him, she said, "Joseph, thee is not where I left thee." He said "Yes, mother, I am." She said, "Is thee sure thee is where I left thee?" He answered, "Yes, mother, I am. If I am not, I will give thee my dollar." She then knew she was lost. He told her to come to him which she did and found he was where she left him.

In those days, Joseph's Uncle Asa Garretson lived down toward Somerton. While he was yet a little boy, Uncle Asa took him down to stay a week with him and help him. On Second day morning (Monday) he took him out to the potato field to pick up the potatoes. He was placed near the road and after a while, Uncle Asa had to leave to go to town, so he was left there to work alone. He said he got very lonesome by himself as he had been used to being with the other children, the time seemed long. Along about the middle of the week, Uncle Asa started hauling coal and took him with him and he thought that was so nice and he enjoyed the rest of the week much better.

Another childhood experience when he was small and had to go to the mill on horseback, a neighbor had threatened him where he had to pass in such a manner that his Aunt Elizabeth Wilson went with him to that place and remained there by the bars until he went on to the mill and came back, in order to see that nothing happened to him.

At another time, his grandfather Garretson had to go to the mill. When he was an old man and not very strong, he rode the horse and held the grist on, in a time when the roads were muddy. Father (Joseph) walked along side to help in case of need. As he was going down the hill, where the water works is now located, the horse stumbled and he and the grist both went off in the mud. Father, being too small to be of much help, went and called Lemuel Patterson who lived nearby. This was the same hill on which the boys ran Uncle Jesse down (father's brother), when they called him a red fox.

THE GRAIN FLAIL IN USE

As grandfather was old and too weak to do much work, he would sow the wheat while on horseback. He would tie something over the horses ears to prevent the wheat from getting in its ears, and sowed broadcast. Father (Joseph) and Uncle Jesse had to stay home from school sometimes in order to help flail the wheat and do other things on the farm. Thus they got along until the children were grown.

Joseph had a very mechanical turn and his uncle Asa Garretson had also. Joseph would often go and work with him in his shop. Asa had a carpenter shop and a blacksmith shop. Sometimes he would work with Mason Thomas in his blacksmith shop. Joseph became so competent that he could make or repair almost anything he needed about his farm in after years. They would sometimes borrow things from the neighbors and there was one man in particular who seemed glad to have him do this, as the things were not always in the best of shape, and would sometimes break in his hands. Joseph would then fix them and when he took them home, they were better than when he got them. He finally decided to have his own tools instead of borrowing and fixing up other peoples. Things he had no money to buy, he made for the most part.

Joseph at one time had a Grubber thrashing machine and a horsepower. *(Probably a treadmill type ramp for the horse to operate the machine.)* We saw it used once or twice when he had a small crop or for some reason could hardly get a thrashing machine. He had a burr grist mill to grind wheat for graham flour, which was very good and also ground cornmeal. He would use the horsepower to do this and the sawmill, as he had several different sizes of buzz saws to saw lumber and wood. When he was a young man, he and a neighbor had a saw mill and father used to run the engine. He worked at that for a while and then built a carpenter shop and blacksmith shop for himself. He also did bricklaying and built chimneys and was equipped to move buildings when needed.

Our spring was at the foot of the hill below the orchard. Joseph made what they called a water drawer. In about five or six different places some distance apart, he had poles set about three feet apart at the bottom and about two feet apart at the top and fastened with a cross piece to hold the track or wires on which the pulleys carrying the bucket ran. He had a waxed cord attached to the carrier on which the bucket hung at one end. The other end was fastened just outside of the kitchen door with a handle attached to the wheel, so as to turn it and wind up the cord as it came up, and unwind when we sent it down to the spring.

Sometimes when someone was down at the springhouse, those at the house would send down the butter plate and the cream pitcher in the bucket and the one down there would get the butter and cream and put them in the bucket and then tap on the wires and the one at the house would know to draw it up. When the bucket was sent down for water, it was so arranged with weights on one side that it would tip over and fill up and those at the other end could tell by the sound when it was full. This was always a great curiosity to visitors. It saved many steps and was used until our well was drilled in 1884.

When they were trying to get the Barnesville and Somerton pike, what is now known as route 8, *(State Route 800),* Joseph canvassed the west side and James Edgerton the east side with a paper to get names in order to get it.

Elisha Doudna, a friend in the Richland neighborhood wanted him to come and do some building for him. *(That would be the area around Richland Meeting which was located between Barnesville and Quaker City on Shannons Run Road.)* Others followed and he was kept busy much of the time for some years building houses and barns.

It was while he was working in this neighborhood, that he met our mother, Rosetta Hall. She was the daughter of Joseph W. and Sara Webster Hall, and a great-granddaughter of Mary Doudna, the oldest daughter of the kidnapped John Doudna, who had married Isaac Hall before leaving North Carolina.

Joseph and Rosetta Doudna were married 4th month 29th, 1875. At this time, he was working on the Boarding School building *(Olney Friends School),* and after working on the school house for a considerable time, the foreman of the barn quit. Alfred Brantingham wanted father to take his place so badly as foreman and take up the work where he left off. Father hesitated quite a bit as he felt it to be too much of an undertaking to take up where another man had left off. He was afraid that in such an important job, everything might not come out all right.

When the day came for the raising of the barn, Francis Davis (the superintendent on the job) said to father, "Now, Joseph, I don't want thee to do any work. Just walk along ahead of the men, show them what pieces to pick up and where to put them." There was close to a hundred men to help at the raising and just as the sun went down, the last piece was laid up without a mistake. Father felt much relieved.

After working on the Boarding School building and barn that summer, he and mother went to yearly meeting while it was still at Mount Pleasant. Later they moved back over here on the farm, which he enjoyed so much. But at times he still worked at his carpenter work.

In 1878, 1st month 26th, when mother's great-grandmother, the oldest daughter of the kidnapped boy died (she lacked two weeks of being 100 years old), there were at that time representatives of five generations living. She was a great aunt to our father. He made her casket, as he did such work when called on, and made them out of nice walnut wood which he lined, padded and varnished.

At different times he was urged by the Watt Mining Car and Wheel Company to come and make patterns for them as he was a very good hand to make them. He had made some patterns of cogwheels of different sizes which he wanted for his own use and took them to the company so they could make the wheels from them. He felt best satisfied to stay on the farm with his family.

About 12 years after they were married, our house burned, 4th month 5th, 1887. It was a cold day with a little snow in the air. Brother John was about two months old. We then stayed until it got warm enough, (about five weeks) in one part of Uncle Jesse I. Doudna's house on an adjoining farm which was also a part of the original farm. By that time, we could move into an outbuilding by putting up a lean-to kitchen so we would not have to go back and forth to our work. As soon as they could, they began work on the new house of which father did the greater part. Joseph's Uncle Isaac Doudna was out on a visit from Wisconsin. He and father's brother, Uncle Jesse, helped keep the farm work going. Uncle Asa Garretson, Aaron Frame, James Frame, John Bundy and William Henry Patterson each donated a day or two apiece on the carpenter work.

Father made a contract that summer with James Edgerton, to take our berries to town for shipping. Father was to see that they were taken to the road for him, in order to save him coming in after them. In doing so much of the carpenter work himself and overseeing and helping with the farming, it was fall before we moved in and then it was not all done inside. He could work at that at times in the winter.

Father had just built a new grainery and just got it completed when the house burned. The grainery had a nice airy loft overhead, so we put a bed up there for Taylor Farmer to sleep in, and when we had company to stay overnight, the visiting men and sometimes father would go out there with him, in order to make room for the women folks in the house.

We had a large carriage house with a floor in it which with the lean-to kitchen, we got along very well for the time we lived there. We were very comfortable and happy. After the kitchen had been built a day or two, one of the neighbors came one spring morning while we were eating breakfast and pleasantly said, "Hello, Joe, you are in your new house are you?".

There were seven of the eight children then, as Rosetta B. was born after we had lived in the new house a while in 1889.

As the years rolled on, Joseph and Rosetta, besides raising their own family of eight children, (Mary J. and Sara A., the twins; Asenath Elma, who married Irving E. Bailey; Dillwyn W. who married Edith R. Carter; Lizzie C. who married Alva B. Hartley, Joseph H. who married Nora E. Hartley, John A. who married Marietta Carter and Rosetta B. who married Frank A. Louhoff) they also made a home for at least three old people and three children at times. One of them was Alva Cook, who was there over 12 years. At two different times, there were 12 to sit around our table during Joseph and Rosetta's married life and these were very pleasant times.

As the children married, they all settled nearby, which was a great comfort to Joseph and Rosetta. Father would often say he could go up on the hill above the house and see where each one lived. Thus the time went on with the great favor of not having a break in their immediate family for over 51 years, when a daughter, Sara A., one of the twins, who will be remembered by many for her faithfulness in nursing at the Friends Boarding School, near Barnesville, Ohio, for eleven terms, passed away. She at one time joined the faculty as teacher for a few weeks at their urgent request, when one of their number was sick. For several years, she was a member of the faculty of Friends Indian School at Tunesassa, New York, as girls caretaker or governess. She came home to help take care of her aged parents, which she did for some years, and passed away 5th month 28th, 1926, from this scene of action, we fully believe "to that house not made with hands, eternal in the heavens" aged 50 years, 3 months and 11 days.

As father expressed it "Fifty beautiful years." Then Joseph and Rosetta with their remaining twin daughter, Mary J., lived on together between six and seven years longer. Joseph especially growing more and more feeble until 1st month 21st, 1933, when he passed away at the age of 91 years and 26 days, and we doubt not, is receiving the reward of a well spent life. Our family in the home being now reduced to two, one or the other of brother John's boys lived with us until after our dear mother was done with the trials of time, and on the 26th of 5th month, 1939, was called, we do believe, to join the loved in the Heavenly Home, aged 88 years, 8 months and 21 days.

Since then the home where our dear father spent practically all of his life, *(59864 Hall-Boston Road)* has become the home of his grandson, Kenneth Lloyd Doudna, with his wife and baby daughter, the son of John A. Doudna and the fifth generation from the "kidnapped boy."

Written by: Elma D. Bailey and Mary J. Doudna, Barnesville, Ohio

THE HOME OF SARA DOUDNA
Sara Doudna 1846 – 1912

Recollections relating to one of the homes of the original Doudna farm, two miles south of Barnesville, Ohio. The home of Sara, the youngest child of John (III) and Asenath Garretson Doudna, and granddaughter of the first owners and first settlers on the farm, John (II) and Miriam Hall Doudna. The writer, Ella Galloway, is one of the third generation reared on the land of these ancestors and pioneers.

My mother, the above named granddaughter (Sara), lived the sixty-six years and five months of her life on this farm land. About twenty-six and a half years of this time at the home of her parents (her mother was left a widow before Sara's second birthday); about twenty-nine and a half years where John A. Doudna now lives, and ten years on that part of the farm where three daughters of her brother Joseph W. Doudna now lives. (Formerly the Edgerton, then the Thomasson farm.) My parents, John III and Asenath Garretson Doudna, were married 12th month 10th, 1872, but began housekeeping in the spring of 1873 in the house on Boston Road and this was my birthplace (4-9-1874) and my home until nearly twenty-one years old.

As to the work that was going on around me, in the late eighteen seventies, I remember very little, but I believe that mother and grandmother together, continued weaving carpets at various times during that period in the building which was used for that purpose at the home place. When this building was moved down to the ridge field to Uncle Jesse I. Doudna's land to be partitioned, plastered and finished for his dwelling house, I think the weaving loom was not used for some time, but Uncle Jesse soon moved to Morgan County, Ohio and the loom was set up again, on the upper floor of his home, and mother wove carpets there for a few seasons and later at our own general purpose work shop. This building was built for, and first used for home evaporating of fruits and sweet corn, but was soon used for many other purposes.

I do not remember how many seasons our evaporator was used, but more or less, I think, nearly every season for at least fifteen years. That always made work-a-plenty for all of us, but most for mother because the work was somewhat on the order of kitchen work, a kind of extension of kitchen work. Mother's good management was necessary in order to get it done successfully.

When we were drying sweet corn, she did most of the cutting of the corn. This was done on a slaw cutter, which was attached to a heavy board on curved metal legs, bent cabriole fashion, and elevated so that a large pan could be placed under the cutter. The corn was then spread on the cloth-covered, wood framed wire trays, and the trays were rotated in the three track drying box, each fresh tray being placed on the lower track nearest the small furnace. About half way in this course, the corn on each tray was scraped from the cloth, from the corners to the center, until all was loosened and then it was spread again to finish drying evenly. Close watching and regulating of the heat was necessary in order that no corn was scorched or the least bit overheated or discolored. Mother looked after all of this or else directed.

The other part of the work was keeping fires, husking corn and removing the silk (all of it) after which the ears were placed in a large basket (a round heavy splint bushel basket) and this suspended in a kettle of nearly simmering hot water, where it remained about fifteen minutes and then was carried to the drying house for cutting.

In the first few years we also dried a good bit of fruit. Apples, peaches, cherries and raspberries. Apples turned out best, and indeed were very nice and that way was a great improvement over sun drying and oven drying.

A great deal of wood chopping was required for these fires and for the wood burning cook stove which we used until after the house was remodeled. I can remember no time when we did not have an ample supply in the wood boxes ready for use. Most of the time there were large piles all around the wood yard.

We usually made as much maple syrup as we could each year. This required labor quite out of proportion to profit.

There was no cellar under our house, but there was a good springhouse nearly half way between the old home and ours, which we used for a number of years for keeping milk, cream, butter, cottage cheese, and so forth in the summer months. It stood north of the farm road some distance above the filled in bridge, in a cool sheltered place, where there was a strong flowing spring, and there were a number of trees all around the banks on either side at that time. A real "Shady Dell" location.

When I was quite young, my parents built a good sized cave, or cave cellar. The greater part of the field stone used for the walls were hauled from Uncle Jesse's part of the farm, a good deal of which was very stony and also steep or hilly. I believe there was one high point which the family called "Mt. Pisgah." Several years later this cave was enlarged and much improved. The sod and top covering was removed, then center pole and side poles, plank and other timbers were replaced with new lumber. The walls were built higher and a cement floor laid. We then had a good roomy cave. It was well ventilated and was kept whitewashed inside and likely was a more sanitary place for keeping milk, milk products and various other foods than many a cellar under a dwelling.

At this home we had a dug well. It was not more than twenty-eight feet deep, but the water was very clear and cold and nearly free of lime deposit. It was considered the best drinking water anywhere along the Boston Road, for many people came to our well. It had a good sized well house over it and the water was drawn with "oaken bucket" and windlass.

In the 1880's there were a great many people who passed by on foot and many who rode horseback, including a good many women. They rode on side saddle and wore the long full gathered black cambric, and other material, riding skirts.

An amusing incident that I recall occurred about the mid 1880's, when an intoxicated horseback rider returning home from town (Barnesville), long after dark, fell off his horse when he attempted to ride in at the front yard gate, at John G. Halls. Hearing some disturbance outside, our neighbors went outside with some caution until they learned what had happened. The man was helped upon his horse and started on his way again in the right direction. When he gave his name, he was asked if he didn't live at Boston. He indignantly replied, No, he wouldn't be caught dead in Boston, he lived in Temperanceville. (Two small towns, not far apart some ten miles south.)

These are a few recollections relating mainly to the 1880's, and here I will mention briefly the dreadful winter we passed through in 1880 and 1881. There was an epidemic of diphtheria that fall and when I had going to school just five weeks, my first term, I was taken ill with the disease. In about three weeks I was recovering when my younger sister was more severely stricken. She too appeared to be nearly out of danger, we thought, in about three weeks. But she suffered a relapse and in another week passed away at the age of four years and four months. Not long after that, mother took the disease and was very ill. In the early spring, the baby sister died at the age of eleven months. We had sickness all through that winter which was, as I remember, a very cold winter with deep snows.

Mother liked the outdoor work better than work indoors and she was especially interested in having trees planted wherever space could be spared. There must have been, in the early 1870's, few fruit trees of any kind around our home, but a young orchard was soon planted above the highway, nearly opposite the house, and came into bearing long before I was grown up. The good varieties of apples and many peach trees and other kinds were planted time to time. A few of some kind or other nearly every year.

We also raised small fruits for market, first strawberries, and later blackberries and red raspberries. Our farm was a small one and it was necessary to try to make the most out of the land we had. I believe it was fully demonstrated here that all hands can keep just as busy on a small farm as on a large one.

The 1890's are often referred to as the "Gay Nineties" and the 1840's as the "Fabulous Forties," but the terms for either period were not equally applicable to all parts of the country, and of course did not originate in that broad meaning. For ourselves and most of our neighbors, there was only normal change in the 1890's, I think, with respect to our work and other activities. We were still living in the "Horse and Buggy days" and even in the next decade there seemed to be hardly more than the shadow of coming events and great change, then near at hand.

No doubt several of the cousins who remained on the land, first belonging to our great grandparents, have written about the later times around the old environs from their personal experience and knowledge. They have also written about many other circumstances and events of earlier times which naturally were more often mentioned at the old home which was also the life-long home of Uncle Joseph W. Doudna, where books and papers, early writing and records, deeds and such were kept and were available for reference.

I will add that mother lived the same active life to the last at her later home, and we had noticed with little difference in her good health and remarkable energy, her ambition, initiative and determined effort at all times, under any difficulties; characteristics which she possessed in marked degrees.

Only three years before her death, her home burned down destroying much of its contents. This happened the day before Christmas in 1909. Mother then had great inconvenience for several months in temporary living quarters, and also much extra work during the time that preparation was made for building a new house. This was the only way she was willing to consider.

Timber for building was cut and sawed on the farm and prior to building the dwelling house, a good sized building was put up for a temporary home on the site of the house that burned, where the oldest part of that house had stood for eighty-eight years, with additions built in 1833 and 1858. Carpenters were working at this house at the time of the great meteoric display in 1833.

The new house was built on higher ground above the lane or farm road, to the west and north of the other location, and in sight of the Boston road and where mother's two former homes were in plain view. *(Location, Section 19 & 20 Warren Twp.)*

Once more the work was done as it had been undertaken, and mother lived in the new home, but hardly more than a year and a half. Her death came unexpectedly, December 3, 1912, after a short illness with pneumonia. It was near dawn of that day that she passed away into the "Silent Land, where toil shall cease and rest begin."

Written by: Ella L. Galloway, daughter of Sara Doudna

MY PIONEER GRANDMOTHER – ANNA HALL EDGERTON
(1795 – 1876)

It seems a long time ago since I heard my grandmother, Anna Hall Edgerton, tell her grandchildren stories of her own childhood and of the pioneer days in Ohio. Her old age was spent in the home of her daughter Sarah, my mother, who had three sons and two daughters. I have heard my father say that he had "lived with her for twenty years and that he had never heard her speak ill of or to anyone" surely a remarkable testimony from a son-in-law who knew her in the intimate give and take of daily living in a family composed of three generations. To the day of her death at eighty-one years, her back was straighter than that of any of her daughters and she enjoyed company, even when her memory had begun to fail, so that she could not be sure of the names of the visitors. She received them very graciously, hoping that some indication as to who they were would appear in the course of the conversation. If the desired lead was given, she would slip out of the room and ask some other member of the family in a gentle whisper, "Who is it? Who is it?".

Her memories of earlier days, as is so often the case with older people, were clearer than those of later years, so that she gave to us children a vivid picture of her experiences from the time she, as a little girl of seven, moved with her family from North Carolina to Ohio. Her parents, Joseph and Christiana Peele Hall, were comfortably settled on a farm in Edgecombe County, North Carolina, and Friends there pled with them not to undertake the hazards and discomforts of the long journey. Their conscience, however, was uneasy with the use of slave labor. They wished their children to grow up in a country free from its effects and when the Northwest Territory was opened on such terms as made settlement practicable for small landowners, they resolved to remove thither. Joseph Hall and one of his older sons went out to Ohio on horseback in the spring of 1802, purchased a considerable acreage near what is now Harrisville, raised a log cabin and barn, and returned to North Carolina for the rest of the family. The wife and mother, Christiana, who was a semi-invalid, made the trip of some 600 miles in a two-wheeled cart, lying on a feather bed slung hammock-wise from the four posts. They had two other carts of their own and had besides, engaged a neighbor to accompany them, bringing most of their household goods and supplies. Unfortunately, he had been paid in advance, so that when, in the last stage of the journey, they encountered a teamster homeward bound, the neighbor unloaded their possessions in the woods six miles from the new home and left them to shift for themselves. This was the more difficult as they were among the first settlers in that part of Ohio and were obliged to cut down trees and make a road for part of the way. One of their possessions we still have in use, a sturdy walnut chest that must have been heavily loaded for the journey. In due time they arrived safely and wintered in the log shelters previously erected for themselves and their stock. The two buildings had been located near two convenient springs of fresh water. The choice of the home spring was a fortunate one, though entirely accidental. One morning when the weather was beginning to feel warmer, Anna, my grandmother, was walking around the barnyard among some loose cornstalks. Feeling something move under her foot, she looked down and saw a rattlesnake, still torpid from the winter cold. When the men investigated, they found a cave in the rocks above the barn spring which contained 60 rattlers. Had the home been built where the barn was located it seems likely that someone of the family would have been bitten before the danger would have been discovered. As it was, seven-year-old Anna never forgot the day she stepped on a live rattler and escaped unharmed.

In the year 1810, when she still lacked two months of being fifteen years old, she was married to my grandfather, James Edgerton, whose brother Richard, her sister Mary had married. She had been her father's housekeeper since she was eleven-years-old when her delicate mother had passed away. James was at this time twenty-four, a minister in the Society of Friends, and a man of such settled character and reputation that Joseph Hall was entirely satisfied with the engagement, especially as he himself was in poor health and felt concerned to see that this youngest of his daughters should be suitably provided for. His approval as well as his affection is evidenced by his making the trip to Wheeling with her to purchase the wedding dress. After she had selected a simple white cotton material, which he purchased, he himself chose a peach bloom silk of which he bought enough to make both dress and bonnet to match. Anna, although so young, had already reached her mature height. She was straight and tall with auburn hair and must have been a striking figure in her beautiful costume with short sleeves and long gloves up to the elbows, and bridal slippers on her feet. The meetinghouse at Short Creek was made of logs and was heated by a charcoal brazier which rested on a central stone. *(Short Creek Meeting was located in Jefferson County, just west of Mt. Pleasant.)* As the wedding was on the 10th of Fourth Month, artificial heat was still required and grandmother used to tell with quiet humor about the sermon that was preached over her on her wedding day. At that time, a Welsh Friend, Mary Wichel, was travelling through Ohio on a religious visit. From the various incidents related of her, she seems to have been something of a character. Unused to the monotony of pioneer food, she grew weary of a steady diet of poultry. At one home where she was staying, she looked out of the window and saw them trying to catch a chicken for dinner. She raised the window quickly and called, "Let the chicken go and catch a pig!" Hearing of the intended marriage of so young a girl, she expressed her disapproval and, being present at the ceremony, preached about "the proud and naughty daughter of Zion." When she was questioned afterward as to what she meant, she replied "it was because of the way the bride switched her silk dress around the charcoal brazier." In telling us the story, grandmother used to add that Mary Wichel herself had been married in her ninetieth year and that it always seemed to grandmother "just as bad to marry in one's second childhood as in one's first." After the wedding feast, Anna Hall Edgerton rode pillion behind her husband to her new home in Somerton, passing by forest paths through what is now Barnesville. *(pillion – a pad on a horse's back behind the saddle for another person to ride on.)*

Most of her new neighbors were squatters without much education. She was often lonely as her husband was frequently away at night. He was a surveyor and went to the river to see to arrangements for settlers taking up new land. In her isolation, however, Anna Edgerton did not forget the amenities of life. Quaker women in those days wore caps over their hair both at home and under their bonnets when they went abroad. Grandmother used to tell how she got hold of a cap pattern cut rounded under the ears, instead of square cornered and tied under the chin. She made herself several caps in this new Eastern fashion and was wearing one when her father came on a visit. Joseph Hall might buy a peach bloom silk, but he was shocked at this new style in caps and said to Anna, "I never thought that a daughter of mine would have worn such a thing."

At one time, Grandfather Edgerton was bitten by a copperhead snake. As she ran for help to some of the neighbors, Anna must have remembered the time, years before, when she had stepped on a poisonous snake and got away unharmed. Acting on the advice of older and more experienced women, she put the warm flesh of a newly killed chicken on the wound. Her husband recovered but was ever afterward conscious of discomfort at the same time of year as that when he had been bitten.

Eight children were born to Grandfather and Grandmother, five daughters and three sons. Grandfather had built a two-story brick house with a central hall, but had not nailed down the floor of the living room when he was seized with a mortal illness. A terrible epidemic passed over that part of Ohio with fatal consequences in many homes. It was a medical conviction of the time that fever patients must not have any liquids, and those nursing the sick kept them in an agony of thirst, until they died or got better. Sometimes there were not enough nurses to maintain this careful watch. One boy, during this epidemic managed, it is said, to crawl away unobserved to the maple grove where he drained a bucket of sugar water. He was one of the very few who recovered. Grandfather and his two oldest sons died, as did also an adopted boy, Vernon, whom they had taken to raise. Grandmother was thus left with five daughters and one son, David, a boy of ten. The young widow had the farm to manage and six children to feed and educate. Fortunately, she had early known responsibility and she met the heavy burden bravely. Twelve years after her first husband's death, she remarried and had one more daughter who died early. Of the Edgerton children, my mother, Sarah, was the last of the daughters to leave the parental home. Sarah married Samuel Walton, my father, and went to Philadelphia to set up housekeeping. After two years in Pennsylvania, they returned to Ohio. Grandmother came to live with them and so it was that the lives of Sarah's children were enriched by my mother's memories of Pioneer days.

Written by: Anna Walton, Moyland, PA

EDGERTON HISTORY
James Edgerton, Sr. – 1764 – 1825
His son, Joseph Edgerton - 1797 – 1865

James Edgerton Sr. and his wife, Sarah Cox Edgerton removed from North Carolina to Belmont County, Ohio in 1805. They located on a tract of land on Captina Creek about three and one half miles southeast of Stillwater Meetinghouse.

Soon after coming to the state, he built a mill for grinding grain for the community. The mill was run by water power as most other mills were in those days. This mill was sold to Isaac Patten some twenty years later. Their son Richard, born in 1786, married Mary Hall, daughter of Joseph and Christiana Peele Hall, in 1808 and located on a quarter section of land about two and one half miles from Barnesville, and not far from Ridge Meetinghouse.

Two years later his next younger brother James married Anna Hall, a sister of his brother Richard's wife. They began their married life on a 160 acre tract of land one half mile east of Somerton. These brothers and their wives must have been frugal and industrious, for we find each with large families housed in substantial brick houses.

In the spring of 1828, Richard died of typhus fever. Within three weeks, his brother James and two of James' older sons were removed by death of the same disease. The two bereaved sisters labored faithfully to keep their children together, and gave them as good an education as other Friends children could get in those days. Both the brick houses mentioned above have been destroyed by fire, so there is little left to mark the places, once hallowed by the presence of the brave spirits of those who labored there.

When James Edgerton and Anna Hall were married in 1810, the bride was not quite fifteen years of age, and could neither read nor write, but she was well developed and skilled in the work of those early days and wove her own linen and blankets. The young couple had arranged to be married the day following Monthly Meeting, at which they "passed Meeting." The procedure probably originated from a desire of Friends to prevent any unwise or hasty union, and by making it public so there would be no question in regard to its legality. The parties were to stand up first in Men's Meeting, and then in the Women's, and declare the "Continuance of their intention of Marriage" with each other. They asked for an appointed Meeting, but Women's Meeting refused to grant the request and they had to wait until the regular Meeting the next week. The bride's family had made provisions for the wedding dinner the next day, and the groom was thirty miles from home, which meant much more than now. It was thought the Women's Meeting was influenced by a ministering Friend from England. Perhaps she thought the bride was too young, and would be older in another week. This English Friend was married when she was very old, and the disappointed bride, in recalling the event in after years, said she "thought it was better to marry in first childhood than in second."

Joseph Edgerton, whose wife was Charity Doudna, like his brother Richard settled in Ridge neighborhood where he continued to live until late in life, when he removed to Iowa. *(Ridge neighborhood refers to the area served by Chestnut Ridge Meeting located south of Barnesville on Chestnut Ridge Rd.)* He was one of the favored ministers of Ohio Yearly Meeting *of the Religious Society of Friends.*

In those early days wild turkeys were plentiful, and those people had a novel way of catching them. They would build a pen out of fence rails, five or six feet high and tightly covered on top. Under the bottom rail, a trench was dug large enough to allow a turkey to enter the pen. Corn was then sprinkled in the pen and in the trench. The corn would lead them into the pen, and trying to find a way out, they would look above and miss the way they got in. Frequently, several would get in at one time. When dressed and taken to market, the sale price was usually a quarter.

    James and Sarah Cox Edgerton's descendants are numerous and many of them have figured largely in the history of Ohio Yearly Meeting since its beginning. Some of the more prominent ones are: Joseph Edgerton, Unice Thomasson, Rachel E. Patterson, Abigail Vail, Rebecca Dewees, Jesse Edgerton, Walter Edgerton, Rachel E. Cope and Esther Fowler, all ministers.

                                        Written by: James Walton, Barnesville, OH

AARON FRAME
1815 – 1896

Aaron Frame was born in 1815 near West Grove, Harrison County, Ohio, where his parents, William and Ruanna (Thomas) Frame, settled soon after their marriage. When he was eight years old, his father was taken away by death, leaving a family of four sons, Aaron being the oldest, and the youngest only a few hours old. Aaron could remember riding behind his mother on horseback to attend Yearly Meeting at Mount Pleasant, when a boy.

Aaron Frame's farm "Jolly Run" near Harrisville, OH

In 1836 he married Talitha Thompson and settled near Georgetown, Ohio, where he owned a small farm and a saw mill which was operated by water power from a stream running through the farm. The house which he built on this farm is still standing. Here ten of their eleven children were born, all except the youngest. Three of the children died in infancy.

In 1856, Aaron and Talitha Frame moved to Iowa, being attracted there by cheap land and feeling the need of more employment for their growing family. There was no railroad so far west at that time, so the eldest son and an uncle drove their team across country, taking what they could in the wagon, and the rest of the family followed by steamboat. They started from Wheeling, West Virginia, going down the Ohio river and then up the Mississippi to Muscatine, Iowa, the trip taking two weeks. They were met at Muscatine by the sixteen-year-old son, Thompson, who had gone before. In 1860 the beloved wife and mother was removed by death, leaving a family of eight children, ranging in age from nineteen to four years.

In the fall of 1863, Aaron Frame was married to Achsah Smith, of Guernsey, Ohio. In the spring of 1864 they sold their Iowa home and came to Barnesville, Ohio, where they settled in the Stillwater neighborhood, near Pigeon Point, or Mt. Holly. The farm had been owned at one time by Issachar Schofield and they bought it from his son, Jonathan Schofield. *(This farm is currently owned by Olney Friends School across the lake from the school, off Sandy Ridge Rd.)*

On this farm there was a commodious two-story log house which had probably at one time been two houses, later joined together by a hallway between. One part, used as a dining room, was two steps lower than the other. A one story frame structure added at the west end adjoining the dining room, served as a kitchen. The walls of this part were ceiled inside with boards. There was a small pantry in connection with the kitchen and a convenient dish cupboard opened through from kitchen to dining room. At the back of the house there was a porch, one side of which was a shed for storing fuel. Changes were made from time to time and finally the house was weather boarded on the outside.

There were three open fireplaces in the house, one in the parlor at the east end, with a chimney serving for both of these. There was a cook stove in the kitchen, the pipe going into the chimney at one side of the fireplace. The dining room had a swinging crane for kettles and they sometimes used a dutch oven there for baking by covering it with hot embers.

A large brick oven outside was used for the regular baking. The women of the family would get the bread, pies, etc. ready, then put them in the heated oven and clean up the kitchen while the baking went on. The floors were all of natural wood, without paint or varnish, and my mother used to tell us how they liked to scrub and scour the wood because it cleaned up so nicely and looked so well when done.

A closed stairway in the hall led to the second story where there were two large rooms and one small one. No way of heating was provided for these bedrooms. They were separated by board partitions and instead of clothes presses, there were large wooden pegs in the walls at convenient places for hanging clothing. The stairway was built of cherry timber and enclosed with cherry boards. When the house was torn down, Uncle William Frame used some of these boards to make the top of an extension table and another smaller table. The wood took a fine polish. The walls of the main part of the house were simply the hewn logs with strips of chinking and plaster between and had to be whitewashed every spring. The joists and floor boards of the upper story made the ceiling for the rooms below.

Nearby was a small house for Aaron Frame's mother, for whom he had long provided a home. There was also a house built over the spring which was at the west end and in the upper story of this building were rooms where Achsah's father and mother, Samuel and Elizabeth Smith, lived for a time. Beneath, in back of the spring, was a cellar for keeping vegetables from freezing in the winter. In a room below the spring was a trough for the water to flow through, making a cool place to keep milk butter, etc. in summer.

In earlier days, when Issachar Schofield lived on the farm, a school was kept in this upper part of the spring house. Aunt Florence Frame tells of her grandmother, Increase Dennis (afterward Increase Thomas) teaching this school. She also relates an amusing little incident which her grandmother used to tell her. The Schofields would sometimes leave their little son Jonathan with the teacher while they were away from home. To keep him from wandering, she would pin his clothes to her dress or apron. One day she was sewing and not finding a pin handy, she took a few stitches instead. The child had a habit of investigating from time to time to see if he was still fastened. On this occasion when he discovered the stitches, he burst into a loud wail, "Oh, I'll never get loose! I'll _never_ get loose!"

Also west of the house was a sorghum mill. Sorghum molasses was made here in the fall and maple molasses in the

spring. We grandchildren loved to go to Grandfather's with a load of cane. A horse was hitched to a sweep which furnished power to turn the great rollers that pressed the sap out of the cane. The sap was conducted by a trough to the boiling shed below. Here a long shallow pan was set over a brick furnace. We liked to watch the sap bubbling and steaming in this pan until it became thick enough for the delicious molasses to spread on our bread. It had to be watched closely and stirred with a long wooden paddle and the scum taken off occasionally. We were sometimes allowed to boil some of the molasses to make taffy. The pulling of this was fun when it did not stick to our fingers, which it was apt to do if we did not run out of doors once in a while to cool it off.

In the year 1875, while engaged in building a new house on the farm, Aaron Frame was again called upon to give up his bosom companion, which was a check on the building for a while. But after a time the house was finished. The children had all settled in homes of their own, but his aged mother was still under his care, and with a housekeeper they moved to the new house. The mother passed away some years later at the age of ninety-three. The old house stood for many years longer and was occupied at various times, once by the family of a colored man, Mark Peterson. Among the white families was that of Lee Price. Also Wilmer Hall, from Richland, and his wife lived there for a time just after their marriage, occupying only the old parlor.

In the year 1885, Aaron Frame and Lavina Wright, of Ypsilanti, Michigan, were married. They were permitted to live congenially together until the year 1896 when Grandfather passed away suddenly. He had felt for some time that he might go this way, as he was aware of a heart weakness.

And so "One generation passeth away and another generation cometh." Is the world any better for our having lived in it?

Written by: Sarah C. (Bundy Holloway) Cooper, granddaughter of Aaron Frame

Aaron Frame's farm with Olney Friends School in the background.

FRIENDS MEETINGS IN BELMONT AND GUERNSEY COUNTIES, OHIO

Concord Meeting, East end of Colerain Township, Belmont County, Ohio, near center of Section 7. First Meeting on logs, a log house built in 1800. First church in Belmont County.

Quarterly Meeting opened and held at Short Creek 1807. Monthly Meetings under it Concord, Short Creek, Plymouth, Plainfield, Stillwater.

Ohio Yearly Meeting established at Short Creek 1813, about one mile west of Mt. Pleasant, Jefferson County, Ohio. Yearly Meeting House built at Mt. Pleasant 1815-1816.

Stillwater Meeting. In 1803 a cabin was built by James Vernon near the French or Township graveyard and in it convened a Friends Meeting. It was the first gathering for religious worship in Warren Township. Ruth Boswell preached the first sermon and business was transacted.

In 1804 a log house was built in the northeast corner of what is now Stillwater graveyard, the first house in Warren Township for worship. Another room was added in 1805 for the women's meeting.

Stillwater Preparative Meeting set up spring of 1805.

Stillwater Monthly Meeting, a division of Concord, reported to Short Creek Quarter in 1807. Fully organized 1808.

In 1812 the brick church was built about 300 feet south of the log house and it was enlarged in 1823 or 1824 to take care of the Quarterly Meeting. Hosea Doudna was Janitor.

Stillwater Quarterly Meeting opened 11-28-1821.

Stillwater Meeting House built for Yearly Meeting, 1878.

Friends Boarding School built one mile east of Barnesville, Belmont County, Ohio in 1875. Rebuilt after the fire of 3-31-1910.

Friends Meeting House at St. Clairsville built 1809-10. Meetings held 1807 at other places.

Barnesville Meeting House built 1875. 30 x 40 ft., two story, $3000. School upstairs. *(this was on the corner of Lincoln and South Streets.)*

Captina Indulged Meeting 1808; Preparative Meeting 1816.

Chestnut Ridge asked for Meeting 11-1811, granted in 1815.

Richland asked for Meeting in 1809, granted in 1816

Stillwater Quarter 1854 divided and Pennsville Quarter set up 1854. (Harvey Smith gives 1842.)

Plainfield Monthly Meeting made up of Plainfield and Flushing 1808.

Stillwater Minutes lost – 1817 to 1826

Stillwater grounds held by Friends from 1804. Contain 10 acres frin Cory.

First Friends school built in 1806 near the northwest corner of Section No. 1, southeast corner of Warren Township, Belmont County, Ohio.

Submitted by: W. V. Webster 1-31-1942. Most of the above history from Joseph Garretson, Sr. and Jonathan Schofield.

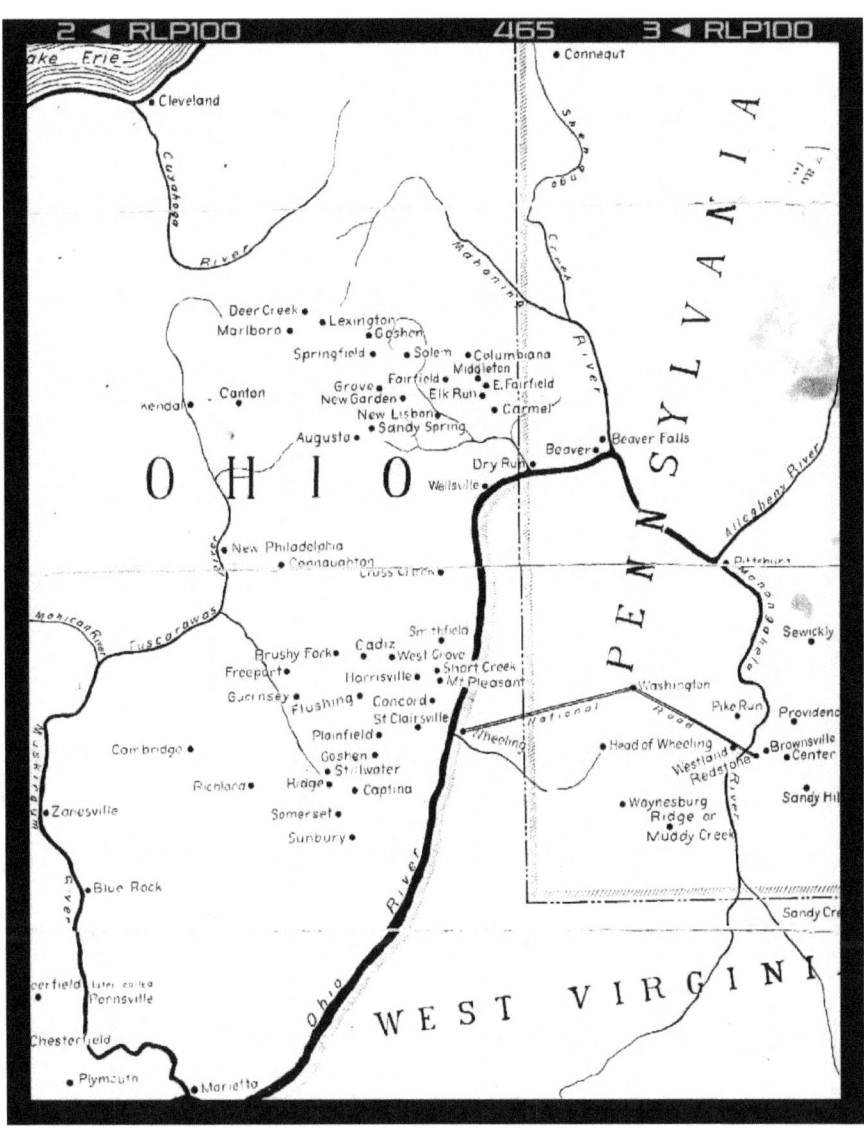

FRIENDS BOARDING SCHOOL
"OLNEY"

This collection of word pictures, of the homes and people of Stillwater Quarterly Meeting of the olden times, would not be quite complete without a sketch of Friends Boarding School.

Schools were one of the early concerns of these pioneers, lately come from Virginia and the Carolinas.

Moses was learned in all the wisdom of the Egyptians, and Paul sat at the feet of Gamaliel, but not till the burning bush and the "light shone round them from Heaven" did either reach full possession of his powers. So Friends believed religion and education must go hand in hand.

The wonderful Friends Yearly Meeting House at Mt. Pleasant was built or completed in 1815 and soon after, the subject of a boarding school was discussed. It did not materialize until 1837, and was situated not far from the Yearly Meeting House on a farm of seventy-four acres. The minutes say "It was to be a finishing school for the youth of both sexes."

Friends' peculiar contribution to education of that day was that they gave thought to their daughters as well as their sons. These first years, boys and girls must be kept entirely separate, except for Meetings and lectures, even had separate dining rooms. When it was decided for all to eat in one room, one of the teachers thought it was so improper that she would not go down to the first meal.

One day while sitting in Meeting, the cry of fire was heard, and all went out to find the leaves in the woods near the barn had caught fire. It was soon put out. When the astonished officers saw the boys and girls working together in distress, one said, "I am afraid fires will be started water will not put out."

Boys and girls of today can hardly picture the primitive arrangements of that time. Only tallow candles for light, not even a cook stove, as cooking was done over a wood fire, or in a Dutch oven. They had to wash on the porch, their towels often freezing. One of the first students writes, "We did not think of these things as hardships, but felt we were enjoying a great privilege to be there."

It was with real regret in 1874, owing to doctrinal differences, the Supreme Court of Ohio decreed that this building be given to another branch of Friends, but the school itself was not given up. Stillwater was soon decided as a promising center for Ohio Yearly Meeting and the present site selected upon which to build a new Boarding School. It was an unsightly wooded field, from which the best timber had been taken. We can but marvel at the vision and foresight and courage of the Friends of that day. They worked together to collect funds, fell trees and commence to work. The brick

was burned on the grounds. The Laundry was built first and Francis Davis and wife moved in and boarded the hands. Francis managed the building of the school house and barn.

The school building was the size of the present one, but had three stories. School was opened on New Year's, 1876, although the halls were still strewed with lumber and shavings and many of the doors were not hung.

There was no furnace, only stoves and grates, but a happier band of students would be hard to find, even today. The next winter they had the largest enrollment, 109, and we wonder how faculty, helpers and all were housed in the one building. The first graduating class was in 1879.

During the early years of the school, they graduated twice a year. In the Winter term of the first class were Wilson Steer, Martha M. Holloway, and Anna Walton, all are living today. In the Spring term were Anna C. Llewellyn, who is now deceased, Mary C. Bundy, who is living and Emma Holloway, deceased.

In the spring of 1910, the school building was burned, but again there were worthy Friends with courage and foresight, and immediately steps were taken for rebuilding. The outer walls were intact, and the present building was erected similar to the former one, only two stories to comply with State law for schools.

Separate dormitories were necessary and other buildings were added. A home for the Principal, a cottage for helpers, one for the farmer and his wife, a laundry and a power house. The latest addition is a modern gymnasium. So that it all forms a desirable school plant, where faculty and students and work and recreation help to develop the "true Christian way of life."

May we of the present day, meet the needs which arise in this war torn world, with brave courage shown by our worthy forefathers.

The name "Olney" was given by Louis Taber, who was a highly valued teacher and lecturer at Mt. Pleasant a hundred years ago. He was much interested in the new school at Barnesville, Ohio, and gave some lectures here and wrote the poem "Olney Green" for one of the first Literaries. He was a great admirer of the poet Cowper, whose home was named Olney. The school has been familiarly known as Olney ever since.

Written by Sarah Pickett Walton, Barnesville, OH   (1942)

SOME HISTORICAL SKETCHES OF FRIENDS AT THE RIDGE

Having written the following account for Chestnut Ridge School Literary in 1917, without thinking it would attract the attention of others so much as to request me to have it published, which after repeated importuning to do so, I offered it with just a little addition for publication in the *Barnesville Enterprise*, if the editor is willing to do so.

Chestnut Ridge Meetinghouse

Joseph W. Doudna

In the early days of Friends Society at Chestnut Ridge, Joseph Patterson, a member of Friends Society, and an early settler there, entered the southeast quarter of Section 13 in 1808 for his future home. Friends soon became so numerous there that the need of a meeting for worship was felt and also a place of learning for their children.

Accordingly, a request for a meeting was granted and it was set up on the 26th day of 11th Month, 1811. A log meeting house and a log school house had been built on the lands of Joseph Patterson, where the present meeting and school house now stand. The first school house had greased paper windows and both it and the meeting house had open fireplaces.

In the year 1812, a school was taught by John S. Williams, and the writer of this has understood that when the spelling class stood up to spell, it was so large that it reached nearly all around the inside walls of the school house. The next school in 1813 was taught by Joseph Garretson for a term of six months, at one dollar and fifty cents per quarter for each scholar, and to be paid for, if the subscribers so wished, in wheat, corn or buckwheat, delivered in Carson Thomas' mill for the first of the term and the second half to be paid in cash at the expiration of the school.

A meeting for worship and a school being now established, Joseph Patterson, in 1816, sold to his friends four acres on which the buildings stood for $32.00. It being one of his last acts in leaving this goodly heritage to his friends.

The time was now drawing nigh when he was to be taken from works to rewards, which took place in the year 1816, and he was the first person to be buried in the graveyard at Ridge, being buried there at his request. He with others of his friends believing that a monthly meeting would soon be established to take care of the interests of the society at that place. This was done about the year 1820. Joseph Patterson was buried in the open ground without any enclosure, so his friends put a rail pen around his grave until it could be enclosed with more ground for a burial place.

Now after a lapse of 100 years, can you who are young scholars going to school (1917) in this nice comfortable room, with its nice large glass windows, realize how much better off you are than our ancestors were when they were going to school in the first school house with its slab benches to sit upon, without any back to lean against when tired, or glass windows to let in the light. The writer of this used to sit upon the described benches, when a scholar here during the winter of 1860-61, and from their appearance (the benches) looked old and substantial enough to have served in all the schools at Ridge from the beginning down to that time.

Our teacher that winter was Mary Crew from Columbiana County, Ohio, who took such a deep interest in our studies, and so much concern in directing our steps in the straight and narrow way that those rude benches did not seem hard to sit upon under such pleasant circumstances.

But now the time was drawing near when the good old school house and its long remembered benches, which did not detract from the happiness of the pleasant school hours that winter at Ridge, had to share the fate of all things here below that finds here an end, no matter how good and useful they have been, and give place to the one which you now occupy.

This one was built out of brick and other material, as far as they would go, which had been first used to build Friends Meeting House at Somerton, that was left vacant after the meeting had been laid down there.

In 1863 Friends took the Somerton Meetinghouse down and hauled enough of the suitable material up here to help build this house, which was completed about the beginning of the year 1864. Thompson Frame taught the first school in this house in the forepart of that year. After this, schools were conducted here pretty regularly, until about the year 1896 when school children became so few and far removed from this neighborhood that school teaching at Ridge was abandoned. The present school commenced with a new teacher and a new generation of children in a newly repaired school room, which had become very desolate and forlorn for want of scholars and teachers to keep the good work going, which we hope may now be kept on for another hundred years under the same good management which characterized the Society of Friends at the beginning.

Contributed by Elma Doudna Bailey

(Note: This Meetinghouse and school is located on Warren Township Rt. 28, east of State Route 800 South of Barnesville; approximately in the center of Section 13.)

OTHO FRENCH HOME HISTORY
1777 – 1856

Otho French was among the first pioneers of Warren Township. He was born in Frederick County, Maryland in 1777. He did not have much of an education as his parents were poor but very respectable.

In the year 1800, Robert Plummer, a neighbor, asked him to go "west" with him and assist him in the selection of some land for entry, and he would sell French a part of the land so taken up. They could not, in those days, get less than a section of land. Otho accepted the proposition and they started on their journey. At Marietta, Ohio, they heard such glowing accounts of Section 10, Warren Township, that they got someone to point out the section line that led to it.

Following this line north, they reached Section 10 and knew as soon as they reached it, so vivid had been the description given them at Marietta. They made the entry and returned home. Robert Plummer and his family came at once in 1801. The country was all timber, and with few if any roads. It is said it took the Plummers five days to come from the open road where Morristown now stands, to the present Plummer homestead near Tacoma, Ohio. The way had to be cleared as they came.

Otho French married a short time after he returned to his home in Maryland, and they came to Warren Township in 1802. Robert Plummer, as he had agreed to do, sold him the southwest part of Section 10 on easy terms. He at once put up a crude log cabin but soon built a hewn log cabin where they lived for some time. Later he built a brick two story house, two large rooms

downstairs and two up. Small windows with small panes of glass, two doors in the front and two in the back. A well was dug at the front of the house near the northeast corner and water was drawn by a windlass. There was a cellar under the entire house, and in the northeast corner, an opening was made in the foundation about two by three feet, even with the top of the well, which opening made a deep shelf and here they kept their milk and butter, a primitive refrigerator.

There were two or three steps up to the doors on the first floor. Large open fireplaces were in the downstairs rooms. Each room, both upstairs and down had a large closet. Shelves in the downstairs closets were used as cupboards, and in the upstairs, one shelf the length of the closet and hooks below for clothing. The ceilings were very low and the doors so low that a tall man had to stoop to pass through. The closed stairway was narrow with only space for one person. The steps were straight and rather steep to a landing, then two more steps to the second floor. Under these steps was the cellar way.

The cellar has never had to be cemented as it has a solid stone floor. So this house "built on a strong foundation" has stood straight and solid all these years. It must have been built about 1815; we have not been able to learn the exact date. *(This house is located at 62158 Tacoma Rd.)*

There were many wild animals in this new and unsettled country and Otho French was a noted hunter and trapper. The outstanding feature of his whole life was his strong opposition to "spiritous liquors." The State of Maine had passed a temperance law, the first in the United States, and Otho French wanted Ohio to adopt the same law and was so strong for it that he had a sign over his front door, "Hold on to the Maine Law forever."

He kept drovers and their flocks overnight, but they were always asked the question, "Are your stock fed on brewer's grains?" If they had, they were never allowed to stay. One evening a drover stopped. He was asked the usual question and replied "no," but in some way Otho had learned he had not been told the truth, and although supper was on the table, they were not allowed to stay.

My mother used to tell me, when she was a little girl, she was passing with her father on horseback and she saw Otho standing at the front door gently pushing a drover away, and was telling him he could not stay, as his stock were fed on brewer's grains.

When he was on his death bed, he asked his family to have engraved on his tombstone, "Hold on to the Maine Law forever," which request was granted and that tombstone can still be found in the "French" or township graveyard, one fourth of a mile southeast of Tacoma, Ohio, across the Baltimore and Ohio railroad tracks. *(On Bailey Road just off of State Route 147.)*

Otho French died in 1856 into his 80th year.

Written by: Anna Bailey Patten

Otho French was not a Friend or a member of Stillwater Quarterly Meeting but he was so closely connected with the early history of the Friends of Warren Township, we feel his history should be recorded here.

THE GIBBONS FAMILY

The Joseph and Penina Williams Gibbons family moved to Warren Township, Belmont County, Ohio from Somerset Township in the spring of 1855 as per arrangements with Somerset Monthly Meeting of Friends for the care of Catherine Flanner who owned a 25 acre farm, and where the first improvement to be accomplished, was the building of the barn by Joseph Williams, brother of Penina. The barn still is in everyday use. *(This property was located on the southern section of Section 13 and 14, Warren Twp. on Chestnut Ridge Rd.)*

The family lived in the old log house where Edward and his sister Lavina were born. This old house was moved back to make room for the large frame house of ten rooms and an attic, with a cellar under the entire house. This house was built in 1868. The lumber being shipped from Bridgeport and heavy timbers hewed out from local timber and the newel post and hand railing all hand worked, made from cherry and walnut.

A thing of wonder in those times was the cellar dug in sandstone and the walls contain locally quarried stone, 11 feet 8 inches by 2 feet square. The water well that was dug in such hard stone, the first man to try it failed and then a neighbor Jehu Bailey offered to dig the well until water was found and it is one of the best wells of soft water in all the countryside. The water standing 3 ½ feet and self-draining, assuring fresh water at all times.

The stone was quarried on the former Crew farm, out on the Ridge, east of the new house and one cut of stone was over 40 feet in length and when being cut into proper lengths, they were hauled with oxen and horses, with the large high wheeled carts, to the building site. The old house was moved back but the family continued to live in it while the new house was being built.

Penina never had a stove until they moved into the new house, the cooking and baking being done in the open fireplace. The winter of 1856 was the biggest snow that anyone remembers of having, as far as we know at this time.

The old house had no glass windows. Greased paper and tallow dripped being used. Later candles were used for lighting and this was thought to be a wonder.

Written by: Edward V. Gibbons, the only survivor of Joseph and Penina Williams Gibbons, late of Warren Township, Belmont County, Ohio.

WILLIAM GREEN
1798 - 1862

William Green came to America in 1813 from England. He married Rachel Hoyle in Richmond, Jefferson County, Ohio, in 1821. She lived first in Philadelphia and moved to Richmond, Ohio before 1820. It was twenty-one days coming out to Ohio and she made her first trip back to Philadelphia, years later, in twenty-one hours.

Our grandparents *(William and Rachel Green)* moved to Barnesville before 1826 and conducted a store in partnership with Benjamin Hoyle. The building had a fronting on Main Street, the lot extending to Church Street. They also owned three acres adjoining the B&O Railroad Depot.

Upon retiring from the store business, grandfather bought several small farms that comprised the 245 acres our father, James Steer bought in 1864. This land adjoined the farms of Robert Plummer and Robert H. Smith, one half mile west of Tacoma and belonging now to Walter Skinner.

The first home on the farm was at the spring where Joseph and Ethel Wylie now live. *(62144 Homestead Drive in Tacoma.)* He built the new house *(62242 Tacoma Rd.)* in 1855 and was a useful member of Stillwater Meeting for forty years. He died in 1862, at the age of 66. Rachel Green died in 1882 at the age of 83.

Rachel was the mother of eleven children, seven of whom lived to maturity and six to the old age. *(Four died young.)* They were Hanna, Sarah, Joseph, Lydia, Rebecca and Mary, with John dying at age 39.

Written by: Anna M. Hoge and
William G. Steer

JAMES STEER HOME
1790 – 1862

This house was built by William Green in 1855, and was very much like the English plan. Our father, James Steer, was born at Colerain, Ohio in 1827. His father and grandfather camefrom Lowden County, Virginia in 1812.

He and our mother, Mary Green, were married at Stillwater in 1853 and were the parents of eight children, two of whom died in infancy. Their names were Anna M., William G., Joseph G., Rachel G., Elizabeth, and Charles, the latter passing away in his twentieth year.

Standing: Joseph Hoge, Louisa Steer, Charles Steer, Ella Steer, D.C. Bundy, Elizabeth Steer Bundy.
Seated: Anna Steer Hoge, James Steer, William G. Steer, Mary Green Steer, Rachel Steer.

Anna is at present in her 88th year, William G. in his 86th year and Elizabeth in her 80th year, and all are members of Stillwater Meeting.

One of my early recollections of our moving to Barnesville, was that I went with father when he took a four-horse load of goods. The way four horses were handled in those days were, the driver rode on of the wheel horses and drove the leaders with a single line called a jerk line. When wanting them to go to the right he would call "GG" and to the left would call "Haw."

Father was about five foot ten inches and weighed around two hundred pounds. In his prime, he was considered the strongest man in Warren Township. Before the cradle came in use, he had reaped 40 dozen sheaves of wheat with a sickle in a day. In the winter of 1874, with four horses, he hauled all the logs to the mill for 125,000 feet of lumber to build the Boarding School *(Olney Friends School)*. After he was 86 years of age, he committed to memory a great many poems which he often recited when in a company. When at the celebration of the 100th anniversary of the building of the Yearly Meeting House at Mt. Pleasant, he stood on his feet and recited a lengthy poem. He died suddenly, while on his feet, the second of Third Month 1917, in his 90th year.

Our mother was born in 1828 and died in 1903 in her 75th year. I don't think any greater tribute could have been paid to her life and character than that expressed by one at her funeral, when quoting the passage, "Her gentleness hath made me great."

Our parents moved from Colerain, Ohio, in the Eighth Month of 1864, and bought the farm which father owned for fifty-three years. Five of their children were born at Colerain. Our brother Charles, in 1864 at the home of our grandmother, Rachel Green. Her home was with us until her death in 1882. It was through the influence of Asenath Bailey and herself that the monthly meeting was established at Richland, sometime in the eighteen seventies.

It has already been stated that the James Steer home was built in 1855 by our grandfather William Green, of which the following is a description. He no doubt followed the English plan of having all the needed rooms under one roof. This making the house 106 feet long. The first section was 40 feet square, with a cellar the same size. The walls were made of nicely dressed stone, as were the seven and a half foot pillars that supported the floor. One stone in the wall is ten feet long.

The milk room adjoining the cellar was ten feet square, the walls being the same as in the cellar. The steps, both inside and outside were also stone, all of which were quarried on the farm. In the milk room was a trough eight feet long, three and one half feet wide and eight or ten inches deep in which was set the pans of milk. It being cooled by water from a well in the kitchen.

Rachel Steer
James Steer   Anna Steer Hoge

The second section was 17 by 17 feet and two story, as the first section. The roofs on these were flat and covered with tarred paper and gravel. This not proving satisfactory, a raised hip roof was soon put up.

The first section contained eight rooms, 17 by 17 feet with 9 foot ceilings and halls 6 feet wide on each floor. Each of these was heated by small coal burning stoves. The first winter we lived in the home, someone thought there was an unusual smoke in the house, so our mother, on going upstairs at once, began stamping on the floor to give warning that there was fire. My uncle John Green, who lived in the home called to me "Come, Willie, quick, and help get water for the fire." Something had been put in the unused flue to stop it had caught fire from a spark and dropped down, burning a hole in the floor.

The rooms on the first floor were provided with double swinging doors so they could be converted into two rooms 17 by 32 feet, one on each side of the hall. The second section lapped only five feet on the first and contained the kitchen and pantry and store room for provisions. This was built up one step above the other floors but was set down even by William Frame when Oscar Bailey owned the home.

The kitchen had four doors, two opening on the outside and also had the open wood fireplace and crane on which to hang the pots for cooking.

The extension, 45 by 17 feet, and a story and a half contained the wash house, coal house, chicken house, and carriage shed. This has a pitch roof with an attic over two rooms and a shop over the carriage shed. The room for chickens extended to the roof, having the roosts in the top and a long ladder for them to reach the roosts. There was a back stairs leading to two sleeping rooms over the kitchen and pantry. There was no way of getting from one section to the other until a door was put in in 1885.

In the first section were two doors leading to a rear porch, 36 by 10 feet and one door in front to a portico, so called, 8 by 10 feet and two steps from the ground. The roof to this was supported by four posts, 10 by 10 inches. There were forty-four windows in the house, all having two sash with 8 by 10 lights *(window panes)*, except four windows in the attic with hinged sash, had but one light. The five windows in the front having sash on each side, one light wide. One thing that has been omitted was that there was a heavy trap door in the flat attic room that gave a good chance to get a good view of the surrounding country, being able to see Morristown, seven miles away.

It had also been neglected to say that the frame of this house was heavy hewn timbers, such as were used in the construction of large barns built many years ago. In recent years, the main sections have been covered on the outside with asbestos shingles, adding much to the durability and appearance of the home. We have been told that the present owner expects to remove the 45-foot extension, which would add greatly to the appearance of its construction and if properly cared for, this house should last perhaps as long as the pioneer brick houses.

In conclusion will say that we made soft soap and used a Dutch oven that father had made. Also the flail grubber and horse power thresher, the sickle, scythe, cradle, "Walter A. Wood mowing machine;" the Kirby harvester, with one big wheel and a platform for a man to stand and pull the grain back with a long rake before dropping it, a self-rake and dropper before the advent of the binder, *all these were used in harvesting.*

Written by: Anna M. Hoge and William G. Steer, children of James and Mary Green Steer

JOHN HALL
1784 – 1854

John Hall, my paternal grandfather, was born in Perquimans County, North Carolina, the 24th of 10th Month, 1784. He died 5th Month 22nd, 1854, at the age of 70. His wife was Phebe Webster, the daughter of John and Hannah Plummer Webster, born the 24th of 11th Month, 1786 in the Little Britian Township, Lancaster, Pennsylvania, and died the 23rd of the 8th Month 1855 at the age of 69.

John Hall came from Wayne County, North Carolina to Ohio in 1805 with his father, Isaac Hall and mother, Ann White Hall and sister Anna Hall. The brothers were Isaac and Moses.

The children of John and Phebe were: Cyrus, Isaac W., Thomas, John P., Nate A., Eli, Jesse and Eliza.

John with his father and family settled on a place about three miles west of Barnesville, Ohio. The following year, John, being 21 years of age, decided to to west, along the valley of the Leatherwood and located a farm. The land was covered with timber. Mostly walnut, hickory and oak. He soon built a cabin for himself; during this time he slept under a white oak tree. Later on, he built a brick house, finishing it in the spring of 1828. It was two stories with one story on the east side. *(South, Section 13, Millwood Twp., Guernsey Co.)*

He was the first settler in Millwood Township. The brick was burned for the house nearby where the house was erected. Many squirrels played on the scaffold while the house was being built, as there were many wild animals here when he came. Deer, wolves, bear and wild turkeys were numerous. John A. Hall was a fine marksman and brought down many a deer and wild turkey, which provided him with an abundance of meat.

In the fall of the year, the ground would be covered with hickory nuts. The fine big walnut trees would be very valuable if we had them today, but had to lie and rot on the ground because there was no way to take care of them.

The house had a very big fireplace and a large mantle. The fireplace would take in 5 foot logs. The windows were not unusual as they had six panes above and six below. There was a fine spring, which was one inducement for him to build his cabin there. The spring house is probably 10 feet by 20 feet, but am not sure if it has cemented troughs. It may have been changed since my grandfather's day.

They made soft soap by leaching wood ashes. Grandfather had a maple sugar camp and made sugar. He had a trough hollowed out of a buckeye log in which he caught the maple juice and he used it as a shelter by holding it over his head when it rained. They raised some sheep and spun some wool. Some of the machinery is too far removed in time for me to remember.

John Webster moved to Ohio in the fall of 1806. Part of his family stayed with John Hall until they got their two story log house built. It was built where the cut for the Baltimore and Ohio railroad now stands. The house was torn down to make way for the railroad.

John Webster had ten children. He bought 800 acres of land, so as to give 80 acres apiece to each of his children. Part of his family stayed in the cabin with John Hall while they finished their house.

One of his daughters, Phebe, married John Hall, thus providing a mate for the one who dared to carve his home out of the wilderness. As I said before, his principal reason for building his cabin where he did, was to be near the fine spring which he had found. What kind of a spring house he built, I do not know, or whether he had any at all for a while. The one I described is the one now in existence.

Grandfather died several years before I was born. The things I know about him were told me by my father and uncle.

Written by: Elvira Hall, Quaker City, Ohio (The only remaining grandchild of John Hall.)

THE THOMAS HALL HOME
1840 – 1886

Thomas Parry Hall was born 11-22-1840 near Quaker City, Ohio. His father, Nathan Hall, was born 12-18-1809 in Wayne County, North Carolina and came to Ohio about 1825. His mother, Deborah Parry, was born 4-7-1814 near Quaker City, Ohio.

His wife, Rebecca Webster Richardson, was born 4-3-1843. Her mother was Hanna D. Vail, who was born 7-5-1810 in Fayette County, Pennsylvania, and died in Barnesville, Ohio, 1-9-1884. Her father, Samuel Webster Richardson was born in (Little Britian Township), Lancaster County, Pennsylvania, and died near Malta, Ohio, 9-12-1849.

Thomas Hall married Rebecca Webster Richardson 4-5-1865, and they went to housekeeping on a farm near Quaker City, Ohio. The children were: Margaret V. Hall, who was born 3-15-1866 at Quaker City, Ohio, and the following children born at the Sandy Ridge home: Wilford T., 8-29-1869; Blanche D., 5-22-1874; Everett and Elma, 6-11-1878; Elsie H., 5-22-1880.

On 3-18-1867, the Halls changed their residence to Sandy Ridge, east of Barnesville, Ohio. *(Located in NE Section 2, on Sandy Ridge Road.)* There was quite a little snow, and Ezekiel Grier let them go through his farm, which made it much shorter distance to come across to the Pultney Ridge Road. A few First-days after they had moved to this new home, Hosea Doudna rode his dun horse down to spend the afternoon, saying he just came down to see what kind of neighbors he was going to have.

They bought the 234 acre farm of John Wehr and wife, and agreed to pay $80 per acre. The house was built by Asahel Thomas, which was a one and one half story frame with an unusual arrangement. From the front door you entered a 10 ft. wide hall – it is said they wanted it wide enough to drive a load of hay through. On one side of the hall was a parlor and sitting room, and on the opposite side there were two large bedrooms, each 11 foot ceilings, and each of these rooms was provided with a grate. *(fireplace)* Then at the back of the house, with one step down, were kitchen, pantry, back porch, and two small bedrooms – all with a low ceiling. From the large hall, a wide stairway led to a small hall upstairs, and from it, a very large front bedroom and a small back bedroom with large side garrets at the sides. Just one clothes closet in the house!

We had dug a well with an iron pump on the back porch and a rain barrel to catch the soft water at the side of the house. The windows were six panes to the sash, except two long narrow-side of the front door. We had a cellar under most of the house within steps from the hall; also an outside entrance, but in the winter we had to use candles or a lantern to see, as in the winter the windows of the cellar were closed.

The barn was built on a hillside so it was really a three story building. From the front there was an approach and a very large barn door to open to drive in with the hay or grain which was stored in the mows. *(Mows were the lofts in the main part of the barn.)* The next floor was used for sheep stables with an entrance there. On the ground floor we kept cattle, and here there was a dug well with a wooden pump so the cattle could be watered there from buckets if the hill was too icy for them to go to the watering trough.

What the house lacked in convenience was made up somewhat in the situation for it had a fine view in all direction. Tommie and Bettie Hall welcomed people to their home, and if they happened there at mealtime they were asked to share the meal prepared. For some time, mother just had a dinner horn to call the family together at mealtime, and they decided to get a farm bell. Mother made soft soap and father peddled it in Barnesville, and in this way they paid $8.00

for the bell from money made that way. Father believed when women had meals ready, they should not be kept waiting, and when this bell was installed, he made a rule that if anyone was late after the bell rang, they would have to go without the meal. Soon after, father was at the lower part of the place at dinner time and some of the men thought he would not have time to get back promptly, but he had a good horse that brought him in time.

They set out peach and apple orchards, also one pear and a quince orchard. Once when father was showing a man through the peach orchard that was laden with fruit, this friend said, "They are very nice, Tommie, but they will all rot." An Iowa cousin went with father to the quince orchard and the fruit looked so nice, and when they returned to the house, the cousin asked his mother what kind of a man Tommie Hall was that he took him around among the quince trees and never asked him to taste any of the fruit.

Our parents were among the largest berry growers for several years. One and a half acres of strawberries, and twenty-five acres of raspberries, which required about 50 pickers – a large per cent being colored folk.

They raised lots of melons and, as father was generous, he asked boys in from the neighborhood to come and eat melons in their season. He did not have vines pulled or destroyed.

They raised Shorthorn cattle and I remember that mother did not get much butter from quite a quantity of cream churned by dash churn. Sheep were raised extensively, and I remember just once being allowed to go to Jesse Bailey's farm, joining ours, to watch the process of sheep washing. They had a pen for the flock with a lane from it to the dam in the creek, and the sheep were driven into the water, then let them out on the other side to another pen. Then sheep shearing was an annual event. Father was an extra fast shearer and mother often folded and tied the fleece.

Thomas P. Hall died 11-14-1886 and the family remained in the home for six years following, then sold the farm at about $37 per acre in 1893, and bought a little home joining, belonging to Beulah Roberts. Here our mother died 3-30-1926. How lightly through the mist of years, my quiet country home appears.

Wonderful progress has been made in science, medicine and transportation, and so many developments in our modern life to enjoy, but am glad I was privileged to be brought up in the horse and buggy days, and our parents took turns with other neighbors in caring for the sick in our community. I am glad we had chores to do in the morning and evening and we did not feel it any hardship to walk to school.   Written by: Elma C. Hall, daughter of Thomas Hall.

ANECDOTE OF SCHOOL DAYS OF WILFORD T. HALL
1869 – 1958

My grandfather, Wilford T. Hall, tells of the many delights of a growing boy, walking to school at No. I, with his sister Margaret. They started in a southwestern direction from the barn of the Thomas P. Hall home, down the lane towards Peter Sears. This lane was lined with very large fruit trees extended almost the length of their place.

One of the large apple trees in Peter Sears' farm was considered the largest apple tree in Belmont County. It is known that Prudence Williams went on horseback to Redstone, Pennsylvania for the trees when planning to plant the orchard, and brought the trees back and set them out herself. *(This was probably located in the NW section of Warren Township Section 2.)*

The last of Prudence's trees was blown down on 7th Month 10th, 1896, and by measurement taken a few years before, was found to be 9 ft. 4 inches in circumference at the smallest point between the roots and forks, 10 feet and eighteen inches above the ground. It had four large branches, one of which measured 4 ft. in circumference, another 5 ft., another 5 ft. 2 inches, and another 5 ft. one inch. These measurements were taken 18 inches from the junction of the forks.

The big apple trees were laden with many varieties such as, Hubbards and Sheep Nose. The large peach trees were laden with juicy fruit. All of the fruit was perfect and required no spraying. The sweet apples hidden in the deep blue grass, so deep that in late winter they could be kicked out, cold and delicious. The walk then continued through a maple camp with perhaps a few sips of maple sap. All these things made the walk to school seem most too short.

The school was located in a beautiful grove, and at that time was one of the best schools in the township. *(Warren Township No. 1 school, also known as Maplewood, was located on Pigeon Point Rd. (TWP 182) in Section 8 near the border of Section 2.)*

With the money earned as janitor, which included the care of the teacher's horse, my grandfather bought his first watch.

On their way home from school, grandfather and his sister Margaret often stopped to see grandmother Anna Sears (Peter Sears' mother) and having her feel them all over to see how they were growing, as she was totally blind.

Written by Harold L. Holloway, Jr, Wheeling, WV (son of Harold and Helen Hall Holloway)

Sarah (Sadie) Stanton Hall and Wilford T. Hall

My father, Wilford Hall, recalls an incident when his father, Thomas P. Hall, was putting up hay on John Bundy's place *(61744 Bailey Rd.)*. Grandfather Jesse Metcalf came along and after dinner the two grandfathers talked together. Grandfather Bundy showed him a new bottom he had put in a half bushel measure. The bottom, although not just real tight, served the purpose quite well. Grandfather Metcalf didn't say much, but in a short time, Grandfather Bundy found out Jesse Metcalf was a "cooper" by trade. He took the bottom out and put in a tight one. At the next opportunity he showed grandfather Metcalf the measure saying, "Jesse, when I showed thee the half bushel measure, I didn't know an old cooper was peering at my work."

The story is told that on a severely cold day, William Bundy and his crew of men went over to his brother John's barn to assist in flailing grain. The grain which was spread on the barn floor was threshed out by beating with a hand flail. Despite the vigorous exercise, William and his men got cold and went to the house to get warm. When they returned, John had his coat off and his sleeves rolled up, reclining in the hay fanning himself with his hat. The apparent inference that William and his men were soft made William so angry he jumped on John and gave him a good "choking" to even the score.

Written by Helen Hall Holloway, Wheeling, WV

ELIJAH HANSON
1798 - 1876

Grandfather Elijah Hanson went to Meeting on one First Day, during very cold weather, and found one other Friend in attendance. These two men held the Meeting on the steps, for the scriptures say "Where two or three are gathered …". By thus conducting the services, it was not needful to report to Monthly Meeting, "No Meeting held that day." Mother *(Deborah Hanson, Bundy, Stanton)* does not know the name of the man who was with grandfather when the two of them held Meeting on the steps.

This meetinghouse was on Captina Creek, near the site of a Methodist church and cemetery, and a portion of the Susanna Scribner Hanson farm.

Grandfather Hanson often talked of the meteoric phenomenon of 1833 which he witnessed.

About the year 1810, my grandmother Eliza Hanson went to school in the frame meetinghouse which stood on the present grounds of the Ohio Yearly Meeting. My mother's school days started in a log house in Goshen Township in 1846. Her desk was a board laid on top of pegs stuck in the wall and their seats were benches without backs.

Written by Mary C. Smith, Granddaughter of Elijah Hanson

DAVID BALL

In the Southland and Plymouth neighborhoods there are a number of houses still standing that were at one time the homes of the early settlers of these Friend *(Quaker)* Communities. However, a few if any, are now living that are old enough to give information concerning the why and wherefore, as well as the process of these particular places becoming the homes of Friends. *(Plymouth Monthly Meeting was located in Morgan County. Many Quakers from Belmont County moved to Morgan County in the 1800's.)*

Our own great-grandfather, David Ball, came to Malta township in Morgan County in 1835 when our grandmother Gaynor Ball (Burgess) was a child of nine. I have visited the scene of their early home and have heard much about it. Had I been wishing to write about this some three years ago, both father and Uncle Nathan could have given much of the value, but as they are now gone, I am not altogether certain about many of the details. I thought I might have secured some information from an old neighbor of the family, who still lives in the community, but since we must so plan trips to try to save tires, and the time in which to gather facts was limited, I have not attempted to write about homes that I had in mind at first.

Nevertheless, since my interest has been aroused, I hope I may be able to gather some information about some of these later for my own satisfaction. In thinking of someone who could tell of one or two of the homes I had in mind, Alden Hobson was asked for information. As he and his daughter Edith Hobson Burr mentioned facts about their home, we felt that although it was not one of the really old homes, there were reasons for its description being interesting, so I am giving briefly what they have given me about their family as connected with this home, along with my comments.

Elizabeth Burgess

P.S. I had waited for a reply to a letter inquiring about the Edmund Fowler home. It was received the 24th but I can give little even yet. I had hoped to secure some photographs to accompany this.

THE THOMAS HOBSON HOME

Thomas Hobson was born in Jefferson County, Ohio, on July 7th, 1812 and died at Bartlett, Ohio, on June 8th, 1899.

His wives were, Unity Johnson, who was born April 11, 1811. They were married on November 28th, 1839 and she died March 13th, 1856. Mary Stanley was his second wife. She was born April 9th, 1823. They were married September 30th, 1857. She died on November 28th, 1879. His third and last wife was Eliza Worthington who was born February 6th, 1831. They were married on July 27th, 1882 and she died about the year 1905.

The children of Thomas and Unity Johnson Hobson were:

Benjamin J. Hobson	Born 7-18-1841 and died 12-17-1907
Mary J. Hobson Conrow	Born 3-13-1843 and died 7-18-1921
Sarah A. Hobson Masters	Born 10-15-1844 and died 8-28-1909
Dorothy Hobson Stratton/Ashton	Born 5-14-1847 and died 3-31-1934
Dr. John A. Hobson	Born 7-2-1849 and died 2-21-1913
Belinda Hobson Binns	Born 8-9-1851 and died 7-23-1915

Thomas Hobson, whose parents came from Virginia, made his home in Jefferson County, Ohio, until his oldest son Benjamin was a lad of nine or ten years old. For some time after coming to Jefferson County, the family lived on what was later known as the Thomas Bowman farm. In about the year 1873 a carpenter was secured to build a new house within a few rods of the Plymouth Meeting House. *(This was located at Smithfield in Jefferson County.)* The site chosen was a very desirable one, furnishing a fine view of a wide scope of country side and the nearby view of the meetinghouse, with the beautiful grove of forest trees on the slope leading to it.

The house is a well-built frame of two story height, consisting of four rooms downstairs and three upstairs. The windows are quite large of the four pane style. There seems to have been nothing especially unusual, except that between the kitchen and dining room were built folding doors. The purpose of these was to provide space to set the long table for the dinners, which the Hobsons provided for Friends at Quarterly Meeting time.

This custom must have clung as a pleasant memory for many Friends. In that day of slower travel, Quarterly Meetings were important events for which considerable preparation was made. They furnished not only spiritual enlightenment but supplied social needs.

Near the house is a well from which water was, and still is, drawn with a windlass. For the storage of fruit and vegetables, a sawdust house was made a short distance from the kitchen door. As to the house and farm work, they made soap, raised sheep, spun and wove cloth. Suits were cut and made at home. The sickle, scythe and grain cradle were used.

Alden, Thomas Hobson's grandson, remembers his father Benjamin, telling about the first threshing machine he ever saw. It was while Benjamin was still a small boy living in Jefferson County. No doubt his astonishment at such a machine encouraged the owner to elastic speech hoping to arouse even greater curiosity. Benjamin was told that the machine sheared sheep and in order to see the wool, he was taken to see the straw coming from the machine.

This house was the home of Thomas Hobson the remainder of his life, but shortly after his death the place was sold. However, in 1906 Alden Hobson bought the property. Perhaps it will not be out of place here to give a brief description of the house which had previously been his home. It was near a quarter of a mile away and had been the home of Benjamin Hobson since about 1862. The house had been built by McCagey Emmons. An old carding mill sixteen feet square had been moved some distance. To it had been added a log structure of equal size. Here the water supply came from a spring at the spring house. This home also was noted for its hospitality.

When Alden moved his family to the Thomas Hobson house, it became the home of the second, third and fourth generation of its founder -- for Benjamin was included in the family. At the present time in this home with Alden is living his daughter, Edith Hobson Burt with her husband and two children, Betty and Harold Jr. Thus again this home is housing three generations -- the third, fourth and fifth.

The Plymouth Community was favored when it was chosen as the home of the Hobson family because of the good influence that has been spread by its members. At least two were placed in positions of unusual responsibility.

Dorothy Stratton Ashton was matron of the Boarding School near Barnesville, Ohio, for some time. Because of her understanding and interest in young people, she was a valued counselor as long as health permitted her to share with others the wisdom of her ripe years of experience.

Dr. John Hobson became associated with Flushing Hospital in 1875 and gave many years to relieving the ailments to which the human body is heir.

In this home which Thomas Hobson established, both he and his son Benjamin, passed on to that "House not made with hands" and were laid to rest in the Friends Cemetery nearby.

For many years there has been no Plymouth Meetinghouse but the Hobson home still stands. Although this house is not especially pretentious in appearance, it is attractive and very home-like for it has experienced that "Heap O' Livin' " that makes a house a home.

Written by: Elizabeth Burgess. Many facts given by Alden Hobson and Edith Hobson Burr.

BENJAMIN HOYLE
1797 - 1875

Benjamin Hoyle was born in Yorkshire, England, 6-11-1797. His father John Hoyle, was a husbandman in the parish of Pontefract, where Benjamin received his education in the Friends School. John Hoyle's first wife and mother of all his children, having died, he married a second time and in 1815 the parents with seven children and two grandchildren, stepped on a sailboat for America.

The voyage was tedious and not without danger. The Captain, unacquainted with the Gulf stream, found himself within its current and helpless. In daytime, the wind blew them westward but at night the current carried them back eastward. Water and food became very scarce. Of the former each person was limited to one gill a day for all purposes and for the latter they were considering killing and eating a dog which was on board with them. In this extremity a waterspout suddenly appeared so near that the Captain feared they would be drawn into it. He fired cannon through the center of it to disperse it. Presently there was a heavy rain with many fish evidently dropped from the waterspout.

Hailing a passing boat, he was told to sail across the Gulf stream and presently they reached Philadelphia after a voyage of fourteen weeks and five days.

Our next trace of them is in the records of Plymouth monthly meeting, when the parents and five children, including Benjamin presented a certificate from Pontefract monthly meeting in England, which was accepted at Smithfield, Jefferson County, Ohio. They were apparently considered solid members and their names soon are found on various committees. At twenty, Benjamin was on a committee to prepare monthly meeting minutes for recording and to prepare a certificate for removal.

In 1820, Benjamin and Tabitha Grimshaw, also born in England, were married at Smithfield. The next year he was companion to Mildred Ratcliff, on a religious visit to Indiana. The next year, he was assistant clerk to the monthly meeting.

He took out his first papers for citizenship in 1826. He seemed to lose interest and did not get his final papers of naturalization until 1840. In 1827 he moved to Barnesville, Ohio, where he and his brother-in-law, William Green. opened a general store. He was head of Stillwater meeting, a recommended minister in Ohio, and made several trips to the seaboard in which he combined business with meeting interests. He bought stock for the store in town, wrote once that he wanted to "get salt at Pittsburg if it can be accomplished so as to have it waggoned from Wheeling, West. Va. by the bacon wagons." Also he bought Bibles and Testaments in Philadelphia to sell in Barnesville.

Business over, he turned to visitation meetings, where he frequently felt occasion to preach, or even to add his comment at times in the business period. During the turbulent times of the Hicksite separation, he said in one letter that the clerk of a certain yearly meeting had suggested that Benjamin Hoyle might better keep his seat.

On one trip he fell ill and visited a doctor who "gave me 20 grains of calomel mixed with one of Epecacuana, which indeed did rouse my system."

He became a widower in 1828. The next year he bought 45 acres from Jonathan Taylor who had it in a patent deed from Thomas Jefferson, President and James Madison, Sec. of State. He added to it from time to time until he gave up the store to devote all his time to farming. He married Mary Millhouse of Stillwater meeting in 1830. A letter which he wrote to her needs to be labeled to recognize it as a love letter. His penmanship was as precise as his language which is prim and subdued as became an Englishman. His son said many years later, that he was very reticent, never talking about his early days unless directly asked. For that reason, very little can now be told of his life.

Three children were born to the second marriage. Hannah Hoyle Smith born 1834, Benjamin Hoyle Jr. 1837, and William in 1847. Two children had been born to the first wife, Tabitha. They were Sarah, born 1821, and John, born 1827.

On his farm, he made a specialty of sheep and turnips. It was an English habit to have a large flock of sheep and to feed them on turnips. He also raised the best wheat to be found in the neighborhood. Sinclair Smith, who had just bought a marvelous big Kirby reaper, used it first on Benjamin's wheat fields and reported it was extra nice and they had cut the whole fourteen acres in one day. Previously the Hoyle's had used scythe, sickle and cradle, and had a homemade fan mill for separating chaff from the grain and clover seed. A salesman wanted to sell him such a fan and when he was shown the one in use, tried to collect royalty on it. But the Hoyle machine was older than the life of the patent so the salesman gave up his claim.

The first house which we know is the present two story brick, completed in 1843. An old Dutch oven was still standing in the 1880s, but is now gone. One old hoary landmark remains at this writing (1942) -- the old sickle pear tree up in the garden. An elderly man born in 1816, once drove past the garden where a workman was busy and asked for a pear, saying he remembered that the tree was planted when he was a little boy. It is now well over a hundred years old, the most aged fruit tree in this part of the State. The trunk is now an empty shell and cannot last much longer, but it bore fruit in 1941.

The old farm became divided to make homes for Barclay Smith and Benjamin Stanton, and the original boarding school farm was made from this land. The present campus was once a maple grove and the trees were tapped for sugar water.

Benjamin and Mary Hoyle were superintendents at Mt. Pleasant boarding school from 1842 to 1847. He was clerk of the Ohio Yearly Meeting for twenty consecutive years, 1838 to 1857. This long term was partly caused by the inability of the representatives to agree on any clerk and by the rules of the yearly meeting, the former clerk held over until there could be unity.

During this time the Gurney separation took place. Benjamin and Mary Hoyle were frequently seen driving on First Day (Sunday) after meeting to visit members of the meeting. Starting out for a social call he often found a fitting word of advice or exhortation given him to deliver. He was a real "Pastor to his flock."

When the inability of age came upon them, they went to their daughter, Hannah Hoyle Smith to live out the remainder of their lives. In 1873 he attended his last yearly meeting and following is an account of his farewell, written at the time:

"Benjamin Hoyle now arose and delivered what was probably his farewell communication to the Ohio Yearly Meeting, reciting that he had attended it for about fifty year, in which time many valued friends had been members of it who had been gathered to their everlasting rest. He had remembered the words of a worthy friend who had said that there was a danger in those who were promoted from station to station in the church -- feeding upon it and being lifted out of the Lord's hand, and he cautioned his friends against being elated with appointments and thus allowing themselves to be lifted out of the Lord's hand.

"He then dwelt upon the text 'Hear ye me Asa and all Judah and Benjamin the Lord is with ye, be with him, and if ye seek him, he will be found of you, but if ye forsake him, he will forsake you', repeating parts of the text three times and leaving it as his farewell to the meeting.

"He took his seat, much affected and great tenderness spread over the meeting in thus receiving the last weighty and impressive message from their ancient friend now worn and weary and soon to be released from the scene of his earthly trials and tribulations.

"Before the business of the day was entered upon, Benjamin arose and walked feebly down the steps of the gallery where he stood for a few minutes weeping. Then gathering strength from his rest, he left the meeting with many a strong man brushing away the tears from his eyes and probably no one in that room with heart so cold as to be indifferent to the occasion."

He died 2-3-1875 and was laid to rest in Stillwater burying grounds.

Written by: Laura J. Hoyle.

DR. CAROLUS JUDKINS
1767 - 1854

The first physician to locate in Barnesville, Ohio, was Dr. Carolus Judkins. He was born in North Carolina in 1767. On reaching manhood he read medicine and began practice near his home folks, but as he was opposed to the principles of human slavery, he determined to move to the then Western wilds, where slavery was unknown. In the year 1810 he came with his family and brother, Joel, to Barnesville. The trip was a long tedious one with horse and wagon.

On reaching his destination, he erected a cabin and an office on East Main Street where he lived and followed his profession the remainder of his days. His field of service was a radius of twenty miles around Barnesville, visiting his patients on horseback.

In 1820 he formed a partnership with Dr. James Stanton, but after two or three years Dr. Stanton moved to Mt. Pleasant, Ohio. Dr. Carolus Judkins was born a member of the Friends meeting of North Carolina and we find in the old minutes of Stillwater Monthly Meeting Fifth Mo. 1811 the following: Received a certificate for Carolus Judkins and wife Charity and their children, namely, Thomas, Jesse, Joel, Anderson, Elizabeth and James, from New Garden Monthly Meeting, North Carolina, dated 30th of Third Month 1811.

He was an active member in the early days of Stillwater Quarterly Meeting. An anecdote is told of his faithfulness as a doctor to his work.

Friends Yearly meeting was in progress, and as his patients were none of them dangerously ill, Dr. Judkins went to Yearly Meeting held at Mt. Pleasant, Ohio, leaving his partner Dr. Stanton in charge of the sick. Among the sick was an old black man, Robert Peters, who when Dr. Judkins left was in the worst condition of any. Dr. Judkins had not been in Mt. Pleasant forty-eight hours when near the close of the second day Dr. Stanton put in appearance. Judkins asked him at once about the sick. Stanton replied, "All out of danger but Peters and he will die anyway, so I thought I'd come to the meeting, too." Without a word Judkins mounted his horse and riding all night arrived at Peter's home by daylight. He found the old gentleman much worse; but by prompt treatment restored him to health.

Dr. Carolus Judkins died Oct. 24, 1854, in the 87th year of his age and was buried in the Stillwater Friends burial ground.

Written by: Dr. D.O. Shepherd, Barnesville, Ohio.

SOME HISTORY OF WOOL, FLAX AND NETTLES IN LEATHERWOOD VALLEY
(From Cyrus Hall's History of Leatherwood Valley)

Ann, the oldest child of John and Hannah Plummer Webster, was born the 6th of Third Month 1779. She was one of the last members of the family that was married, but of that event I at present have no date. She was married to Jesse Chalfant about the year 1823 or 1824. He was a widower and came from Wilmington, Delaware.

Jesse Chalfant was by trade a wheelwright -- or one whose occupation was making and repairing spinning wheels, and reels for winding yarn, and other spinning and weaving machinery, which were then in use in almost every family. In this branch of business Jesse Chalfant was a skilled mechanic. There being much of that class of work to be done in that day, the services of such a man was needed in every neighborhood. At this period when both the food and clothing had to be produced and prepared within the families of the people; the Scriptural problems -- "What shall we eat?" and "What shall we drink?" -- were closely followed and almost inseparably connected with the no less important question -- "How shall we be clothed?" Among the inhabitants of this period a large portion of their clothing was wholly or in part prepared by the members of their own families. Thus the spinning wheel and reel, and, in a large number of families, the loom, were household necessities.

THE LARGE—OR WOOL—SPINNING WHEEL

Woolen goods of home manufacture then formed most of the winter clothing of the country people; most farmers kept a few sheep for that purpose. The wool, after being prepared, was carded at the country carding machine, which was then an indispensable institution in every section of country -- as much as the mill for grinding grain. A portion of the wool was sometimes carded at home with hand cards which was a slow and tedious process. The wool after being carded or made into rools, was usually spun by members of the farmers' families. After being spun it was woven into cloth of several kinds as desired by country weavers, of which there were generally several in every neighborhood. This branch of business was generally followed by women, but there were men also who followed the business of weaving.

SMALL SPINNING WHEEL

There were factories in almost every section of country that did spinning, weaving, dyeing and finishing of cloth; but for want of more improved and efficient machinery their work was tedious and comparatively expensive and they received only a limited patronage.

The culture of flax for textile purposes, was also carried on very extensively throughout the country during the early settlements and even up to near the middle of the present century (1850). Flax, being used in a multitude of ways, filled a place as much if not more important than any other material in providing clothing for the common people. It was spun and woven into linen, which formed one of the staple articles of summer clothing. It also was used to some extent for the chain for linsey and other woolen goods. The principal part of the sewing thread then in use was spun directly from flax. The culture and manufacture of flax was a thing that took considerable time; it was a tedious and, in some respects, laborious business. After the flax was raised and the seed had been taken off, it was spread thinly upon the grass to be "rotted" as it was termed, which caused the woody part of the straw to be easily broken and separated from the fiber. This took a period of from one to two months. This was done in the fall or early spring as the hot sun would injure the fiber. Then came breaking and dressing, or cleaning the fiber of the coarse or woody portion of the straw.

The old flax brake is now a relic of the past; it was a clumsy implement and was made with five horizontal bars, two above and three beneath, the under set being stationary set in heads at each end and mounted upon legs of convenient height. The upper set were set in heads in like manner, the head at the back end being in the form of a roller, leaving the front end free to be moved up and down the two upper bars working between and nearly touching the three under bars. The operator took the flax in bunches as large as he could conveniently handle in one hand and holding it under the brake moving it backward and forward between the bars. At the same time, with his other hand, he raised the upper section of the brake and brought it down with a heavy stroke, shaking and knocking it from time to time as the work progressed.

After being thus broken, the flax was then dressed or "swingled" as it was termed. This was usually done by another man, as two persons could work together to the best advantage. This was done by taking each hand of flax as it came from the brake and holding it across the end of an upright board (the end of which had been dressed to a smooth blunt edge), and striking it with a large wooden kirtle, with both an upward and downward stroke until it was cleaned or sufficiently freed from the shives or small pieces of the broken straw. In this way two men could usually break and dress from twenty to twenty-five pounds per day. This work was usually done during the cold and dry days of winter when the farmers were most at leisure. The flax, if not sufficiently dry, was dried over or around an open fire. Many of the older citizens recollect the old *Family Almanac,* where at the head of each calendar month was a picture illustrating the principal kind of work set apart for that month -- or properly belonging to that particular season. For the month of January, two men were always represented breaking and dressing flax, with a boy drying it over a fire. For the month of December, two men were always represented in the barn thrashing grain with flails.

Concerning Nettles and Their Uses Among Some of the Pioneer Settlers

The nettle is a perennial plant that formerly grew in great abundance over all or most of the northern United States. It is partially covered with minute sharp hairs or prickles, which are in a measure poisonous. Upon coming in contact with the skin, they cause a painful, itching, disagreeable sensation. At the time of the first settlement along the Leatherwood Valley, the nettles grew in patches -- some larger ones covering acres of ground, some smaller confined to a space of rods, or even a yard or less. Nettles would dominate and smother other plants. Wherever they grew, they seemed to be in entire possession of the soil to the extinction of all other plants. In a rich moist soil such as shaded forest with sparse undergrowth of bushes and small timber, they would frequently grow to the height of three or four feet and occupying acres. Nettles, of course, are propagated from seed more or less, but the plants increase and spread from suckers -- forming a thick network of roots near the surfaces of the soil. In the early stages of its growth, hogs will eat nettles with a relish -- nearly if not equal to red clover, the young shoots being very succulent, tender and easy of mastication; thus the swine were made to feel themselves at home in the enjoyment of the forest life amidst a patch of luxuriant young nettles and as they frequently destroy those young germs which probably tended to check and diminish its spreading growth. Upon once being nipped off, it does not so readily start again as is the case with some other plants, especially the grasses.

I was informed a number of years ago that Jane Shannon, widow of George Shannon -- one of the three first settlers in Warren Township, who soon after his coming there was frozen to death while hunting -- that Jane Shannon, being left at the head of a family in straightened circumstances, manufactured a long web of linen from the textile fiber of nettles. At the time, they lived in Belmont County, a few miles northeast of Barnesville. She had care of an interesting family and possessed a genius and an energy peculiar to those whole-souled pioneer women who figured in the early unwritten history of southeastern Ohio. With her inventive powers -- which were equal to the emergency of the times -- she had a quantity of those nettles mowed or cut with a cradle and left exposed to a process of "maceration," as was the custom in rotting flax and hemp. After this process, the stem or woody part which forms the interior of the stalk, becomes brittle and the fiber or lint becomes somewhat loosened from exposure to alternate sunshine and rain. When this process of rotting is done, it is then broken and "swingled" in the same way that flax is. The stalks are larger and the shives are separated with less labor. The fiber is finer, softer, stronger, more pliant and silk-like than flax; and is capable of being drawn into a finer thread by the spinning wheel. The little spinning wheel was used to spin all kinds of linen or thread, whether made of flax, hemp, or nettles. Thus, when the fiber of those nettles was prepared to be drawn into thread, this diligent woman -- with the labor of her own hands, assisted more or less by the members of her family as the case might be -- spun and wove a long web of fine linen, ample for all domestic purposes in the family.

Several members of the family of Jane Shannon that were thus raised under these adverse circumstances and amid the privations to which the rising generation of that period were subjected, became prominent citizens and held responsible positions in society.

The youngest son, Wilson Shannon, the first white child born in Warren Township, who in his youth wore clothing such as heretofore described, later became governor of Ohio and an ambassador to foreign courts, thus gaining a state and national reputation.

Ann (Webster) Chalfant was a Great-Great-Aunt of the contributor.

Written by Debora Webster Dearing, 2699 Indianola Ave., Columbus, Ohio.

HISTORICAL REMINISCENCES OF THE JOSEPH EDGERTON FAMILY
Joseph Edgerton 1762 -

Note: Prepared for and read at an Edgerton reunion 9-25-1891 by James Edgerton.

It has been laid on me to give at this time some items of unwritten history concerning some events in the life of the family to which I have the honor to belong. A very striking feature of my remarks on the reminiscences of the past sixty years will be the contrast between the present times and that of forty or sixty years ago in respect to the manner and the expense of living.

When our father Joseph Edgerton, son of James Edgerton Sr., settled on this place in 1818, the country was almost an unbroken forest, and the wolves were quite numerous and troublesome. The neighbors united to hunt them down, and found a den about a mile away on the Leatherwood hills. It was not certain whether the old ones were inside or not. Therefore, they decided that grandfather Doudna would crawl in, light in one hand and gun in the other and rope tied around one foot by which his comrades on the outside were to draw him out on signal of danger. Thus equipped, he dragged himself in about twenty feet and was awarded by finding a nest of several young ones but no old ones. These cubs they secured and used as decoys to draw the parent wolves, and in this manner succeeded in shooting one or both the parents.

We had no friction matches in those days, and if we let the fire go out we had to go to a neighbor for a supply. Grandfather lived a quarter of a mile away, and usually burned good hardwood -- maple or sugar-tree wood. As a result, he was in a position to furnish fire, so some of us were dispatched there to get hot embers. In those days, everyone did their cooking by open fire in a large fireplace, so we seldom lost fire. If we did, and couldn't get fire from a neighbor, we knew how to make it by striking flint and steel which, we always kept on hand.

We seldom lost fire when the weather was cold and a fire was kept up all of the time; but we lost it sometimes in summer. A fire of green sugar wood, covered well with ashes when not in use, kept very well. Many a time I have gone for fire when grandfather would open his pile of ashes and divide his stock -- giving me a generous share, which I would carry home on a shovel. Then, too, our light at night for reading or sewing was from the open fireplace, and if an extra task of the kind needed to be done at night, a supply of light wood must be provided. This was secured from an old tree or some such place and stored in one corner. The tallow candle was kept only for extra times or for use when company was present. Our oil of today was then unknown although it was at that day stowed away in natures storehouse waiting the light of science and the inventive genius of man to find and utilize it. Indeed, when I first went to Mt. Pleasant Boarding School in 1845, our light for studying at night was a lard oil lamp swung overhead and raised or lowered by a pulley. There was one such lamp in a room, the balance of the light being supplied by candles.

I also well remember the first cook stove brought into our house. It was of the Hathway patent. The peddler begged hard and finally got them to let him put it in to try but it was thought too expensive a luxury and he had to take it out and they returned to the open fire for cooking and the tin reflector for baking.

This article was a case made of tin about twenty inches long, a little like a miniature house or shed set with the open side to the fire. It was equipped with a pan similar to the bread pans of today. This would soon bake a loaf of bread or a couple of pies if placed near and in front of a good hot fire. A more advanced contrivance was the Dutch Oven out in the yard. Made usually of mud, it had to be heated to a certain degree, then the bread or whatever was to be baked, put in and shut up tightly to bake as the oven cooled. I remember very vividly my honor of getting oven wood, which had to be very dry and split up fine. A modification of this oven is still in use, particularly by bakers, but we never see nowadays the old mud oven out in the backyard. It stood on four posts set in the ground and on them a floor laid of split puncheons covered with a thick coat of mud to keep them from burning. The oven was made of mud piled on wood and arranged so that when the wood burned out it would leave the oven of dried mud. This possessed the great advantage of costing little except work, and that was a grand item in those days -- when it was harder to get a shilling than it is now to get a dollar.

We were glad to get six and a quarter cents a pound for butter then and many things which now sell readily at paying prices would not sell at any figure. Wheat, so important to us now, was not then found to any great extent in any farmer's storehouse, and would commend only twenty-five to fifty cents a bushel. I well remember when father had a few bushels made into flour, which he thought we could spare -- and he had to haul it to Wheeling, W. Va., in order to sell it.

There was a tread mill in the neighborhood to which I used to go to get our family breadstuffs made and I well remember one time in the fall of the year when our father was away from home and the water was so low the mills could not run. I would have to get up way before daybreak and go to the mill and wait until someone came to join teams *(of horses)* so as to have force enough to run the mill. In this manner we got our corn and occasionally a grist of buckwheat ground. In the latter case I would have to put the product into a sack and carry it into an upper story and bolt it by hand. Compare this with the present mode of producing breadstuffs.

In the matter of clothing there was nearly as marked a difference. We would raise flax, pull it, thresh the seed from it, spread it out on a clean piece of grass, rot, and when sufficiently rotten for the hard stiff part of the stalk to break easily, it was put away in a dry place until time to manufacture it. Then if the weather was too damp for the stalk to break up readily, it had to be dried by fire. For this a frame was made over a pile of burning logs on which the flax was spread to dry, but great care was necessary to keep it from catching fire.

To break, skutch, spin, and weave the lint was a job for the farmer's family in those days and nights also. In the cold winter evenings, mother would get her wheel in front of the large fire and spin the evening away in the manufacture of sheets as well as clothing such as skirts, pants, etc. -- save what few dimes we could raise and lay away to pay our taxes or other necessary bills.

The item of fruit has also changed. A peach orchard stood on the hill in sight where we now are, which was planted in 1805 and bore abundantly. It was very difficult to realize anything for the fruit and I have seen neighbors come with ox carts, beat off the peaches, put them in their carts, and take them home. The sugar bills were of the indispensable variety and father would make any exchange he could to secure a supply. I remember his coming home with a lot of maple sugar cakes at one time. These were very large -- having been molded in some vessel which made them big enough to weigh ten or twelve pounds each -- and it seemed a problem how best to get them reduced to a state to be used. Father finally got the cutting box from the barn and sliced the sugar on it. In subsequent years we secured sugar water from this grove of maple trees, and made our own maple sugar. We hauled it to the cellar where there was a large open fireplace and evaporated it in iron kettles, and thus procured the season's sweet.

Submitted by: Sarah Maxwell.

ANECDOTES CONCERNING CHARLES LIVEZEY

Charles, son of Jesse K. and Elizabeth Patterson Livezey, raised a colt that proved to be one of those good family horses. Such were designated because of their quiet, gentle disposition and a valuable trait in those days when used so much by women and children as well as the men.

His wife, Elizabeth Smith Livezey, could harness and hitch her to the surrey, if necessary, and drive her wherever she wished. The children, Albert, Walter, Jesse and William would play around her and walk under her body when so inclined, without the least fear of danger and she never betrayed their confidences.

When they got old enough to help care for and work her, she was more responsive to their commands than those from an older person. For a number of years, she was the only horse on the ten-acre lot. Consequently, she pulled the surrey to take the family to meeting at Stillwater twice a week and very often to the Boarding School, as well as elsewhere.

Near the meetinghouse, the road forked -- one lane leading to the meeting house and the other to the school. When nearing that point, if someone would say, "Nelly, we want to go to meeting," or "Go to the Boarding School this time," she always took the right road. If in the evening, without being told, she took the road to the school, apparently having learned that we did not go to meeting that time of day.

When the time came that an automobile was bought, old Nelly still had her same home and master as long as she lived.

Written by: Elizabeth Smith Livezey, Barnesville, Ohio.

MEMORY LANE BY ISAAC HALL

In writing a bit of early history, I will say that anything I may offer will be from memory alone.

I was 71 years old on the 12th of March 1942, so my memory goes back to practices and things that might be a new subject to the younger generation. At this particular time, sugar and sweets are a much talked of subject. No doubt there are many young folks who do not know that even in my time, no one, even with plenty of money, could buy granulated sugar.

My first recollection of sugars was "Orlenes" sugar, a very dark sticky coarse grained kind, that would become so juicy in the bottom of the grocers' barrel that the last had to be carried home in water-tight containers. Then there was light brown, which exposed to the air for a short time would become as hard as sand rock.

But I invite the younger generation to go with us, down "Memory Lane" to the time when but little sugar was used in canning or for fruit butters. My grandfather, Cyrus Hall, was the first white child born in the Leatherwood Valley. After growing to manhood he married Ellen Strahl. They built a home on the hill, one mile south of what is now Quaker City, Ohio and planted what was then considered a large orchard. In this orchard were many sweet apples of several varieties. These were used for making sweet cider to be used for sweetening fruit butters, etc.

Back in that time, many people travelled long distances on horseback, with a cotton grain bag with a gallon jug in each end thrown across the back of the saddle (or maybe a sheepskin) to my grandfather's, to try to buy, or beg, enough cider to sweeten "a sturring" of apple butter.

Grandfather had three sons. The older of the three, Edward -- who was my father-- learned the art of maple sugar making when quite young. Grandfather at one time had about two hundred sugar trees (hard maples). When there was a good run of sap, all four men were quite busy at least part of every day and well into the night, as long as the season lasted -- that being until the leaf buds were ready to swell.

A good-sized log house was built near the middle of the camp. An open fireplace extended entirely across one end and in this fireplace were hung four sugar kettles. Some of them weighed 250 pounds. At that time, buckets were scarce and expensive, so by each tree was a trough made from half of a poplar log about three feet long. The sap boiled down to a light syrup after the kettles had been filled up many times.

This syrup was allowed to cool and settle, usually overnight. Then it was strained through a heavy woolen cloth. Next, a well-beaten egg together with a pint of rich milk was added, and allowed to come to a slow boil. The milk and egg all left the syrup, and came to the top in the form of an ugly looking scum. This process brought up the dark particles of woody substance and left the syrup a bright golden color. This produced a product that I am certain will never be excelled, if one is looking for a top dressing for either griddle cakes or hot soda biscuits.

On the farm where I now live, there were at one time about forty large sugar trees, but scattered over a wide area. We called it the sugar camp. There I served my apprenticeship.

Some may think that in order to make maple syrup, or maple sugar, one must have a great number of trees, expensive outfits, etc. They are wrong. On our lawn are sugar trees that were planted in the spring of 1914. This spring I tapped four of the larger ones. On good sap days, they produce 1 1/2 gallons per tree. Four gallons of sap should make one jelly glass of thick syrup. Five gallons should make a dessert dish of dry maple sugar. You might ask, does it pay? The answer depends entirely upon what kind of pay you are looking for. Sell at a profit? No. Who would want to sell anything so good. Is it profitable to make and keep? Yes, for "it's good to the last drop" and the "memory lingers on."

Some people may have "raised cain," before the advent of maple sugar making, but the raising of cane for molasses making came much later.

Six miles southwest of Quaker City and on the Seneca Fork of Wills Creek was in the early times the Joseph Burson farm. On it was the first clearing and permanent home in that part of the valley. On the Burson farm, no doubt, was the first cane patch in this part of Ohio.

The following year cane was raised in many places in Guernsey and Belmont Counties. The Burson farm is now covered by the water in Seneca Lake.

Written by: Isaac Hall, Quaker City, Ohio. *(grandson of Cyrus Hall)*

THE PATTERSON HISTORY

(The following Patterson Family chart is inserted to assist with the following story.)

William and Keziah Patterson's son, William Patterson Jr. married Elizabeth Ladd Patterson

    Their children: Silas Patterson married Rachel Starbuck
        Talitha Patterson married Stephen Bailey
        Jeremiah Patterson married Elizabeth Plummer
        <u>Exum Patterson married Anna Doudna</u>
        Rachel Patterson married John Plummer
        Sarah Patterson married Micajah Binford
        Jared Patterson married Angelina Binford

<u>Exum and Anna Doudna Patterson</u>

    Their children: Phebe Patterson
        <u>Elizabeth (b. 1821) married Jesse K. Livezey</u>
        Mary Patterson
        John Patterson
        Sarah Patterson

<u>Jesse and Elizabeth Patterson Livezey</u>

    Their children: Charles Livezey married Elizabeth Smith
        John P. Livezey
        Oliver Livezey
        Joseph Exum Livezey
        Albert Livezey
    <u>Anna Livezey married John Hall</u>

<u>John and Anna's daughter, Elizabeth Hall married Silas Hartley</u> and she is the author of this article.

As near as I can tell, the Pattersons came to Concord Meeting (now Colerain) from North Carolina in 1807 and later moved to Stillwater Meeting one mile east of Barnesville, Ohio.

Sarah Patterson, daughter of William and Elizabeth Ladd Patterson married Macajah Binford, on 2-4-1804. Jared Patterson, son of William and Elizabeth married Angelina Binford 1-2-1808. Silas Patterson, son of William and Elizabeth, married Rachel Starbuck 5-4-1814. Some of their descendants are Lindley P. Bailey and Allen Bailey. Jeremiah Patterson, son of William and Elizabeth Ladd Patterson, married Elizabeth Plummer 12-16-1812. Rachel Patterson, daughter, married John Plummer 3-27-1817. Exum Patterson, married Anna Doudna, 11-27-1818.

Talitha Patterson married Stephen Bailey 9-14-1808 and had six children, Elizabeth, William, Benjamin, Exum, Stephen II, and Rachel. Some of the Fishers in Barnesville are descendants of their son Benjamin Bailey who married Lucy Crew. Burkharts flower gardens is owned by Vernon Burkhart, a great grandson. Some of the Skinners on Stillwater are descendants of Rachel who married Louis Naylor.

Stephen Bailey II married Martha Edgerton; their descendants are Rosella Bailey, who married Jonathan Binns, and Ida Bailey, who married Harvey Binns.

I have heard mother Anna Livezey Hall tell of the years of long ago about great grandfather, William Patterson Jr. He had what was called "White swelling," so was lame. His mother Keziah and others were at a quilting bee. The company was talking about this one and that one who were going to get married. Keziah Patterson said, "My poor lame Billy, there won't be anyone have him." Elizabeth Ladd was present and spoke up, "Yes, I will." Grandmother Keziah said, "I intend to see it shall be so." They were married in 8-22-1781, and raised a large family.

William Patterson, son of William and Keziah, married Elizabeth Ladd, and came to Stillwater Meeting in 1808; later they moved to Ridge Monthly Meeting. They bought a few acres of land just south of the road leading to Ridge meeting house and on Number 8 road. *(currently SR Rt. 800.)* A new house and barn have been built in the past 25 years. The old log house stood near a spring about 100 feet northeast of the present one. I have heard mother say "One First Day (Sunday) morning grandfather Exum was eating his breakfast. He looked up in time to see Anna Doudna on her way to meeting. "I believe I would like to walk with Anna Doudna on her way to meeting," he said. That was the first she knew he thought anything of her. They were married in 1819 and lived in a house almost on the same foundation where Joe Johnson now lives, just south of Sugar Grove School house on Number 8 *(SR 800)*, south of Barnesville, Ohio. *(Sugar Grove was a country school located in the far southwest corner of Section 14 Warren Twp.)*

They had 40 acres of ground that her father -- John Doudna -- gave them. Elizabeth Ladd was the first to speak in the first meeting house built at Ridge. *(Chestnut Ridge Monthly Meeting)* My mother -- her great-granddaughter, Anna Livezey Hall -- spoke her first time in the last meeting held in the same building. It was torn down so a new building could be constructed on the same location.

The meeting grounds were given by Joseph Patterson, who married Hannah Marmon in 1775. They lived where Alfred Doudna now lives -- a lane east of the meeting house, to the left. Joseph Patterson was the first to be laid in the graveyard.

Elizabeth Ladd Patterson had a minute (written instructions from the meeting) to visit with some Friends, and while they were away, their son Exum, who lived about one quarter mile away, was asked to take care of their chores. During this time, my grandmother, Elizabeth Patterson (Livezey), was born in a little log cabin near the spring of William and Elizabeth's home in 1821.

Exum and Anna Patterson bought a 131-acre farm in Somerset Township, two miles east of Ridge meetinghouse. This home was near a spring in the bottom land, near a pine tree now standing close to State Route 148. This was a great charge, as great Uncle John died in 1827 and great-grandfather Exum died in 1828, with typhoid fever. In 1856, great-aunts Phebe and Mary both died with scarlet fever. The rest of the children had it. Grandmother Elizabeth Patterson had it so bad that the soles of her feet peeled off so perfectly, that she laid them away for keepsakes. Her children played with them and they had it, too. These soles became so broken, she finally burned them.

My uncle Oliver Livezey had the habit of running with his tongue out. One evening, he was running back and forth on a settee and stumped his toe and fell on the arm of the settee. He cut the artery in his tongue with his teeth. He lived only a few hours as the doctors in those days did not know how to stop bleeding by sewing, like they do now. The doctors used to bleed nearly everyone if they were sick. That was the custom in the early days.

This left great-grandmother Anna Doudna Patterson alone with two young girls and a large farm. They held together until 1848, when Anna married Joseph King of Chesterhill, Ohio. She then went with him to live there. This left grandmother Elizabeth and Aunt Sarah alone.

In 1849 grandmother Elizabeth married Jesse K. Livezey. They lived here a few years but thought the family would be stronger and have better health if the house was moved up on a hill a few hundred feet. This was done by rollers and a horse. The family lived in a different house while theirs was being moved. It took some time to do and it was a slow job. Afterwards, a two story addition, two rooms wide and one deep, was built in front of the old house. I think all of the old part now has been torn down.

In 1889 or 1890 grandfather built a large two story barn, which sheltered a large flock of sheep, cows, and horses. It had large mows of good hay. I have heard people say "Jesse K. Livezey's farm was the best in Somerset Township." He was a good financier and farmer. Both he and his wife were real old-fashioned Friends (Quakers), as well as my father John G. Hall and mother Anna Livezey Hall. Grandfather and grandmother had six children. All died young except mother -- the oldest -- and Uncle Charles Livezey.

Mother was a teacher at Ridge School, Westtown Boarding School, and Friends Boarding School at Barnesville, Ohio. She taught seven terms at Barnesville.

She was married to John G. Hall, who came to the United States when 25 years old, from England. He was born on Paradise St., Liverpool, England. They were married 12-21-1883.

Grandfather Livezey bought great-grandfather John Doudna's farm in the spring of 1884. Father and Mother moved into it in 3rd Month 1884. *(Located in Warren Twp. Sect.7 and Somerset Twp. Sect.12)* They lived here nearly 34 years. Wilmer Hall is now living on this farm. They had two children, Elizabeth and Wilmer Hall.

Elizabeth married Silas H. Hartley in 1907. We have five children and eight living grandchildren. Wilmer Hall married Mildred Rachel Edgerton in 1918, and they have four children and one grandchild. Wilmer lives on the old home place which has been in the family for six generations continually. Elizabeth and family live in the house Amos Barlow built, and is just west of father's and mother's home.

In 1893, Charles Livezey married Elizabeth W. Smith and they went to housekeeping on Jesse K. Livezey's farm until 1898 or 99, then went to Barclay Smith's on Stillwater neighborhood and bought ten acres from him and built a house west of Barnesville, Ohio where his wife now lives. He died 8-20-1927 while superintendent of the Friends Boarding school, of influenza. They had five boys, the oldest died in infancy. There are fifteen living grandchildren. Albert Livezey is the only one living around Barnesville since their marriage.

Aunt Sarah Patterson (grandmother Livezey's sister) married Henry Clay Lewis in 1860, and they had four children (one died in infancy). They have nine living grandchildren and eighteen living great-grandchildren. Aunt Sarah lived most of the time with grandmother and grandfather Livezey until she married. They lived a few years where Charles Meyers now lives, west of where they bought and their son Hiram Lewis now lives. They both died here.

A Dog Story

After Uncle Charles Livezey moved away from the farm, his dog finally got to our home. Grandfather and Grandmother Livezey came to live with father and mother *(John and Anna Hall)*. Grandmother lived only a few weeks and passed away 10th Month 1897. The dog remembered grandmother as she fed him so often. After he came to our house he came in and greeted all but soon went to the hall door and whined. He found all but grandmother. He died a few years later.

It appears that a number of Patterson families moved from North Carolina to Ohio and settled first at Concord Meeting at Colerain, Ohio, then moved to Stillwater Monthly Meeting and later on, some moved to Ridge Monthly Meeting. Joseph Patterson married Hannah Marmon. The man who gave the ground for Ridge Monthly Meeting, Lemuel Patterson, married Hannah Arnold, and lived in a house by the water works.

A son Joshua Patterson married Amy Broomall. Their son, Barclay, married Georgia Connard. Benjamin Patterson Sr. married Jane Bailey, and later married Jane Lowery. The first wife had ten children. One child, William Henry Patterson, married (1) Carry Outland, (2) Elizabeth Griffith-French, no issue. William Henry and Carry had two children. Ernest Patterson, a contractor, married Florence Bailey. They live in Barnesville. A son, Benjamin, married Anna Hardesty. They had four children. Frederic and Edward live in Barnesville. Frederic is an electrician and Edward is manager of East Main Street M.K. grocery store -- besides being prominent in other affairs.

Isaac Patterson married Rebecca Crew, 9-20-1820 and they had eight children, four died in 1836 of scarlet fever. Two of them died within a week. Their son Eli married (1) Phariba Bailey, (2) Tabitha Bailey. Eli lived just east of Ridge school house near a spring. He later built a nice house by the road where another house now stands. The first one burned in the 1890s.

Louisa Patterson (daughter of Eli and Phariba) married Jesse I. Doudna. They had four children. Wallace and Ethel lived and Wallace has two children and two grandchildren. Ethel married Joe Wylie, and they have three living children and five grandchildren. Ruthanna (called Ruthanner) Patterson married Joel Bailey. David Patterson married (1) Eunice Starbuck, (2) Sarah Stewart. The first wife had four children. A daughter, Eva Luzerne, married Allen Bailey. They had seven children. The second wife had seven children and they live in the west.

The Ridge School house was built out of bricks out of the meeting house at Somerton.

Written by: Elizabeth J. Hartley, daughter of John and Anna Hall

JOSEPH PATTERSON
1753 - 1816

Joseph Patterson was born Third Month 18th 1753, and married Hannah Marmon in 1775. She was born Second Month, 27th 1753. Joseph Patterson died 5th Month 7th 1816 at the age of 63, and was the first one buried in the grave yard at Ridge. His wife, Hannah Marmon Patterson, died 2nd Month 9th 1820 at the age of 67.

Their daughter, Sara Patterson, was born Fourth Month 8th 1790, and married John Shoebridge Williams. He was born 7th Month 31st, 1790. They were married 9th Month 16th, 1813. Sara died 5th Month 29th, 1858. John died 4th Month 27th, 1878. John Shoebridge Williams was my father's great-uncle and a brother of his grandmother Elizabeth Williams Garretson.

Uncle John Shoebridge Williams helped build the National Road. In 1826 he became the assistant of C.W. Wever in the construction of the National Road in Ohio -- east of Zanesville. It was his business to superintend the grading and macadamizing of the Maysville Turnpike, which he did during the six years of its construction. That road -- together with the engineering of drover roads in Kentucky and several diverging from the city of Cincinnati and some other roads in this state -- will long remain as marks of seventeen years of labor.

I will copy a little from the *American Pioneer*, which Uncle John S. Williams wrote in 10th Month 1843:

"In my twenty second year, I took up school near Barnesville, where the bright blue eyes of one of my pupils, Sara Patterson by name (the same eyes that do not wear glasses to this day) together with her rosy cheeks, seemed to monopolize in themselves all that was good, bright, or pretty in Euclid, Ferguson, Newton, Bacon, Martin, and a host of other authors that were dear to me. The purpose of my life seemed to be changed. Here let me drop a caution to the fair lasses not to let their eyes shine too sparkingly around, for they know not what harm they might do. How many good scholars in prospect they might spoil, and how much of the course of life might be changed by them."

Later he says, "Ten fine children have in times past sat around my table. Other kinds of wealth I never was adept at either collecting or keeping together. The lack of such a trait of character I shall not regret until it is seen that money bestows merit, or that the value of the man is in direct proportion to the weight of his purse. Having seen some men do more good with one dollar than others with their thousands, the conclusion had been forced upon me, that riches are more frequently detriments than in blessings. This, however, is not the fault of the property, but of those who possess it."

Written by: Elma Doudna Bailey

Bob Peters

When Jesse Bailey Sr., grandfather of Lindley P. Bailey, came to Warren Township, Belmont County, Ohio from Dinwiddie County, Virginia, in 1811 he brought with him a black man, Bob Peters, who joined Stillwater Friends Meeting soon after his arrival, and, so far as is known, was the only black person ever belonging to this meeting.

"Old Bob" was known and honored for his many good qualities and was the best cook around. No wedding was complete without "Old Bob" as cook. His maple sweet cakes, corn pones and roast possum made him famous and were enjoyed by all. Robert H. Smith related to William H. Stanton how "Old Bob" kept his cookie box well filled for the boys of the neighborhood and if he was not at home when they called, they would sometimes climb down the stick chimney of his cabin to get them, though they knew the door was never locked, just to hear him scold about them "ornery" boys that would steal his cookies, but it pleased him and was just what he wanted and expected them to do. Robert H. Smith was one of the boys who ventured down the chimney for "Old Bob's" cookies.

At one time he lived near the present James Walton brick house *(current location of Walton Retirement Home)* and "kept" the Stillwater Meetinghouse.

He died sometime in the 1840s and was laid to rest in the Stillwater burying ground, loved and honored by all.

Written by Anna Bailey Patten, Tacoma, Ohio

EDWARD PICKETT

Edward, the youngest son of William Pickett, was married in 1888, and moved to Omaha, Nebraska, where two children, Warren Edward and Howard Richard, were born. Owing to the declining health of his wife, they moved back to Barnesville, Ohio in 1893. After a year in Barnesville, she passed away.

The boys were cared for in their grandfather William Pickett's home and Edward went to Pittsburg and was engaged in the Life Insurance work. Edward later married again in the Third Month, 1898. He contracted typhoid fever and passed away the following winter and was buried at the Stillwater burying grounds. *(William Pickett's home was located on Pigeon Point Road in the northeast corner of Section 8, Warren Twp.)*

William G. Steer was appointed guardian for the two boys and they lived in their grandfather Pickett's home until they reached manhood.

Howard, the youngest, seemed to be the unlucky one in early life and all of his troubles were on his left side. First it was boils, then while riding a pony, he was crowded against a fence and injured his knee. Later while in a swimming pool, a turtle bit a piece out of his heel as large as a twenty-five cent piece which left a permanent scar. When he was nine years old, I sent him to the barn to bridle a horse that I had borrowed from a neighbor and was thought to be perfectly gentle, but on inquiry found that when young he had a wicked disposition. Soon after Howard went to the barn, we heard an alarming cry and, on going immediately to the barn, 20 rods away found him outside with his left eye laying out on his cheek.

The horse had bit him and the lower teeth had cut the eye open and the mark of the upper teeth was very light on his forehead and disappeared in a few days. A doctor was called at once and he removed the eye. The cavity soon got well and he never had trouble with the artificial eye, except when at Penn State College. He had the artificial eye crushed in the socket and he was in the hospital for some time.

He has lived on the Pacific coast for more than 20 years and his home is now in Salem, Oregon. He has three sons, the oldest is a Marine in the Pacific fleet and another past 21 years of age. He has been successful in business and he and his wife are leaders in religious activities.

Written by William G. Steer, Barnesville, Ohio.

WILLIAM PICKETT
1820 - 1910

William Pickett was the son of Thomas Pickett and Hanna Steer. Hanna was a sister of my grandfather, James Steer Sr. William was born in 1820 at Concord and moved with his parents to Hopewell Meeting, three miles south of Malta, Morgan County, Ohio.

William married Rebecca Worthington when she was sixteen years old. They were the parents of nine children -- John, Mary, Elizabeth, Perley, Isaac, Louisa D., Sara M., Thomas and Anna, the latter passing away when young. With the exception of John, they all were educated at the Boarding Schools at Mt. Pleasant, Jefferson County, and Barnesville, Belmont County, Ohio.

Mary taught at Mt. Pleasant for several years, and all the others had been teachers except John and Thomas. Sara M., the only one who graduated at Barnesville Boarding School, taught for a number of years at Number One Tacoma school in Warren Township, Barnesville Public school, and Friends primary school at Salem, Ohio.

Of the twenty-five grandchildren, sixteen are living, and eleven great-grandchildren are of draft age; two of them are in the Navy. William Pickett had little means when married, so felt the need of economizing time. On one mid-week meeting day, he thought best to stay at home and plow. The first round he made he broke his plow, which to repair cost him more than a week's work. This accident confirmed in him the belief that it was not right to absent himself from attending all religious meetings or worship.

At the time of the Civil War, John, the oldest son was of age, so father and he were taken to Marietta, Ohio when they refused to enlist, and were kept there for some time -- then allowed to return home without having been punished in any way.

With the help of his sons he cleared the land and also increased the size of his farm so it was considered one of the best kept and best fenced in the community. In those days all the fences were rail, staked and double ridered. To build such a fence, they had to first make it eight rails high, set two stakes at each panel, and place the two riders. These rails were made of the best walnut, poplar, and oak. The virgin soil was very productive.

Father told me that he grew 100 bushels in three crops in succession or 1,000 bushels on the 10 acres. Also, he noted that he was the first one to use bran to feed stock -- that the millers previously had always dumped it into the river. I am reminded in connection with this, that one evening he had loaded a wagon with sacks of wheat to take to the mill, and the next morning, found his wagon on top of the barn with the wheat in it. This was a Halloween prank.

In the early time of the Boarding School at Mt. Pleasant, a brother, Thomas Pickett, was a student. One day near noon, he received a telegram telling of his brother's serious illness. There was no railroad in Morgan County then, so the only way of travel was by steamboat on the Muskingum to Zanesville. Having to wait until morning for the boat, he started on foot and was soon picked up by a farmer and taken several miles. Then he again walked on until a man in a high wheeled one-seated sulky overtook him and stopped to ask where he was going. On learning from father the urgency of getting to Zanesville in time for the train, the man informed him that the only help he could give was to allow him to hold on to the back of the cart, which offer he readily accepted. In this manner he ran for some time though it required an effort to keep up with the speed of the horse. By being thus assisted, he was able to travel the 28 miles in time for the train to Wheeling, W. Va. It was after night by the time he had reached the boat landing that crossed to Martins Ferry and no boat was running on account of the heavy ice floating in the river. Although it seemed a hazardous thing to do, he saw no way but to endeavor to cross on the floating cakes of ice, which he was favored to do without an accident. We need to remember that the only light to guide him was the reflection from the blast furnaces. It was still 12 miles to Mt. Pleasant. Yet he travelled on to the home of Asa Raley about half way and soon learned he was too late to see his brother alive.

William and Rebecca were faithful in the attendance of all their meetings, driving to Chester Hill, 12 miles away over unimproved roads in all kinds of weather. Their only conveyance was an open-top spring wagon. Those who never have had such experiences can hardly realize what it meant to drive that 24 miles and attend meeting the same day.

By 1883, their home meeting being kept up by only a few persons, and two of their married daughters -- Mary P. Taber and Louisa D. Steer -- living near Barnesville, they decided to sell the farm and move there. They bought the Joseph Doudna farm, which was formerly the Joel Dawson farm, located one-half mile from the Stillwater Yearly Meetinghouse. Father was then quite lame and not able to manage the work, so his son Thomas and wife lived with them for four years, after which he had to depend on hired help until 1896, when Louisa and I returned after living nine years in California.

Rebecca Pickett passed away in 1904. The farm was sold, so father and the two sisters -- Elizabeth and Sara M. -- went to live with us in 1907. The home we had bought at Tacoma was formerly the home of William and Jane Stanton. *(62085 Tacoma Rd.)*

William told us of one autumn when he failed to get his apples stored before winter. Instead, he covered the piles with corn fodder and the apples wintered in good condition. He was a man of strong character and a very useful member of meeting. Though having little education, he would often repeat a selection he had committed to memory while following the plow. William and Rebecca were faithful attenders of meeting when able. They were both in the position of elders here and in Pennsville Quarter, Morgan County. She passed away in 1904 and he in 1910, the day after his grandson Louis J. Taber and Edna Bailey were married.

William and Rebecca had been married more than 65 years and were laid away in Stillwater burying grounds, as were all of their children except John and Thomas. The former was buried in Colorado and the latter in Omaha, Nebraska.

Written by: William G. Steer, Barnesville, Ohio. *(married Louisa Pickett)*

THE PLUMMER FARM

Back in the last of the 18th century when Friends (Quakers) were freeing their own slaves, but were surrounded and hectored by neighbors who would neither agree with them nor welcome such free thinkers among them, these friends were casting longing eyes to the regions about them for a land where freedom of speech and conscience might still be exercised. At this critical juncture, the great Northwest Territory was opened to settlement. Slavery there was prohibited, and the country was beautiful and rich, full of hills, meadows, rivers and, most of all, forests. It is no wonder the heartsick Quakers thronged towards it willing to face all sorts of heavy labor and privations.

The first Friend, and the fourth person, to settle in Warren Township, Belmont County, Ohio, came from the Plummer family, which traces its ancestry to Wales in the late sixteen hundreds. Its first representative to settle in Ohio was Abraham Plummer, born in 1736 and who married Sarah Ward in 1762, in Calvert County, Maryland. The mother is not mentioned as being in Ohio, but Abraham Plummer accompanied by his son Robert Plummer Sr. and his family, arrived in the region now called Warren Township, in the late spring of 1801. They hired a wagon and teamster to carry their goods to the wilderness, but rode horseback themselves. While debating where to build, the wife stuck her willow riding switch into the ground near a spring saying "This is where our house shall be." Many years later the old willow tree still marked the spot though the little cabin was soon replaced. The certificate of membership among Friends followed them as soon as it could be arranged. *(This property was located at 62400 Dusty Lane, east of Tacoma, Section 10 North.)*

From the records of Concord Monthly Meeting 11-19-1803, a certificate was produced for Robert Plummer, Rachel his wife, and children, Elizabeth, John and Abraham from Pipe Creek Monthly Meeting dated 13th of 11th Month 1802, which was read and received.

Abraham Plummer, then 65 years old, promptly "entered" the land and in 1802 received the patent for same, granted by Thomas Jefferson, President, and James Madison, Secretary of State. These three adults -- with the children, aged respectively 6, 5, and 2 -- lived as one family. Having arrived late in the spring they built a hurried summer home of logs and poles, cut and placed by Abraham and Robert, and chinked by Rachel, the latter's wife. The roof was made of hickory bark, the first layer being placed with the sap side up, and the second laid so as to break joints of the first, with the bark side up. When exposed to the sun, this green bark became so shriveled and drawn together that rain could scarcely penetrate it. The floor was dirt, and the door a quilt. The window had greased paper for glass. They hastily cleared a small space and raised a crop of corn. The nearest to have it ground was Morristown, six miles away, through the wilderness.

By autumn they built a more substantial home of heavy logs. The ambitious builder put a little porch at the front door to sit on which innovation placed this cabin in a class by itself, and

Plummer Cabin 1950

Rachel held up her head in pride that her house was the only one in the neighborhood to possess such a feature. This last log house is still on the "Plummer Farm," and has for many years been used as the "shop" -- housing all sorts of carpenters and mechanics tools. It has been boarded over inside and out but a little chipping away of this shell reveals the original logs.

The oldest part of the present dwelling also was built by Robert Plummer Sr. In the big kitchen fireplace, recently re-opened, the cooking was done in pots hanging on the crane, in utensils covered with ashes on the hearth, a reflecting Dutch oven, long legged skillets, and so forth.

He dressed the stones and built the spring house and deep stone trough into which the milk crocks were set to be surrounded by the cold water, and erected the log smoke house in the rear of the dwelling, both of which are standing at this writing.

He set aside in 1802, the next year after his arrival, an acre of ground for burial purposes, *(The "French Cemetery" on Bailey Road)* intending to make it the property of Friends so that a meetinghouse could be built on it, so rapidly did the settlement fill up. In the meantime, James Vernon built a home in 1805 near the burying ground, and this house was used as a meetinghouse. This was the first gathering for religious worship in the township. Shortly afterwards, the trend of settlement having moved southward, the first meetinghouse was erected on the land where now stands the yearly meeting house. Consequently, the intention of Robert P. Plummer Sr. was not carried out, but the plot became a township burying grounds. We do not have the date of the death of Abraham Plummer, but one or the other of these two is buried in this acre donated by Robert Plummer Sr. and we suppose it was the former, as he passed out of the records rather soon. In those days no stones marked the graves of Friends. *(Records show Robert Sr. and wife were buried at Stillwater burial grounds.)*

ROBERT PLUMMER, JR.
1813-1894

After arriving at the new home, two more children were born to Robert and Rachel; Mary C. in 1809 and Robert Jr. born 1813. The latter was just one-year-old when Robert Sr. died. The widow Rachel, presently married Caleb Engle. In the course of time the farm became the property of Robert Plummer Jr. and his mother again a widow, lived out her space of life with her son's family.

In 1836, Robert Jr. married Jane Bailey (born 1817), the daughter of Micajah and Mary Bailey. They raised eight children out of nine. The house not being commodious enough for such a family, he added more rooms to the old part as can be readily seen.

Part of the original farm was disposed of to the Belmont County Children's home. The remainder was purchased in 1940 by Charles and Ellen Morlan and were presented to the Friends Boarding School as a gift of love. Both were members of the Boarding School Committee.

Notes: A maple sugar camp was operated on the place and also cane was raised for sorghum molasses made for themselves and neighbors. Lye was leached out of wood ashes and

homemade soap was for a long time the only kind they knew. Flax and wool were both raised and processed at home for wearing apparel. Weaving of cloth, carpets and bed spreads was an almost daily occupation. When trees became scarce, a coal mine was opened "down in the woods" which still is in operation.

The story came by word of mouth that so dense was the forest and undergrowth when the first settlers arrived, that it took them three days (some say five) to cut their way from Morristown to their destination, about six miles away. Corn had to be ground at Morristown, flour had to be hauled from St. Clairsville, and the nearest neighbor was a mile away.

The name of Robert Plummer Sr. is seen often in the Stillwater Monthly Meeting minutes. He was the first recorder of births and deaths, being appointed in 1809.

Robert Plummer Jr. used to go once a year to buy shoes in Barnesville for his brood. He guessed at sizes, brought home a big sack full of various kinds, dumped them on the floor and told the children to fit themselves. They were all straight shoes, no rights nor lefts, so that by changing each day from one foot to the other, they wore longer.

When the early trail became a road, it passed immediately in front of the house, dividing the farm. Drovers and tramps were frequent guests and none were ever turned away. But the latter were granted but one room (which frequently had to be de-loused) and to this day it is still called the "tramps room," where they were locked in. The droves of cattle were turned into the fields.

"Aunt Martha Leek," a neighbor, and Rachel (Plummer) Engle, both spent their last years at the old house. As was pretty general in those days both smoked tobacco in pipes. It used to be the duty of the oldest granddaughter to fill and light these pipes. A mischievous tale is told of one of these old ladies. We do not know which.

One night she had a "boy-friend" who was apparently staying overnight. They sat one on each side of the big fireplace in the living room. It got later and later. Conversation languished and died. Finally, she said "I wish thee would go to bed, I want to take my smoke." He replied, "I have been waiting for thee to go to bed so I could take mine." So both lit their pipes, visited as they smoked and puffed the smoke up the chimney so the family would not know how long they sat up.

Once in the earlier days when it was customary for Friends as well as others to use a "home brew" of some sort to regale the harvest hands. little Robert Plummer Jr. was sent to the fields with the jug. His curiosity was aroused, probably more than once on the way and he sampled the contents. They found him in a drunken stupor. Horrified at what had happened, his stepfather banned forever any intoxicant on the farm.

About three months after Rachel Plummer became a widow, Caleb Engle, who was recently a widower with several children, met her at meeting and expressed some sympathy for her. He also hinted that they might possibly become interested in each other. She was offended at such a suggestion but he added "Oh, I know thee isn't thinking of such things yet, but thee's still young and goodlooking, and somebody is going to get thee. I wanted my name in first." He not only got it in first but last also and in two years they married. The families mingled till her youngest child said many years afterwards that there was such harmony they could never have told which parent claimed which children.

Compiled by: Laura Hoyle, Cambridge, Ohio.

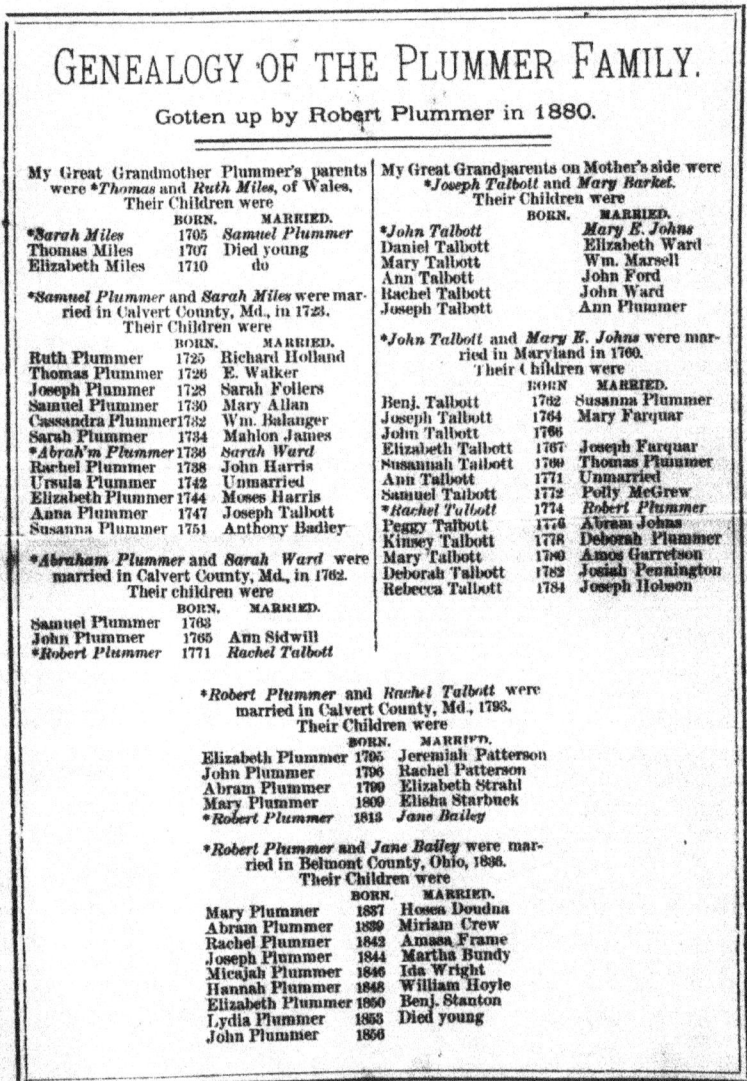

A QUAKER CENTENNIAL

Mt. Pleasant, Ohio, May 5th 1900. This year forms the centenary of the first meeting for worship of the Society of Friends in Ohio, and the Northwest Territory. This meeting was held five miles from this place at Concord, and was held under the spreading branches of a tree. Those who formed the gathering sat on newly hewed logs. It was held near the tent of Jonathan Taylor, who afterward moved to Short Creek near this place and then the meetinghouse was moved here. *(Location, Colerain Twp. Section 7)*

The first meetinghouse was built in 1804. Among the early settlers in this section, the Society of Friends formed a considerable portion, in regards to numbers and influence. By their industry and thrift, they soon transformed the wilderness into a community of prosperous homes. Their intense religious fervor and fidelity to defend convictions of right made them a strong power in shaping the contour of thought about them.

These Friends streamed to this section from Pennsylvania, New Jersey, Maryland, Virginia and North Carolina. Those coming from the south sought a more rigorous climate that their children might grow up free from slavery associations. In 1806, the Society was prosperous and they purchased ten acres of ground, and one year later the Short Creek Meetinghouse -- 45' by 70' -- was built at a cost of $2000.

In the beautiful burying ground at that place are to be found generation after generation of worshippers. In 1807, the Short Creek Quarterly Meeting was organized, consisting of the five monthly meetings of Concord, Short Creek, Salem and Miami, Ohio, and West Branch in Iowa.

The Ohio Yearly Meeting was set off from the Baltimore Yearly Meeting in 1812 and the first yearly meeting was held at Short Creek a year later. During the years 1815-16 a large meetinghouse capable of seating 2500 people was erected there. *(Mt. Pleasant Meetinghouse located at Mt. Pleasant, OH)*

The Friends settled here in such large numbers and spread out to points for miles, that they still predominate these communities. This was an underground railroad station, and as early as 1817 slaves would get across the river and strike out for this place, and be helped on to Canada. These fugitives increased year after year, and as none that ever got to Mt. Pleasant were ever recaptured, this station became famous. The first anti-slavery convention in Ohio was held here in 1837. In 1821, Benjamin Lundy who lived here then, began the publication of the "Genius of Universal Emancipation," the first genuine abolition paper in the United States. The records of 1814-15 tell of the marriage of Lundy to Esther Lewis.

The mother of Anna Dickinson lived here. Shortly after 1830, Benjamin Ladd, a Quaker, established two colonies of manumitted slaves at Hayti and near Stillwater. Edwin M. Stanton's grandparents were early settlers here.

The late Congressman Updegraff and the present Congressman J.J. Gill came from this stock. One of Mr. Gill's ancestors established the first silk mill in the United States here in 1841.

Abbie Flanner, the Quaker maiden with whom Fits-Green Halleck had a romantic leap-year correspondence in verse in 1836, lived and died here. This place has furnished eight members of the state legislature, two state senators, three lieutenant governors and Benjamin Stanton, once a member of the U.S. Congress from the Bellfountain district. The millionaire Senator William Sharon of Nevada was born near here.

Copied from: *Barnesville Enterprise* of May 10, 1900. Submitted by: Elizabeth C. Hartley.

JONATHAN T. AND ABIGAIL STEER SCHOFIELD

Jonathan and Abigail Schofield moved from the Aaron Frame home to the brick one-half mile below the Boarding school before 1863. There is no history of when this house was built. It was two stories with six rooms and a lean-to kitchen built over a good spring.

It faced the east and had two doors on the front and was well lighted as all the early built homes were. It burned about the year 1894. The occupants, Perley Pickett and Rebecca Schofield Pickett barely escaped with their lives.

Uncle Jonathan was the first agent here of the Provident Mutual Insurance Company of Philadelphia, Pa., when it was established in 1865. Our father failed to pass the physical examination when examined for insurance and yet lived to be nearly ninety years of age.

The first story of the barn was built in 1863 and was used for a place to crush cane for molasses. The mill was a large horizontal one getting the power from four horses attached to sweeps in the basement. This crushing was operated the entire twenty-four hours. Our Aunt Abigail did the work at the boiling shed.

About 1865 or 1866 the other story was raised on the barn. Amasa and Thompson Frame did the carpenter work. This required a large force of men to raise the bents *(sides)* when put together; the bents were forty feet long and sixteen or eighteen feet high. Strong poles with spikes in the end were used to assist in the raising when the bents were too high to use hands. It was found that while the work was in progress, that a mortise was not in place in the sill of the basement, so another had to be made with all possible speed so as not to keep the men waiting too long.

When the boring machine was brought, Peter Sears, an uncle of William H. Sears, offered to use it. Though not a very strong man in appearance, he was not lacking in energy and quickness and rapidly completed the work. Though this occurred more than seventy-five years ago (as of 1942), it is as vivid to me as though it had been yesterday.

Uncle Jonathan Schofield had one daughter, Rebecca, who died in Pittsburg, Pa., in 1899.

Written by: Anna M. Hoge and William G. Steer.

ANECDOTES OF NO. 1 AND NO. 2 SCHOOLS

(Number One country school was on a hill south of 60160 Pigeon Point Rd. Number two school was Tacoma School located on Bailey Road.)

No. 1 and No. 2 Schools were supported and taught mostly by Friends. My mother, Deborah H. B. Stanton, taught at No. 1 as early as 1862 and 1863. The effect of the Civil War was felt in the school. The younger children had more time to play besides recess and noon. These were about six or seven years of age and they would line up on each side -- one for the North and one for the South -- and fight with stones. They called the two parties Butternuts (the Southern) and the Unionists. Mother could only stop the school battle while in the building for as soon as they were out they were at it again.

While Mother taught at No. 1, they dismissed school one day because of Morgan's raid. He was supposed to be headed for that section. It was interesting to note that those who sympathized with the South made as much haste as anyone to hide their horses. One party hid his horses by cutting trees across a small hollow and putting the horses under it, similar to a cave. During the time my mother, Deborah H. B. Stanton, taught at No. 1 and No. 2, she had eight step-children and me as pupils -- but not all at one term.

When I taught at No. 1 the average attendance was 50 during the winter term. The winter term was for five months and the older pupils did not go during the spring and summer. These schools had a teacher and an assistant. Old No. 1 building stood about 100 ft. southwest of the present brick building. Some of the teachers were: Sara Bailey, Lindley Bailey, Pearley Pickett, Joe Bundle, Mary C. (Bundy) Smith, Sarah (Stanton) Hall.

Related by Mary C. (Bundy) Smith, and Contributed by: Dorothy L. Holloway, Wheeling, W. Va.

Copy of a Letter to Margaret Bailey -- From Anna Sears

My dear Niece;

We were at Isaac Stubbs on a visit a short time ago, and Elizabeth had these writings of thy father read. She also said thee had said thee would like very much to have them. My granddaughter Anna Milhouse heard it and said she would copy them for me, which she has done and we are about to send them to thee by Tilman and R.E. Patterson, as they talk of starting to Barnesville, Ohio soon, or tomorrow evening.

I suppose thee has heard of the peaceful state of thy father's mind during his last sickness.

I am still here at Robert Millhouse, and they are all very kind to me which makes it a pleasant home.

In much love to thee, Edmund, and the girls, I remain.

Thy Aunt Anna Doudna Sears

(Aunt Anna Sears was a daughter of the kidnapped boy -- John Doudna -- and a sister to Uncle Henry Doudna, who was Margaret Doudna Bailey's father and Sara M. Bailey's grandfather.)

The following extracts are in Henry Doudna's own words, except when it seemed better to leave out a word or words to bring out the meaning intended more perfectly or grammatically, and very few were changed at all in what we wrote for we wanted it as nearly as possible in his own words.

To my daughter, Margaret Doudna Bailey

A short account of some particulars of my past life, I thought it might be proper to relate for the encouragement of others in some such travail.

I may say by the account of my parents, that I was born in the County of Pitt in the state of North Carolina, within eleven miles of Pamlico Sound. I was raised in those parts where there was no preaching of the gospel, or scarcely a profession of any sort of persuasion, for at the burying's of the dead, some man that could read pretty well, used to take the Bible and read a chapter and then they covered up the corpse.

I well remember that when my grandfather John Knowis was buried, a man by the name of Jorden Shepherd read the sermon. Although I was only eight or nine years old, I well remember a great many words of the sermon as it was called, and I noticed his eyes as he read along. How he raised them off from the reading and turned them to the grave, which I thought was some profit or good to the dead, as I noticed him doing it many times. I have thought of these things many times since, and have often wondered if he had lifted his eyes towards heaven, whether that would have had the same impact on me as it did to see him cast them to the grave. I thought then that he did that for some good to the dead. Now it appears as plain to my view as it did then, though nothing but a child. I have heard say, "train up a child in the way that we want it to go and it will scarcely ever depart from it all."

My parents taught me better things. I have had to thank them many times for not allowing me to use any profane words or go to frolics or dancing -- although they were not clear of them themselves, especially on my father's part. He was brought up a sailor and without any education. I have heard them say when he was married to my mother that he did not know his letters and never went to school a day in his life. Yet, before he died, it appeared that he knew the Scriptures throughout by heart. James M. Round of Barnesville, Ohio, told me that he would not begrudge a vast sum if he could know and remember the scriptures as well as my father.

We lived in North Carolina awhile until the Revolutionary War. My father was drafted, and by consent of both my parents, he chose to hire, and they paid away almost everything they possessed. *(It was an accepted practice to hire someone to go to war in one's place.)*

At length the war ended. Then sprang up some persuasions of Methodists and Baptists, whose meetings for worship I frequently attended. It did not appear to me that their mode and manner of worship and the ground work of their religion, did agree with the little manifestations that were revealed in me. There appeared something within me that told me to get a wide, well-rounded perspective on religions before I joined any. So I went on without accepting any specific religion until I was twenty years old.

By this time, my parents heard of a settlement of Quakers, about sixty miles distant. By this time, they had heard some accounts of such people and had read some accounts of them in some books. My father took a journey out to see them, and when he came among them, he was very pleased with their comeliness and order. He attended one of their meetings, which suited him so well that he came and made ready and moved within twelve miles of Contentny meeting house. My parents, brothers and sisters then became members.

By request and birthright, I have had cause to look over the different professors of Christ. How many would be willing to stand their ground in the world if there was to arise some invasions of a very high power, which was going through the country destroying all who professed the name of Christ? Those who stand undaunted and unshaken at the point of the sword and muzzles of gun are the true volunteers of those who profess Christ.

I knew for my own part, it was a great while before I could appear permanent enough to stand it, for I often brought it to the bedside as I could get it to try my punctuality by, when at the same time allowing myself but one night to try it in. Supposing that the sun had set to rise no more with me. This has been the case many, many times and caused the floods of tears to flow from my eyes and bedew my pillow, before I could witness a submitting of this permanent standing which says "come life, come death, come whatever may come, and welcome, if I have my blessed Lord and dear Redeemer on my side, I care not who is against me.

For blessed be his Holy name forever, for He made Himself manifest to me in various ways, even when the devil was putting his bait and feeding me on Deism, with a scrupulous opinion of a mediator, He was pleased in his great and ever blessed condescending mercy, to lead me away in the vision of the night and show himself to me and his standings that it might assert me in reality.

For He (Christ) was standing a little space below the great Creator of heaven and earth, between him and the crowd I was in, standing of the outside with the dreadfulest feelings that every mortal had to be sure, my tongue is not able to express, nor my pen to write, though it appeared to be in profound silence.

But they all appeared to be walking up to him and turning off, without one word spoken, and it appeared to me that it would be my turn next. Oh, my knees and all my joints appeared to shake and shudder as though they would come apart, but at last I heard the joyful news that I might go away now, my time was not yet come.

Blessed be His adorable name forever which I have cause to praise for unfolding those hidden mysteries to me in various ways. I believe there is a portion of grace sown in the hearts of all who come to mature age. If rightly attended to, but for the want of this early cultivation it has caused me so much hard work, so many sleepless nights as well as days, to regain the lost time, that it has caused me to pen down a little of my experience and knowledge by such neglect in order that it may be a caution and invitation to all young and tender minds, that it may meet with, not to neglect so great and important a work that procures an increase of riches that will make a dying bed easy and judgement pleasant, where we shall all appear sooner or later to receive the reward of our works done in this life.

Written by: Henry Doudna and contributed by Mary J. Doudna, Barnesville, Ohio.

ANECDOTES OF ANNA DOUDNA SEARS AND HENRY DOUDNA

When Aunt Anna Doudna Sears was a young woman, one day she saw a strange man passing along through the field near their yard. She immediately thought he would be her husband. The man proved to be Peter Sears Sr. -- from Virginia -- who afterwards married her.

Uncle Henry Doudna did not come from North Carolina when the others came. He had not yet decided to come, although everything seemed to point that way.

> "Even in the early morning
> He could hear the rooster crow
> And it seemed that he was saying
> You must go to O-hi-o."

Uncle Henry, we have been told, walked back to North Carolina for the money ($800.00) when the farm there was sold. On his return trip, a neighbor took him part of the way, among people that did not know him. The money was wrapped up like a package, in some old thing. So anyone where he stayed at night would not know it to be of any value, Uncle Henry would casually throw it on the ground.

HOME OF BENJAMIN AND ESTHER SEARS

Benjamin and Esther Sears bought their home, and moved to it on the Sandy Ridge road, two and three quarter miles southeast of Barnesville, Ohio, about the year 1854. In this house they spent the remainder of their lives. Benjamin (my father) contacted consumption in the fall of 1856 and died in the Eighth Month of 1857. Esther, my mother, lived until Second Month 1905.

It is not known just what year their house was built but it is one of the early houses in Warren Township. Henry Doudna, son of the kidnapped John Doudna, and brother of Hosea Doudna, and my grandmother, Anna Doudna, built the original part twenty by twenty feet, one and a half stories high. The house was built from large poplar logs hewed on two sides so they were seven inches thick. When the logs were set on edge, they matched together at the corners so perfectly that the joints would almost hold water when torn down in 1903.

The plates were doubled mortised to receive the rafters, which were halved at the comb and fastened together with wooden pins. Later a board kitchen -- twelve by twelve feet square -- was built on the east side and a double bedroom -- twelve by twenty feet in size -- was built on the south side.

Henry Doudna built the house for his son Joseph, who lived in it several years. Joseph Bailey then occupied it a number of years; Benjamin Sears bought it from him. The original farm contained 160 acres. The tax on the 160 acres and Henry Doudna's personal tax for the year 1828 was $3.28 and six mills. Since then it has been cut up in small tracts, but this part has remained in our family since 1854 and is still my home, where I was born.

Henry Doudna built two wonderful buildings before he built this one. They were a house and a barn. The house was a frame structure veneered with brick fit in between the studding. A part of it was two stories high and one part was one story high. The barn was a large frame building made entirely by hand. He had gone into the woods for the timber and made the lumber from trees he cut down. The frame was all hewed, rafters split or hewed and fastened with wooden pins. The floor was made of split logs and they were pinned down. The weatherboarding was split and nailed on with nails that he made. That is all the nails that there are in this building.

The lath for the roof was split and the roof was made of chestnut shingles fastened on with wooden pins. These did not go through the lath but hooked over in such a way as to hold them firmly in their place. I well remember seeing a section of the original roof in place. These buildings were on a part of the original 160 acres that he kept for a home and was located about forty rods north of our house.

A well had been dug at our house before father bought it. They had started to dig at the side of the porch, but after going down until it took forty loads of stone to fill up the dry hole, the diggers were discouraged and stopped work there. A "water smeller" with his forked stick found water ninety feet from the kitchen door, after going down forty-three feet. This cost, by careful estimates, as much work as walking almost to California and back. But the well produced very good soft water and never goes dry. For a long time, water was drawn by a windlass and rope.

Later a pump took its place. In the "Horse and Buggy" days, travellers made the old well a stopping place to get a good drink, as it was so close to the road.

When the old house was torn down in 1903, we erected a new one over the same cellar. It was two stories with eight rooms, pantry and a bath room. This was equipped with all modern conveniences, except gas.

A very peculiar accident took place on the farm, in the Seventh Month 1927. I was quietly mowing, when suddenly I felt a sharp sting on my head. I stopped the team and looked all around but could see nothing that could have caused it. I then took off my straw hat and putting my hand to my head felt the blood. I examined my hat and found two bullet holes -- one where the bullet had entered and the other where it had come out. Evidently, it had been shot high in the air from the other side of the hill from where I was, and as it came down, it struck me, cutting a small furrow in my scalp. I went to the doctor. He put a bandage on it, and gave me a "shot" to prevent lock-jaw. In a short time, it was well again and gave me no more trouble.

HOME OF PETER SEARS - 1807

This house was built by Thomas and Prudence Williams in the year 1807, and is located at about three and a quarter miles southeast of Barnesville, Ohio, near one-half mile west of the Sandy Ridge Road. The house is still standing erect, but is not inhabited.

The original house was twenty-two by twenty-two feet and two stories high. It was made of logs hewed on the two sides to be seven inches thick. They were set on edge, "chinked and dobbed", and plastered. Later a one story addition on the north side was added. It was fifteen by twenty-two feet and was divided into two rooms for the kitchen and bedrooms. There also was a "meal room" and a porch on the east side, which was nine by twenty-two feet.

The house is located on a hillside about five rods from a wonderful spring where a log milk house was built. The property was occupied by the Williams family for several years before it became the home of Peter and Phariba Sears. Here they raised four children: Benjamin S., Mary B., Sarah D., and Edwin W. Sears. Edwin passed away in Sixth Month 1925, the last of the family. Phariba died in 1878 and Peter in 1898. The children continued to live in the old home until 1903, when they sold it and moved on the public road nearby.

I remember seeing Charleyn Cole putting a tin roof on the house fifty-five years ago (as of 1942), and it is apparently in good condition yet.

Phariba wove many yards of carpet and material for clothing, as they made their own clothing. Peter was a very kind man and did not believe in sacrificing convenience and comfort for outside appearance.

On one occasion, a man living a mile or two away, had the misfortune to break his leg. Peter went to his assistance to render what help he could. The man was taken to his home and laid on his bed. In getting him comfortably fixed so he could stretch his broken leg, the footboard was in the way. Peter got a saw and was about to saw off the board when the owner objected. Peter said, "It is in the way of making thee comfortable and I am going to saw it off," which he did.

They built a frame barn thirty by thirty-six feet with basement and drive way overhead, which was an asset to the property in years past. They were lovers of fruit, and planted a large apple orchard and dedicated considerable space to other fruit of all kinds that are grown in this latitude.

Years ago a pine tree that stood in the yard about ten feet from the house was struck by lightning, but no one in the house was hurt.

Uncle Peter was a brother of my father.

Written by: William H. Sears, Barnesville, Ohio.

Our Old Apple-Tree

(From <u>Heart Sunshine</u> by Sarah D. Sears published in 1909)

Thomas and Prudence Williams were pioneer settlers near the present site of Barnesville, Ohio on the farm since owned by the late Peter Sears.

In the spring of 1807, Prudence went on horseback, alone, to Redstone, Pa., a distance of nearly one hundred miles, a large part of which was a wilderness road. Her purpose was to obtain fruit trees; these she carried home behind her, and planted them herself. The last one was blown down in a storm Seventh Month 10th, 1896. It was a beautiful tree and had grown to a great size. By measurements taken a few years before it was blown down, it was nine feet, four inches in circumference at the smallest point between the roots and forks, and ten feet at eighteen inches above the ground. It had four large branches, one of which measured four feet in circumference, another five feet, another five feet two inches, and the other five feet eleven inches; these measurements were taken at eighteen inches from the junction of the forks. It was believed to be the largest apple tree in Belmont County.

This summer day, the winds at play,
   O'er hill and valley free,
With ruthless strife, have cost thy life,
   Our dear old apple-tree.
Thy giant form bowed to the storm
   And to the woodman's stroke—
We built a fire—thy funeral pyre—
   And deep regrets we spoke

From out our heart, from thee to part;
   That now no more appears
This landmark true, the cycles through
   For almost ninety years.
And so tonight, sweet memories bright,
   Around our hearts are cast,
We fondly deem their golden gleam
   In memory long shall last.

In childhood hours, among thy flowers
   Of pink and white we've played,
And 'neath thy dome our play-house home,
   Our childish hands have made.
And while I write, this summer night,
   Beside thy funeral pyre,
In fancy fond, I see beyond
   Thy brightly beaming fire.

I seem to hear, while far and near
   Resounds the woodman's stroke
From wooded hill and vale, until
   Falls many a sturdy oak.
The forests vast are felled at last,
   And then I seem to see
The corn-fields wave above their grave,
   The wheat-heads swaying free.

The picture bright with golden light
   Before my view appears;
'Neath Fancy's guise the homes arise
   Of sturdy pioneers.
With honest work—no room to shirk—
   The acres broad were tilled;
And night's sweet rest was doubly blest,
   And hearts with praise were filled.

The butter churned, the cheeses turned,
   The busy loom and wheel,
From rise of sun till day was done,
   The housewives' care reveal.
One woman-heart did well her part,
   And wise the plan she chose
To make the wilderness rejoice
   "And blossom as the rose."

With courage rare that few now share
   She journeyed all alone
'Mid perils deep o'er rocky steep,
   On horseback to Redstone.
With money earned from butter churned
   As trophies then she bought
Some fruit trees rare—both apple, pear—
   And with her safely brought.

Her woman-hands, the record stands,
   Then planted every root;
Long years they grew, and furnished too,
   Rich stores of goodly fruit.
She passed away her record they
   For four-score years and ten,
Of interest kind that noble mind
   Felt for her fellow-men.

Not weak and blind, like those we find
   Who plant no shrub or tree
For fear that they will pass away
   Before the fruit they see.
Far nobler they who strive each day,
   To bless their fellow-men;
Not questioning who, if false or true,
   Or whether kith or kin:

Whose joy is keen that some will glean
   From seeds their hands have sown;
Nor know the strife, the narrow life,
   That lives for self alone.
A lesson deep thy life shall keep
   Through all the years for me,
While sounds they knell—farewell, farewell,
   Our dear, old apple-tree.

By Sarah D. Sears

A HOUSE BUILT ABOUT 1810

My grandmother, Mary C. Bundy Smith, has related to me some of the features of the house in which she was born. Her memories of it date from 1862 to 1865 and on various occasions afterwards when she visited there. It was built in Goshen Township, Belmont County, Ohio, about 1810 by Isaac Patten (William Patten's son and a brother of John Patten). Her grandparents, Elijah and Eliza Hanson moved to this place about 1839.

The house faced northeast. Its main part was a two-story frame, with no attic, but a basement (called cellar then) under the whole of it. Here there was a fireplace in the southeast end, where the chimney that served to carry the smoke from all the heating and cooking units in the house was built. The foundation was of hewn stone. In my grandmother's time, parts of it had been displaced due to erosion by water, and the cellar was practically unused. She recalls occasions when water was ankle deep on the floor. The house was prevented from settling into the basement by props which had been added whenever the declining state of the foundation required it. The weatherboarding was plain boards about eight inches wide. It had no tongue and groove. On the house it overlapped as shingles do.

The kitchen was one story, but had sufficient floor space for the women to cook and the whole family to eat their meals there, which they did. It was as wide as the main house, and built into its southeast end. There was no cellar under it, but there was a loft above it in which items could be stored or people could sleep. It was reached by a stairway from the kitchen and had no fireplace or any entrance to any other part of the house. My grandmother recalls the fireplace in the kitchen as being the biggest in the house. In it, most of the cooking was done, and logs were burned. Those known as back logs, that is those placed to the rear, were often around six feet long and one and a half feet in diameter, while those toward the front (front logs) approximated one half this size. The back logs often lasted four or five days but of course the front ones burned out sooner. The height of this fireplace was four or five feet. A short person could stand in it and look up the flue and see the sky. Two large flagstones formed the hearth. In the other fireplaces in the house, coal was used for fuel. The kitchen also contained a cupboard, two tables and a stove. My great-great grandmother Eliza did not use the stove but her girls did. A large table was used to wash the dishes and another one was moved to the center of the room at meal time. A table that served in this capacity at one time in this house was made of cherry wood and is being used now in the H. S. Webster home at East Canton, Ohio.

The first floor of the main part of the house was divided into three rooms. One was the living room; it was located in the southeast half and one of its dimensions was the width of the house. The fireplace in this room was on the side adjacent to the kitchen. The other part was divided into two rooms which were bedrooms. The second floor was divided into four rooms. There were no presses (closets) in the house, except in the kitchen under the stairs to the loft. Clothes were hung on pegs on the wall.

The inside walls of the house -- instead of being plastered -- were made of boards about four inches wide and nailed on horizontally. The space between these boards and the weather boarding was filled with pieces of wood. The same kind of boards were nailed vertically to form the partitions which were only one board thick. The ceiling was made of the same sort of boards while those in the floor were broader and from a different species of tree. It was covered with rag carpet woven by Eliza Hanson. No paint or varnish was used in the house. Windows were of glass with at least six panes in each sash. The house was torn down thirty or forty years ago (as of 1942).

Written by: Willis W. Webster, Columbus, Ohio, Feb. 1942.

THE SMITH HOMESTEAD - 1813

Thomas and Phebe Smith (Phebe Sinclair) came from Frederick County, Virginia, and entered a tract of land one mile east of Barnesville, Ohio, in 1813.

They first lived in a cabin while preparations were being made for the brick house, now owned by James Walton. This was not finished until 1817. It is two stories with eight rooms and a large one-story kitchen attached. Each room was provided with a fireplace for coal fire.

Coal was found on the lower land on the place, and by removing five feet of dirt, the coal vein yielded about fifty bushels to each square yard of surface. A stone foundation enclosed a cellar under the whole house.

At Thomas Smith's death, the "Plantation" was bequeathed to his wife, and at her death it was inherited by the youngest son, Robert. The three older sons, Sinclair, Jonah, and William, received tracts of land in Guernsey County.

Perhaps the following from the will of Thomas Smith might prove interesting: "Being desirous to settle my worldly affairs, and thereby be better prepared to leave this world, when it shall please God to call me hence, do make this my last will and testament."

"First and principally, I commit my soul into the hands of Almighty God, and my body to the earth, to be decently buried at the discretion of my executor," the document then goes on with distribution of effects.

The brick house, with 240 acres of land, *(Section 9, Warren Twp.)* became the home of Robert H. Smith -- who married Elizabeth Williams 12th Month 4th 1822. Two of their children died in infancy. The following all lived past 60 years of age, except one.

Jonah 1-1-1825	Sinclair 5-19-1831	Robert 3-11-1838
Rebecca 12-16-1826	Ephraim 9-28-1833	William 4-5-1842
Barclay 1-25-1829	Joel 4-11-1836	

This was a self-supporting home. Flax and wool were grown and prepared and woven into linen and cloth. An apple orchard was planted early and great copper kettles of apple butter were made. There were also great quantities of peach butter made. An abundance of wheat was grown, and bread baked in large out-door ovens. Pork and beef were put away and some of the surplus pork was sold in Wheeling, W. Va. Some went over the mountains to Baltimore.

Soft soap was made from surplus fat and wood ashes. Maple sugar was made from the sugar camp. Rag carpets were the rule in those days.

The farm was largely a grain farm. One of the first mower and reaper outfits was a "Kirby" reaper -- with one large wheel, which was pulled by four horses. One man drove and another sat on a stool with rake in hand to push off the grain, which was bound in bundles.

A large barn was built sometime in the 1840s. The top-most floor was made of pieces of oak, 2 x 3, spaced one inch apart. The grain fell through to the next floor where it was gathered and put through a fanning mill.

Later came the tread power grubber. Then came the horse power thresher, made by the Hoyle Company of Martins Ferry, Ohio. Steel plows were hailed as a great invention, so the wooden mold boards and paddle were laid aside.

Smith Stories

One day Robert H. Smith was out in a field by the road when a man came along and called out: "Well, Robert, you are cutting a wide swath." "Yes, we cut 42 feet wide," he replied. The boys were in the field with their scythes, cutting grass.

One field on the farm was largely timbered with chestnut. In the lower corner of the field was a cabin where a charcoal burner named Joab lived. Nearby was a wonderful spring, which went by the name of "Joab's spring" for three generations.

The boys were sent to Mt. Pleasant Friends Boarding School. One night in the chamber some of the boys noticed a tall Smith boy setting up in bed. "What's the trouble, Joel?" they asked. Joel replied, "The bed is too short for all of me to sleep at once, so I'm giving the lower part of me a chance."

One hot day -- as some of the boys were out mowing -- and as they came around to the starting point and stopped for a rest, one of them said: "Fellows, I can't stand this, I'm not going to stand it, I am going to Westtown, then marry some girl over there and live in Philadelphia." That came to pass.

One time when the Friends in the neighborhood were cleaning the meeting house, some of the younger ones threw a bucket of scrub water out the door which struck Robert Sr. in a way to bedraggle him very much. Some altercation issued, which was not very pleasant. Next morning, Robert saddled his horse early and was gone, being back at breakfast time. It was found out later hat he had been to each one of the young people to apologize for being too hasty. He was stern, but had a fine sense of justice.

Written by: Robert H. Smith, Barnesville, Ohio, Grandson of Robert H. and Elizabeth (Williams) Smith.

THE OLD LOG HOUSE OF ELI STANTON – 1835-1885
(This was located on a lane off Sandy Ridge Road beyond 61319, in Warren Twp. Section 3.)

The log house of note here was built by Jesse Bailey Sr. about the year 1812. Eli Stanton bought the log house from him about the year 1856 or 1857. Eli Stanton married Mary P. Bundy 12th Month 9th, 1857 -- a daughter of John and Ruth Patten Bundy -- and set up housekeeping in this log house. Here their three children were born. William Henry, 8th Month 2nd 1860, Sarah B. 11th Month 23rd 1861, and Emma C. 10th Month 5th 1864.

When the house was nearly sixty years old, there was moss on the north side of the roof, the big chimney was cracked and ragged, and part of the cellar wall had fallen down. But it was a home for a happy family -- father and mother Eli and Mary, and a boy and his two sisters full of life and joy -- such as the following recollections will show you.

On October 5th 1864, a little girl came to the home of Eli and Mary P. Stanton -- the old log house among the sun-kissed hills of Belmont County, Ohio. There I lived and grew for four years -- there I learned to walk and talk and take a place in the happy family life. I had one brother and one sister.

The house being old and cold did not bother us. We had a one-story kitchen. In one end was a large old-fashioned open fireplace where the wood was laid on stone. But even if I do remember seeing the sun rise as I looked between the logs, where the chinking had fallen out, I only remember the big red sun, not the cold and frosty mornings.

That fireplace afforded other memories. It was there that I remember getting my hand burned. We had come inside to warm. Aunt Lizzie (Bundy) Frame was with us. I was at one edge and thought it would be warmer if I moved to the other side, by the kitchen stove. Forgetting my manners, I walked between the others and the fire. Someone stepped back and losing my balance, I fell with one hand into the ashes. Mother or someone wrapped it up and I went into the room to cry it out. As I lay there on the floor in the sunshine, I remember seeing the colors of the rainbow flash as the tears dropped on the carpet. Later we wanted to climb the ladder to the loft, over the woodshed to get grapes, and me being a "cripple", I had to be helped.

Probably the same fall, we all had the itch -- a real disgrace. One day when Mother had extra men for dinner, we children -- who had received a thorough application of lard and sulphur -- were hustled to the loft over the kitchen by the back stairway, with instructions to remain until after dinner. One would think most of my life was spent in that old kitchen, but that is where my memories seem to center. The floor was in the cellar. The foundation stones were out of place and probably the door was open or off its hinges, letting in the light.

I have been told that we had an old door for a slide, with one end laid up on the banister around the old porch and a stone at the bottom. Sister Sadie and I climbed up to slide down, no care or thought being given to shoe soles. In some manner, we tipped back and fell on a large stone jar placed under the eaves to catch rain water. We each emerged some the worse for our experience with badly bumped heads.

The next spring when mother was able to care for me, she found some unusual bumps on my chest which they decided had come from cracked or broken ribs, and accounted for my having complained of my chest during the winter.

It seems to me the house was torn down and removed in the spring of 1869. One bright warm spring morning we children went down to watch the men at work. Thus, at four and a half years of age, all had passed out of my sight and only vague memories remain.

Written by: Emma C. (Stanton) Webster; Contributed by her granddaughter, Yvonne Ardel Dearing (9 years old)

ELI STANTON'S SORGHUM MILL

My Grandmother, Sarah Stanton Hall, says her earliest recollections are clustered around the cool shade of the beautifully formed maple tree, which stood near the spring -- a few rods for the back door of the old log house on her father's farm. While still too small to carry a bucket, she derived much pleasure from the privilege of going to the spring to bring back a dipperful of the cool, refreshing water.

Her father's sorghum mill was located just above the spring, and the gently sloping ground was suited exactly to his plan for efficient operation. The cane was hauled from the fields by horse and wagon and neatly piled near the mill. With everything in readiness to keep the mill going, a horse was hitched to the free end of a naturally curved pole or sweep -- while the other end was attached to the top of the mill. The horse was told to "Git up" and traveled in a circle with his hoof prints, and paying slight heed to the shouts of the men and the rattle of the mill which his efforts set in motion by turning gears which revolved two upright rollers. Helpers carried cane to the feeder who fed it between the rollers, causing the light green juice contained in the cane to be crushed out and run into a reservoir beneath the rollers. The crushed cane or "pummy" came out of the rollers opposite the feeder and was carried away to be stacked and later used for bedding stock, etc. From the reservoir, beneath the rollers, a pipe or trough followed the sloping ground away from the mill, and the sweet cane juice ran through this to a flat, rectangular pan, fitted into the top of a stone furnace. The furnace was equipped with doors at one end, and built up at the other end to form a chimney. This furnace was built to a height convenient to the skimming operation, and a roof or shed was built over it to protect the cane juice from rain and other exposure. From a nearby pile of wood, a fire was kept going under the pan of juice, and care was taken to regulate the heat so the juice would boil without scorching. The boiling process caused a thick scum to form on the surface of the juice, and constant attention was required to skim this off with a flat pan open at one end and equipped with a long handle at the other to prevent the skimmer from being scalded by the sugar-laden steam. After the juice was boiled to a certain consistency it was drawn off through a pipe or trough to a second pan where the boiling and skimming process continued until the juice was reduced to a light colored molasses that was sweet to the taste and contained the vigor of the outdoors from whence it came. The finished molasses was drawn off through spigots into a cooling pan and then transferred to various containers for storing.   Grandmother's father, Eli Stanton, used great care in making sorghum molasses, and his product was widely known to be of the highest quality.

In the fall of 1871, Eli Stanton called in Sarah Briggs to assume his responsibilities in connection with watching and finishing the sorghum molasses since he felt it his duty to spend more time with his ailing wife Mary, in what proved to be her last sickness.

The scarcity of sugar during the Civil War led to the growing of cane, which was in great demand as a substitute and became an important industry. For this reason and also because Friends refused to use slave products -- sugar being one of them -- the making of sorghum developed into an important cash income for the farmers and pleased, indeed, were the children of the day when they were allowed a small portion of sorghum for the making of taffy or some other luxury. Great quantities of molasses were hauled to Wheeling, W. Va. in large containers, and sold for $2.00 per gallon during the Civil War period.

In connection with the sorghum mill, my Grandmother recalls some amusing incidents that are perhaps worth recording.

One day, Grandmother noticed several of her father's swine reeling around the barnyard and acting altogether very strangely. An immediate investigation led to the discovery that the swine had found and consumed a generous helping of discarded sorghum skimmings which had fermented in the sunlight. The conclusion was quickly reached that the swine were thoroughly intoxicated and so it proved to be, since they soon recovered their equilibrium and normal health.

Grandmother also recalls that John Hartley was very fond of thick sorghum molasses and made it his business to find work around the sorghum mills in that season. He consumed great quantities of molasses mixed with various other foods and if the molasses became thin or of poor quality he refused to stay on, and sought work where he was sure of thick molasses.

Written by: Harold L. Holloway Jr. and Harold L. Holloway Sr., Wheeling, W. Va.

Anecdote

Many were the happy memories in the Eli Stanton home where for twelve years the three families represented, worked and played in closest harmony.

My mother, Sarah Stanton Hall, recalls "going fishing" with her sister Mary E. Fawcett (Aunt Matie) down at the creek, straining the water through their wide dress skirts and in this way catching the fish.

Hunting the sweet apples and then hiding them for future use was quite a game. Hunting to find another's hidden store was part of the fun.

One time they tapped some trees hoping to get maple sap to boil down for a delicious treat and found they had tapped some beech trees, too.

Written by Helen Hall Holloway, Wheeling, WV

JAMES STANTON

1810-1851

James Stanton was the son of Henry and Clary Patterson Stanton. He was born 24th day of 7th Month 1810.

He went from the vicinity of Short Creek Monthly Meeting to Stillwater Monthly Meeting on the 19th day of 5th Month 1812. He did this with his father and mother and a brother Joseph.

James Stanton appeared before Stillwater Monthly Meeting with Rachel Scholfield on 27th day of 2nd Month 1830. James Stanton and Rachel Scholfield were married in Meeting on the 31st day of 3rd Month 1830.

The children of James and Rachel Stanton were as follows:

David Stanton	born 4th day, 2nd Month 1831
Lindley Stanton	born 5th day, 11th Month 1832
Edith Stanton	born 25th day, 5th Month 1834
Lydda Stanton	born 7th day, 2nd Month 1836

James Stanton's wife, Rachel Scholfield, died 1st day of 9th Month 1836. She was, at death, twenty-five years and twenty-eight days of age. She was buried at Stillwater burying grounds.

Between the years of 1840-1850, James Stanton was quite prominent, his name entering the minutes of Stillwater Monthly Meeting quite often during that time. He served on quite a few committees. He made a visit with Benjamin Hoyle to part of the Monthly Meetings of Ohio Yearly Meeting from 12th Month 1849 to 6th Month 1850.

In the 5th Month of 1843, James Stanton and Charity Bundy appeared before Stillwater Monthly Meeting declaring their intentions of marriage. They were married on the 28th day of 6th Month 1843.

Little is mentioned of James Stanton in Stillwater records until his death, which occurred the 20th day of 1st Month 1851. He was forty years, five months and twenty-seven days of age, when he passed away.

Written by: Dorothy L. Holloway and Harold L. Holloway, Wheeling, W. Va. James Stanton is a great-great-great Uncle of Dorothy Holloway.

Note: Following is the text of the Marriage Certificate of James Stanton and Rachel Scholfield.

Wedding Certificate of James Stanton and Rachel Scholfield

"Whereas James Stanton of Goshen Township, in the County of Belmont, in the State of Ohio, son of Henry Stanton of the County afore said and Clara his wife, and Rachel Scholfield, daughter of Issachar Scholfield, of the County and State afore said, and Edith his wife, having their intention of marriage with each other before a monthly Meeting of the Religious Society of Friends held at Stillwater, according to good order used among them, and having consent of parents, their said proposal of marriage was allowed by said meeting. Now these are to certify whom it may concern that for the full accomplishments of their said intentions this 31st day of 3rd month, in the year of our Lord, one thousand and eight hundred and thirty, they the said James Stanton and Rachel Scholfield appeared in a public meeting of the said. James Stanton taking the said Rachel Scholfield to be his wife, promising with the divine assistance to be unto her a loving and faithful husband until death should separate them and then the said Rachel Scholfield did in like manner declare, that she took him, the said James Stanton to be her husband, promising with divine assistance to be unto him a loving and faithful wife until death should separate them. And moreover, they, the said James Stanton and Rachel Scholfield (she according to the custom of marriage, adopting the name of her husband) did as a further confirmation thereof, then and there to these present set their hands. James Stanton   Rachel Stanton

And we whose names are also here unto subscribed being present at the solemnization of the said marriage and subscription, have as witnesses them to set our hands the day and year above mentioned;

Robert H. Smith	Joseph Stanton	Henry Stanton
Elizabeth W. Smith	Edmund Stanton	Issachar Scholfield
Sarah Williams	Mary Hoyle	Edith Scholfield
Elizabeth Millhouse	Benjamin Hoyle	Cory Stanton
Robert Millhouse	Andrew Scholfield	Jonathun Scholfield
Martha Doudna	Martha Scholfield	Anna Stanton
Henry Doudna	William G. Scholfield	Cidney Scholfield

Following the death of his wife Rachel Scholfield, James Stanton married Charity Bundy, daughter of William and Sarah Bundy, on the 28th day of the 6th month, 1843, in the Stillwater Meetinghouse.

Those present were;

Iona T. Scholfield	Ephriam Williams	Sarah Bundy
Phebe Sears	Joseph F. Doudna	Ezekiel Bundy
Elizabeth Starbuck	L. L. Haloway	Prudence Bundy
Anna Sears	Clishe Doudna	Elizabeth Bundy
Hulda Sears	Thomas Wilson	Ann Bundy
Rachel Green	Joseph Green	David Stanton
Elizabeth W. Smith	John Sears	Daniel Stanton
Rebecca Smith	Henry Stanton	Joseph Stanton
Mary Stanton	Clary Stanton	Thos. C. Parker
Thomas J. Romons		

These facts were prepared for William G. Steer from Stillwater Monthly Meeting minutes by James J. Winder - Friends Boarding School, 1942.

THE JAMES STANTON HOME - 1837

The old and unique brick house built by James Stanton about the year 1837 holds particular interest for the writer because my mother, Helen Hall Holloway, was born there in June 13, 1899.

James Stanton was born near Mt. Pleasant, Ohio, in the year 1811, a son of Henry and Clary Patterson Stanton -- who came from North Carolina in 1800. James married Rachel Scholfield of Virginia on March 31, 1830 in the Stillwater Meeting House, and to them were born two sons and two daughters; David, Lindley, Edith, and Lydia. At the age of 25 years and 28 days. Rachel Stanton was laid to rest in the Stillwater burial grounds on September 1, 1836.

On June 28, 1843, James again said his marriage vows, this time to Charity Bundy. The meeting records show that he was held in high esteem by the meeting and served on many committees, also as a companion to Benjamin Hoyle during his religious visits to Ohio Yearly Meeting in 1849. While living in the home that he built, James passed away at the age of 40 years and was buried at Stillwater on January 20, 1851. After his death, three commissioners were appointed; William Green, Joel Doudna, and John Starbuck, to decide how his land was to be divided. A decision was reached to sell the farm altogether. In 1853 Joseph Stanton bought the house. Some of the later owners were; Israel Wilson - 1858, George Tatum - 1861, and Joseph and Anna Hoge who owned it for 25 years.

From Stillwater Meeting House, we travel southeast on Sandy Ridge Road to Pigeon Point -- now known as Mount Holly -- and continue on to the left and the turn right up a slight grade, at the top of which a road turns sharply off Sandy Ridge to the left. We follow this road down a steep grade and pass the well-preserved and attractive former homestead of Eli Stanton. If we go down another steep grade and then up a slight rise, at the top is spread before us the 151 acres on which the old home of James Stanton is located. Grandfather and Grandmother Hall recall that from this point on toward the house, the road was lined with huge cherry trees -- now gone -- that yielded wonderful crops of large sweet cherries of perfect quality, which sold in town for 50 cents a bucket. *(Located in SE Section Three, Warren Twp.)*

The old brick house which stands on a gentle southward slope, is screened by a closely set row of stately pine trees on the west; a lone pine stands in the front lawn to the north. The house itself, reflects the character of its builder by presenting a plain but very substantial type of architecture mingled with a suggestion of Southern influence. Originally there was a double decked porch running the full length of the frame part on the west side. This porch was provided with a closed stairway leading to the upper deck and access to the back bedrooms in the frame section -- presumably for the use of hired help.

The main foundation measures twenty feet by thirty feet; and averages twelve feet high and sixteen inches thick throughout. It is built of carefully dressed and perfectly squared sandstone of various sizes fit together so perfectly that no mortar joints were used. Even today the walls stand straight and true. The largest stone measures 5 ft. 2 in. long by 19 in. deep by 16 in. thick, and there are many more that approximate that size. On top of this foundation, walls built of hard-baked bricks measuring 8 1/2 inches by 4 inches by 3 1/4 inches rise to a height of 18 ft. 5 inches -- to the eaves and are 14 inches thick. After more than a hundred years it is difficult to find imperfections in either the bricks or mortar joints, and the walls stand true with no indications of cracks or bulges. In the front or north wall of the house there are ten openings supported by sandstone lintels in perfect condition. The top row of openings consists of five evenly spaced windows and the bottom row of four windows with one door in the middle. The window openings measure 5 ft. 6 in. high and 3 ft. 2 in. wide and are equipped with double sash -- each of which is divided into six lights measuring 10 in. by 14 in. The front door measures 3 ft. by 7 ft. and is without question the original, since the paneling is strikingly unique in design.

Entering by the front door, we step into a small hall and face a stairway leading to three bedrooms on the second floor. On our right and left, doors open into large west and east living rooms. Each of the five rooms is equipped with a small fireplace. In the south wall of the east living room we go through a door and down three steps into the dining room and continue on into the adjoining kitchen. Turning to the east wall of the kitchen we pass through a door into the well room. Directly above the dining room, kitchen and well room there were three rooms of corresponding sizes and this section of the house was of frame construction and formed an ell extending southward from the east end of the main brick building. The doors throughout the house are equipped with iron latches of unique design which are placed unusually low. From the well room a flight of steps leads downward to a landing, off of which opens two doors, one leading into the main basement and one to the outside. These doors are supported by wooden frames which are spiked to the stone wall with square, handmade nails. From this landing more steps continue downward into a room measuring approximately 10 ft. by 10 ft. by 12 ft. high, the walls of which are constructed of stones identical to those used in the main foundation walls. A door in the east wall leads to the ground level and there is a window in the south wall to light the stairs and one window in the east wall about 6 ft. from the floor. The joists for the floor above the spring room are hand hewed poplar and chestnut logs measuring 5 in. wide by 8 in. deep.

This room is unquestionably the outstanding feature of the entire house, since it houses a wonderful spring of clear, cool water which rises from the earth and flows into a large sandstone bowl approximately 4 ft. in diameter and at least 2 ft. deep. While most of the early settlers of Belmont County selected a home site near a good spring of water, James Stanton evolved the quaint idea of building his home over a spring, thereby protecting it from outside risks of contamination and insuring its quick and comfortable use during all seasons and any sort of weather. We younger folks have listened many times to our elders reminiscing of "The house built over the spring." What an unusual idea it was and what an extraordinary spring it had proven to be. No wonder then, that gazing into the depths of this beautiful bowl of pure, clear water and beholding our reflected image therein, we should have impressed upon our consciousness the great and everlasting service that nature bestows upon mankind, for we surely know that before us, this crystal pool has reflected the images of hundreds of good people while they tasted its cool freshness.

Joseph and Anna Hoge, who owned the property for 25 years installed a food elevator that raised and lowered from the spring to the floor above, thus saving many steps up and down the stairs. Before them, Israel Wilson installed a pump in the well room that pumped the water from the spring to the floor above. My Grandparents, who lived in the James Stanton home for five years used a long trough constructed to accommodate several milk cans that utilized the overflow from the spring for the purpose of cooling fresh milk. The present owner, a Mr. Wade, has built a modern cement spring house about 30 ft. east of the old spring and is installing a gasoline engine to pump the spring water through the entire house.

The old barn stands today on its original foundation of stones identical to those used in the house foundation and measures 40 ft. by 60 ft. The framework of hand hewed timbers, held together by wooden pins and handmade nails appears to be rigid and straight. The hewn log joists that support the floor are placed close together and most of them are good solid timber.

When we young people of today delve into the busy lives of our ancestors, we wish it were possible to step into the past and sit with them before their log open fires -- listening to the crackle of the burning logs mingled with exchanges of that homespun wisdom which was born of simple living and good fellowship. Then we might grasp more fully the true reasons for that pioneering spirit which built strong characters and contented lives.

Written by: Dorothy L. Holloway and Harold L. Holloway, Wheeling, W. Va.
        James Stanton is a great-great-great Uncle of Dorothy Holloway.

ANECDOTES WRITTEN BY WILLIAM G. STEER

Oxen

When my father, James Steer, bought the grandfather William Green's farm, he also bought the stock which included three yoke of oxen and twenty-five head of three-year-old colts. He sold the latter at public sale the same year and kept the oxen for a few years. He employed a black man by the name of Sam Betts to drive them. *(This farm was located on 62242 Tacoma Rd.)*

One of the first jobs was to have the sills for the barn hauled. They were twelve by twelve and sixty feet long, and came from the "Billy" Doudna farm on Sandy Ridge. Another thing of importance was to deliver the stone for the first bank vault built in Barnesville in 1865.

The oxen were so well trained that the driver could turn the team and wagon on Main Street and not leave the sidewalk. At one time father hauled three loads of coal, one hundred bushels in each, to Barnesville, in one day. The coal digger helped him to load it.

In hauling coal to Number Two (*Tacoma*) school house, *(located on Bailey Rd.)* he only used one yoke of oxen. After getting up the long steep hill and crossing the railroad with seventy bushels he stalled on the track. After going to the rear wheel, with his lifting, helped the oxen to get across the track. The outcome to this incident caused a report to be circulated that father had lifted seventy bushels of coal over the crossing. In his prime, it was said that he was the strongest man in the township.

The names of three yoke oxen were Jo and Jerry, Buck and Berry, and Bill and Barney.

Tramping Out Grain

There was plenty of floor space in the large barns built before and after 1864, so we often used this space to tramp out grain.

The sheaves were unbound and placed in a circle. Then we brought in four or six horses and colts, tieing them two and two. With someone to ride the leaders and another person in the center to keep the horses in place, they soon learned how to go.

Of course it was necessary to keep a large shovel nearby to remove the droppings. It was necessary to use a flail to thresh out that which was not tramped.

The Flail

This was made by taking two sticks of wood about the size of a fork handle. One was four or five feet and the other two or three feet. A knob was made on the end of the longer one and a hole was bored in the shorter one. The two were tied together with a flexible rope or raw hide. Thus the loop on the long piece would turn around when swinging the shorter stick.

An inexperienced person, if not careful in using the flail, if the short piece would sometimes strike him on the head, he need not be surprised.

Sugar Camp

The maple sugar camp was located about three-eighth of a mile from the home of James Steer and consisted of sixty trees so close together that the sap could be carried to the boiling shed -- a log building near the center of the group of trees. The boiling was done in a can made of galvanized iron, nailed to a wooden side; it was ten by three, by one foot deep. As soon as the frost was out of the ground, the trees were tapped by boring two holes three-eighth inch in diameter and inserting spiles, or spouts about twelve inches long. These were made by using the elder from which the pith had been taken.

The vessels for catching the sap were called sugar troughs, and were made by chopping out a place in a two-foot length of log deep enough to hold two or more gallons. In later years, iron spouts on which a bucket could be hung took the place of the more primitive outfit. When the syrup was as thick as we wanted it, it was carried in buckets to the home, which was no easy job at nine or ten o'clock at night, as was often the case.

The syrup was cleared by using a blend of milk and eggs and was never made into sugar except for home use. Just below the camp was a small tenant house not far from the home of Eli and Sara Hodgin before they moved to Otho French house, before 1864.

The tenant who lived in this house died from an attack of Asiatic cholera, it was then thought. As that was long before antibiotics were in general use, father was authorized by the township trustees to burn the house, which he did.

I remember what a sight it was to two small boys like my brother Joseph and me to see the fire.

Sorghum Molasses

During the Civil War from 1860 to 1865 no sugar could be had from the Southern States. To have a substitute, many farmers in the northern states grew sorghum cane and made molasses. I remember that it had been told that Lewis Naylor, a Friend of Sandy Ridge had made as much as five thousand gallons in one season. The most cane father ever raised in any one season was six acres. A colored man and his girls were employed stripping and cutting and got it ready to be hauled to the mill located in the basement of the barn.

The cane was crushed by a sweep mill containing three upright rollers two feet in length and one foot in diameter. The juice was conveyed by gravity in an open spout to the boiling shed, one hundred or more feet below. From the storage bow the juice was drawn into the first pan for boiling, made by nailing sheet iron to wooden sides. It was allowed to boil only a little in one end so that the green scum could be taken off. It was necessary to feed this to the hogs before it fermented or it would make them drunk.

The juice was drawn from the first pan into a settling box and then on to the finishing pan, made of solid cast iron ten feet long, three feet wide with flaring sides one foot high, and an opening in one end two by six inches to draw the molasses into the collecting box.

This was done with a board six inches in width to fit the pan. With the board we shoved the molasses to the end, being careful to have a vessel with juice to follow up the board. This was to keep the pan from burning. One year when we had a large surplus, it was sold in Wheeling, W. Va. for $1.25 a gallon. A day's work was about seventy gallons of molasses. The management at the shed was generally by the women. Our cousins Ruth Bailey was a very good helper.

On the return trip from Wheeling, we met some men on horseback who had just crossed Wheeling Creek and reported the water so high that it would not be safe to cross. Father thought with his strong team, he would try it. So when we came to the stream, I tied the pony that I had ridden twenty-five miles bareback, to the wagon. We got safely across, though the water was deep enough to swim the pony, and came into the wagon-bed.

This was during the Civil War when friends refused to pay the tax. The sheriff told father he was going to take one of his horses the next morning when he started back. At that time, stock was taken and sold by the authorities to get money for the tax. Father was very much worried about what to do as we were taking a flock of sheep to the new home. He decided to go another way and so did not lose the horse.

The Primary Brick School House 1835

The Primary Brick School House was built in 1835 and was in use sixty-three years. The brick used in building this school was made on the Benjamin Hoyle farm, later the L.J. Taber farm.

The plans were made by William Green, whose early life was spent in England. Thus, there was a similarity to the English buildings as there were three rows of seats on each side of the room. Each row was up one step from the row below. However, these were removed not long after we first went to school in 1866, and new desks were put in. James Steer and Sinclair Smith were the donors.

After this change was made, it left the windows so high that we could only see out at one end. There seems to have been a time before 1866 that no school was kept. Peter Sears, the grandfather of William H. Sears, lived and died in the house. The early teachers we know were Isaac N. Vail, Thompson Frame, Lindley B. Steer, Lydia Millhouse, Mary Caleb Bundy, and Elizabeth Smith Livezey.

The building was in good repair when taken down to make room for a more modern one in 1898.

Corn Husking

Sixty or seventy years ago, the manner of gathering the corn was very different from that of the present day. Many farmers, instead of putting it in shock, cut the top of the stalk just above the ear and used it for fodder. They snapped the ears off and hauled them to the barn to husk. When the crops were large and they had large barns, it was placed in long ricks across the floor and the neighbors were invited in to help husk it at night. After husking, a good supper was served quite late at night.

The huskers rested on their knees as close together as they could work and there was always a rivalry to see who could first husk through the pile. It was the task for the older men to rake back the husks as they accumulated.

Around 1860, J.T. Scholfield made a business of hauling the husks to his barn and they were shredded, to be used in making mattresses -- baling and shipping them to Wheeling, W. Va. The power for the shredder was a treadmill large enough for two horses to walk on. A large wagon bed seven feet high and large enough to hold a ton of husks was drawn by a four-horse team to deliver the husks. This had to be done in the winter when the roads were very muddy.

My first ride on a wagon like this was in 1864, when I was eight years old, and we went from the Henry Doudna home on Sandy Ridge to the Aaron home, then the home of Jonathan T. Scholfield.

In the winter of 1880, I was in partnership with Perley Pickett and we carried on the same business. It was the practice in those days for the neighbors to take the Boarding School scholars on a sled ride each winter. It fell to my lot to take twenty-four of the scholars in my load. This wagon bed was too high for them to see out and when the door was closed they were practically in prison.

On our return trip, two miles west of Barnesville, Ohio, the scholars crowded too much to one side and the bed -- being on bob sleds -- upset and rolled the scholars into an adjoining field and pitched me into a fence corner in the snow. No one was hurt.

James Frame

More than fifty years ago, my wife's father, William Pickett, related this incident. James Frame, a great uncle of his, during the Revolutionary War, was brought into the presence of George Washington by two soldiers. He addressed James as follows: "James, what are you doing here?" The reply was these two men brought me here because I refused to bear arms. Where upon the Commander said to him "Many a time have we drank out of the same cup and many a time have we slept together under the same blanket. You are at liberty to return to your home and help produce food for those who are willing to fight."

James Frame told my father-in-law, William Pickett, that he had assisted George Washington when he was a surveyor.

The Steer Name

While my wife, Louisa D. Steer, and I were living in Southern California from 1866 to 1887, one day as I was driving in Los Angeles, I saw on a sign the name Vacy Steer. On making inquiry I found she was an English woman, who later on gave me the following information:

In the 10th or 11th Century, when the Normans first attempted to invade England, they found it difficult to make a landing on the stern and rockbound coast of Cornwall. After several unsuccessful attempts, a safe landing was made and the man who guided the boat was given the name of Steer.

She also informed us that in a little town in Cornwall, the family history had been kept for five hundred years. The first record of the name was found in the period from 1660 to 1665. From that time to the present, we have a complete line of records.

If these records are desired, write to Warren E. Pickett, Washington, PA and he can furnish a copy.

Three Accidents

A Barn Accident

When raising a barn on the farm of James Steer in 1865, there were one hundred and twenty-five men working. Through the carelessness of one man, a beam four by four and eight feet long fell from the top story to the floor striking a large man who wore a silk hat, a glancing lick. It then struck Chalkley Bundy on the head and seriously injured him.

He was carried into the house and placed on the couch where he laid until taken to his home. I was only eight years old, but I remember seeing his brother John Bundy standing by him and I noticed how pale he was. He recovered, and later married Debora Bundy. He died two years after the accident, and it was thought this injury shortened his life.

Another Barn Accident

In the Fifth Month 1879, when moving a barn to what was known as the lower farm, while putting the heavy sections of the roof with pole rafters in place -- owing to a defective worm eaten timber -- the entire building thirty-six feet long collapsed, carrying twenty men down with it. The only one of those who was on the platform who was injured was David Edgerton, who suffered a badly sprained ankle. I was near the eaves and was removing a pin that was in the way, so when the barn spread, I fell through it. Though pinned to the ground, I was able to make known my whereabouts. The men soon removed the heavy sections of roof and carried me and laid me on the lawn. When the Doctor came he found my spine was injured and informed me that I would never be able to work again. After lying in bed for six weeks, I gradually recovered until I was able to manage my farm work. Although I suffered with my back for over thirty-five years, I had it straightened by the first Chiropractor that came to Barnesville.

There were three conditions that saved my life. The tie that was on me was the only one that had drawn out of the mortise. I fell in a hole and also just missed a stake driven in the ground. I have not been insensible to the great mercy and good my dear Heavenly Father extended to me in prolonging my life to advanced age; I am now nearly eighty-six.

A Serious Train-Wagon Accident

I think it was early in the 1880s that my brother, Charles Steer, when crossing at James Walton crossing with a covered spring wagon in which were my crippled sister Rachel Steer, Mary Kennard, and Samuel Test, were struck by a freight train which failed to blow its whistle on approaching the crossing.

All but Mary Kennard were thrown onto what was then called the "Cow catcher" of the engine and none of them were injured. Brother Charles -- seeing that Mary Kennard was not with them -- jumped off and ran back to find her lying by the side of the track, seriously injured. The two that were on the engine were carried on to Barnesville before the train stopped.

When the case came to trial, the evidence by William Stanton was so conclusive that the engineer failed to whistle, that the Railroad Company paid Mary Kennard one thousand dollars and fifty dollars more for repaying the wagon. The remarkable thing about this occurrence was that none of those thrown on the engine were injured.

The Boarding School Fire in 1910

(*In 1910, the Main Building at Olney Friends Boarding School was destroyed by fire.*) The day of the fire, Superintendent James Walton was asked if he thought the school could be continued, to which he replied he did not think it would be possible. The night of the fire, Mary Davis, who had been cared for by William Stanton's family after the death of her husband Francis Davis, passed away, thus making it possible for the Stanton family to move to Pennsylvania as had been contemplated.

A friend making inquiry, learned that the (*Davis*) home would be vacated in ten days and also that, what was known as the Hoge cottage -- now the home of the Fogles -- was vacant. *(The Hoge Cottage was located at 62183 Tacoma Rd.)*

The Superintendent of the Belmont County Childrens Home, Themes Branson, kindly offered to make sleeping quarters if needed after the fire. The twenty-two girls were provided with homes among friends and the seventeen boys occupied the Hoge cottage for sleeping quarters. They were given their meals in the home of William G. and Louisa D. Steer. Louisa Steer had Anna McGrew and Anna Cope Hall assist her with the work.

To have the needed classrooms, the tables and dishes in the dining room had to be moved to one side twice each day. Sina Walton, not being able for her duties as Matron, Louisa D. Steer was employed to take her place. She was assisted by Stella Hall and Inez Campbell.

It required a great deal of work to repair the Stanton home to get it ready for the school. A pipe line had to be laid for several rods to connect with the Children's Home water system, and the plumbing had to be overhauled in the house. At the expiration of ten days, everything was in readiness for the school with the twenty-two girls and the teachers lodging in the building. *(Located at 62420 Tacoma Rd.)*

The exercises at the end of the term were held on the lawn. A large barn door was used for a platform on which the six graduating girls were seated. With all the inconvenient ways of getting along, the teachers thought that the scholars made as good progress as they would have done in the old building. There were two terms held this way, before going to the new building in 1911.

This was a memorable experience and enjoyed by all who had a part in conducting the makeshift school.

CAMM AND ELIZABETH THOMAS

Florence Frame's great-grandparents, Camm and Elizabeth Thomas, being dissatisfied with slaveholding, moved from Georgia to Ohio, settling on Sandy Ridge, in Belmont County, on what was afterward known as the Thomas Hall farm. *(North Section Two, Warren Township)* It was then a new and unimproved country. Selecting a spot near a good spring, they built a crude pole pen to live in that summer while building a more substantial log cabin. Most of the cooking was done outside. The father swung a piece of curved bark across one end of the pen for a cradle for the baby. The mother said it was the handiest cradle she ever had, as she could touch it while going about her work and keep it swinging. There were several older children, too.

When the cabin was almost finished, Elizabeth decided she did not want a puncheon floor, which was customary in those days. Hearing of two men on Captina Creek who had a pit saw, she rode horseback to see them about sawing out some boards for their floor. The men brought their saw with them to a place near the cabin. It was necessary to dig a pit, as one man must go below and the other above, to work the saw up and down to cut the boards. They would be a little rough but not as rough as the hewn puncheon floor.

Later, one of Camm and Elizabeth Thomas' sons, Hezekiah, married Increase Dennis, Florence Frame's grandmother. She was sent from New Jersey, when a young girl, to relatives in Ohio, and did not return. She was very efficient with her needle and when left a widow with four small children, she supported her family by the tailor trade. One year, with the help of one of her daughters, she made 103 suits and parts of suits, all the work being done by hand.

The children of Camm and Elizabeth Thomas were William, Abisha, Ashel (commonly called Asa), Hezekiah, Catherine, Henry Camm, Priscilla, Elizabeth, Camm, Rebecca, Ruth, and Cidney. Asa built the house still standing on the Thomas Hall farm.

In explanation of the fact that two bore the name of Camm, the first, Henry Camm, died in infancy and they evidently wished to keep the name going so gave it to a child born later. This was a custom in the family -- and possibly common to all in those days of large families and much infant mortality. As generations passed, however, it was noted that the second child so named usually died early also, and this gave rise to a sort of superstition, probably one reason for discontinuance of this practice.

The children of Hezekiah and Increase Dennis Thomas were Philip Mason, Eliza R., Phebe Dennis and Hezakiah. The last named died when a very small child.

Written by: Sara Cooper and Lura Frame

SAMUEL WALTON

Dr. Samuel Walton, a native of Philadelphia, came to Barnesville, Ohio, in 1857. He began learning dentistry when he was sixteen, doing only mechanical work for about ten years. He then attended Dental College and graduated in one of the first graduating classes of Philadelphia Dental College.

While doing mechanical work, he purchased his supplies from the S.S. White Co., which began work in basement rooms in Philadelphia, but their business increased so rapidly that long before his death in 1899, their establishment was the largest of its kind in the United States, if not in the world.

In 1854 he was married to Sarah J. Edgerton of Somerton, Ohio. The railroad then known as "Central Ohio" was not sufficiently completed to maintain passenger service. He came by stage coach to St. Clairsville, Ohio, and there hired a team and carriage to use at the time of his wedding. A day or two after that event, while driving down a hill near the Barnesville Water Works, the carriage tongue broke at the point at which the double tree was attached and the short end ran into the ground, instantly stopping the carriage. The team being free, the groom was pulled out on his head. The fall rendered him unconscious but did not permanently injure him.

The bride received a nervous shock, which affected her memory all through a long life. They lived for a time in Philadelphia, and then moved to Barnesville with one son, in 1857. There was no dentist in the little town at that time. They purchased a farm of 100 acres, half of it was inside the town corporation. The house to which the Waltons moved was located on a site which is now the northeast intersection of Walton Ave. and Park Street. It was a frame structure 30 ft. by 26 ft. It contained three rooms and a covered porch on the first floor and two attic rooms above, which were reached by a stairway at the north end. The porch was later enclosed and divided into two rooms, one of which he used as a Dental Office. A lean-to kitchen was also added, with an adjoining shed, under which was located the well with a pump. Nearby was a barn with basement stable.

At that time, what is now Walton Avenue, was a private lane, and the Hendrysburg Road, now North Chestnut Street, was unimproved and often became very muddy. As there was no sidewalk, Dr. Walton tried to maintain one so that his patients could reach his office. Sometimes the road would get so muddy that those horseback riders would use the sidewalk much to the annoyance of the dentist.

For some years after 1857 cattle and hogs were allowed to run at large, so it was necessary for the villagers to protect their yards with fences. It was quite an undertaking for our dentist to follow his profession and manage his farm, as he had no experience in farming. He got his information from farm papers, especially *The Country Gentlemen*. He thus got in touch with new methods, so that he was frequently the first to have some new tool or try some new method. During the Civil War in the 1860s, the Waltons made hundreds of gallons of sorghum molasses -- as much as four thousand gallons in one season. The charge for making the molasses was one-third of the syrup or thirty cents a gallon.

Soon after the close of the Civil War, Samuel Walton joined with James Edgerton in sending to Long Island for thoroughbred cattle. The former got a pair of Ayrshires and the latter a pair of Jerseys. It is thought these animals were the first of these breeds to cross the Allegheny Mountains. He built the first silo in this area in 1886. With the exception of one or two public buildings having steam heat, there were no furnaces of any kind.

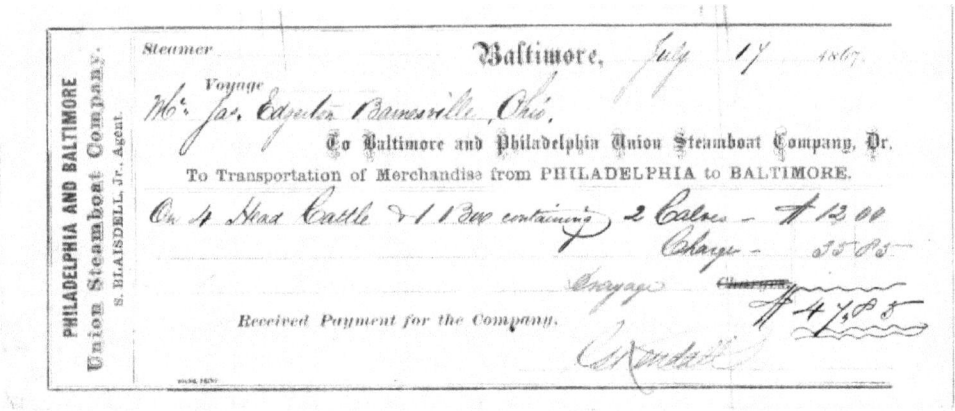

One of the writer's earliest recollections of thrashing was spreading the sheaves out on the barn floor and tramping the grain out with horses and cleaning the chaff from it with a fanning mill. Other recollections are connected with the closing days of the Civil War.

During the Campaign of 1864 when Lincoln was running for the second time, I was out with our men in the field by the highway, when men were returning on horseback from a Democratic Meeting. As they rode along, their refrain was "Hurrah for Old Abe and a rope to hang him." Our men would answer, "Hurrah for little Mack (George B. McCelland) and a rope to hang him." "Hang Jeff Davis on a sour apple tree" was often heard during Civil War days.

This worthy couple were not pioneers in the strictest sense, yet they commenced under primitive conditions and labored to support their family and be useful citizens in the community.

They were especially interested in education, and did much for the Friends Boarding School. They were life-long members of the Society of Friends. Without many modern conveniences, they entertained freely, keeping what might be called open house through the years.

Three of their five children, are still living, each over eighty years of age, now in 1942. We, who call them Father and Mother, owe them a debt of gratitude for consistent Christian example, which always speaks louder than words.

Written by: James Walton, Barnesville, Ohio

THOMAS WEBSTER, SR.
1782-1858

Thomas Webster Sr., the oldest son of John and Hannah (Plummer) Webster, was born at Little Britain, Lancaster County, Pennsylvania, on the 6th of the Third Month 1782. He came to Ohio with his father's family in the later part of year 1806. He remained here for about two years, working with other members of the family. During a part of this time, he made some improvement upon the land designed for his future home -- this being the southeast quarter of Section Number 26 in what is now Millwood Township, Guernsey Co, -- the farm now owned by Norval E. Day.

He cleared a few acres on the site of the present residence and on the hill to the north of it. He planted a small orchard of apple trees on the upper part of this ground. These were probably small seedling trees, either procured from the older settlement in the vicinity of Barnesville or trees raised from these seed. The family brought apple seed and seeds of other fruit at the time of their move here from Pennsylvania.

Thomas, after remaining here for about two years, returned with his brother William to Lancaster County, Pennsylvania, and resumed their labors at the carpenter trade. After remaining there about two years, they both returned to Ohio and ever after resided in this vicinity. When Thomas Webster returned to Ohio, he found his fruit trees so nearly destroyed by rabbits and the ground so overrun with bushes, he abandoned the orchard and started a new one elsewhere.

During Thomas Webster's first residence here -- either just before or after his return from Pennsylvania -- he had an encounter with a bear. My father (Cyrus Hall) left upon record the facts in the case, which I shall reproduce here.

Thomas Webster was out one morning prospecting over his intended future home; he carried his axe in hand. The ground was slightly covered with snow. A large bear came along being pursued by a dog, which manifested the most unceasing vigilance and daring courage. This was reinforced more as Thomas fell in with the line of pursuit, giving constant encouragement to the dog from the shrill sound of his voice, and the threatening attitude of his axe as he gave chase. Thus encouraged, the dog would lay hold on the bear, and hold on checking his speed, by bracing back. The bear was compelled in his onward march to drag the dog by his superior force and massive strength, rather than risk an encounter with the approaching woodsman's axe. Whenever an opportunity offered, the bear would wheel around and smite the dog with his fore paw. The dog, to evade the blow, would instantly loosen his hold and retreat. Thus this noble specimen of the canine race proved true and equal to the present emergency, resuming his hold on the bear on every opportunity.

Thus the chase was continued until they were near the cabin of Michael King. He owned the land east of Thomas Webster's and adjoining Quaker City on the west. As they came within calling distance, Thomas requested Michael to shoot the bear. With that, Michael's two dogs ran up to the bear holding him at bay for the time being. At this juncture, Michael attempted to shoot the bear, but by some means he unfortunately missed the bear and killed one of his own dogs. Thomas got the gun and loaded it with the only remaining bullet Michael had and shot the bear in the flank, without much effect. Thomas happened to have two rifle balls of smaller size in his pocket. He reloaded the gun and shot the bear in the head without killing him. Such was the tenacity of the bear. They finally approached him with an axe, the bear reared up boxing off the dogs. But the ax finally brought an end to this combat.

Written by: Edward Hall, Quaker City, Ohio.

Ancestry of Frederick Stuckey Webster, b. 2-28-1928

Gr. Gr. Grandfather,	Gr. Grandfather,	Grandfather,	Father,
Thomas Webster, Sr.	Thomas Webster, Jr.	Willis V. Webster	Thomas Webster
b. 3-6-1782	b. 10-26-1832	b. 3-1-1861	b. 6-25-1897
d. 4-21-1858	d. 12-1-1913		
m. Anne Gore,	m. Lydia Richardson	m. Emma Stanton	m. Helen Louise Stuckey
m 12-13-1813	m. 4-21-1860	m. 8-23-1888	m. 6-17-1922

JOHN WEBSTER, JR.

From Cyrus Hall's *History of Leatherwood Valley*, and the writings of his son Edward Hall.

John Webster, son of John and Hannah Webster, was born the 19th of Second Month 1791. He came to Ohio with his father's family in 1806. After the building of his father's mill on Leatherwood Creek, his time and attention was mostly devoted to tending and having the care of the mill. John Webster was married three times, first to Albina Gregg of Belmont County. They had three children, namely Charles P., Abner, and a daughter named Albina that died in early youth. They first lived in a cabin that stood near the mill and about thirty rods south of the railroad bridge above Quaker City.

During this period and for some years following the War of 1812, the Friends (Quakers) of Jefferson, Belmont, and Guernsey Counties, Ohio, were almost constantly harassed by military officers and those in their employ for non-performance of "Military Duty" as they termed it -- that is, for refusing to join the army, non-compliance in attending the company, and not attending the General Muster, for the purpose of learning the arts of war. This service included all the able bodied man, and for the non-performance of such service, they were all subjected to fines and penalties. The Friends were willing to abide and suffer the legal penalties of the law under the powers that then existed, with the hope that the people at large might become more enlightened in regard to the magnitude of the evils of war. With the opportunity presented here, a class of petty military officers were created or made up of reckless and unprincipled men of the country, the purpose of which was the collection of muster-fines. This became an organized persecution of the Society of Friends. Under this misguided rule, men were to be found in every Friends' neighborhood ready to collect fines, seizing every kind of property known to a farming community without showing any written or legal authority of warrant of law. Assuming arbitrary and discretionary authority in what kind of property they would choose or best suit their purpose, even bedding, clothes and wearing apparel -- in numerous instances -- were seized upon and carried away. In some instances, it led to the opening of locks, chests and drawers in search of money and seizing upon it and carrying it away when found. The property thus taken was frequently disposed of at a sham sale in a distant part of the county, which was contrary to law. These pretended sales were generally conducted by men who only served their own party and selfish interest. With sales thus conducted, the property would seldom fetch more than would pay the officers for collection, the fines still remaining unpaid. It is believed and has been confidently asserted that all of the fines thus collected and property thus confiscated from the peaceable citizens of the community, not one dollar was returned to the treasury, or turned into the proper channel by which it was to reach the State Department.

Of this state of misrule, John Webster was probably one of the most severe sufferers. After having been harassed at different times by having his personal property seized and carried away, they finally proceeded to sell his land and mill.

Elijah Dyson, the first sheriff of Guernsey County, was a man possessed of a good deal of refined manners, and always made a liberal display of friendliness among the people. He had filled his first term of office creditably as far as was publicly known, but during his second term -- which he was now serving -- he had become perfectly reckless, both in his private affairs and in what related to the duties of his office. He had now become a party to the military swindle and from superior knowledge, combined with treachery and cunning, he became one of their most active and able instruments in devising their plans and in aiding their cause. The dignity of his office was prostituted to partisan purposes, as far as the office of sheriff could be applied to misrule, until his course was finally run.

Sheriff Dyson -- with some others that had become professional fine collectors -- now colluded. They filed a bill in chancery under the plea that there were muster fines standing against John Webster as a member of the 5th Battalion 3rd Brigade and 3rd Division of the Ohio Militia and upon this plea thus filed they procured an order of Court to sell Webster's land and mill. The tract of land contained eighty acres, being the west half of the northeast quarter of Section Nineteen, of Range No. 7, Township No. 9, on which tract the mill and residence of John Webster was situated. The proceeds of this sale were to be applied to satisfy this fine. Under this order of Court, they made sale of the land and mill which was bid off by one of their own partisans, and they proceeded to take forcible possession according to the order of sale. Thereupon they sent twelve chosen men to take forcible possession, some of whom had been fine collectors in seizing on property and carrying it away to satisfy muster fines from the neighboring inhabitants.

During this procedure, John Webster was kept ignorant of what was going on. His wife Albina was dangerously ill when a posse of men came to dispossess them. Three of the most prominent of these were Samuel Scroggins, Samuel Wilson and L.T. Henderson. I name them as I shall have occasion to refer to them hereafter. They held a parley in and about the house where the sick woman lay, in regard to the ways and means by which they were to be governed and what was to be their immediate action. All, except one man, were in favor of showing no leniency or mercy, but planned to carry the sick woman out of doors, as she lay in bed with her infant child. They would possess the household goods and take full and complete possession by locking up the house and forcing the family to leave.

One of the company who had been pressed into the service against his will -- a man by the name of James Garrett -- said that he came there much against his will, but that he would not act any further in this case contrary to his better judgment, in violation of his better feelings, and that he would not dare to see a woman thus misused, nor be instrumental on so flagrant an outrage. From the bold and determined stand he took on behalf of the then terribly distressed woman, they desisted at the present from this undertaking. They left the house and retired to the mill of which they took immediate possession. They took the fastenings off the doors, and put on other fastenings and another lock with bolts.

John Webster, at this time, had become much disheartened from the great pressure that seemed to bear upon him. The idea of having his sick wife liable to be turned out of house and home at any time, and of losing all his estate, prompted him to request his brother-in-law John Hall, to go to St. Clairsville to consult Charles Hammond in regard to the twelve men taking possession of his mill. When John Hall proceeded to make his statement in regard to the matter and what means the men had employed to get possession of the land and appurtenances thereto, Hammond said in reply, "Tell Webster to take twelve other men and throw them out neck and heels." When Hammond heard the whole statement he wrote out a Writ of Ejectment, a species of mixed action which lies for the recovery of possession of real property, and damages and cost for the unlawful detention of it. He gave John Hall instructions in regard to the writ and to serve it himself without any delay, on whom-so-ever had the mill in possession when he should arrive there. On his return home he took one or two neighbors with him, and when they arrived at the mill it was in possession of Samuel Wilson, who ground for such customers as came. When Wilson was told the object of their coming he took up a large butcher knife that lay near as if to assume a threatening posture in holding his possession. But as the paper was being read to him not-with-standing all his former assumed bravery, he trembled and it seemed with difficulty he could hold his weapon, and left the mill as soon as he could do so.

After the men first took possession of Webster's Mill, they left it under the care of Samuel Wilson and one or two others that attended to it. L.T. Henderson, in his exaltations over the success they had in John Webster's case, said "that he would glory in seeing the Quakers despoiled of their goods, and their real property confiscated so as they would be forced to leave the country" -- as there were only a few Quakers in Guernsey County. He promised that when he returned from Duck Creek, he would give them no rest or peace until that end was accomplished. These threats were made in an outspoken manner, in the presence of some of those he had, or intended to, persecute. But this was a boast that was not realized. He and Samuel Scroggins set out for the Duck Creek Saltworks, to procure some salt and upon their arrival at the works, Henderson was taken suddenly ill and died within four days and thus rested from his further labors.

In course of time, the trial came on at Cambridge Court. Charles Hammond of St. Clairsville and Alexander Harper of Zanesville managed and plead the suit on behalf of John Webster, and Samuel Herrick of Zanesville, on the part of the Military officers. The trial lasted several days and was warmly contested. Lawyer Herrick made a plea in Chancery which he supported at great length and endeavored to maintain the legality of the sale of Webster's land by way of Parole evidence to prove that Webster's was the land they meant to sell, that is, the tract of land in Section Nineteen instead of a tract similarly situated, in Section Twenty-four. It was shown and made manifest throughout the trial that the Military had acted illegally in numerous instances on their part, with an intentional fraud and swindle throughout. Webster's property was remanded and legally restored to his possession, and he established in his inherent rights.

John Webster was married the second time to Elizabeth Marshall. They had two children, Susan and Warner Webster. They both lived to mature age but died young. Susan, the oldest, married Dr. T.J. Romans then of Londonderry Township, and died soon afterwards. Warner died in the spring of 1848, unmarried.

John Webster was married the third time to Debora Chambers. They had three children:

Mary Webster	b.	d. 8/16/1835	m. 12/27/1855	Henry Hartley
Samuel Webster	b.	d.	m.	Jane Homes
John Webster, Jr.	b. 12/31/1838	d. 5/8/1906	m.	Eliza J. Perry

Contributed by: Mary L. Webster, Columbus, Ohio. John Webster Jr. was a brother of my great grandfather Thomas Webster.

Homes of Thomas Webster, Sr.

1782-1858

Thomas Webster Sr.		Son of John Webster (the pioneer)	
Born 3-6-1782		Born 12-16-1751	
Died 4-21-1858		Died 3- -1808	
Married 12-12-1813	Anna Gore	Married 6-27-1778	Hannah Plummer
	Born 7-23-1795		Born 4-13-1761
	Died 7-8-1854		Died - -1834.

John, Hannah and their ten children came to what is now Millwood Township, Guernsey Co., Ohio from Lancaster Co., Pennsylvania in October of the year 1806. Thomas entered the S.E. Quarter Section 26, Township 9, Range 7 of the Seven Ranges of Congress Land sold at Steubenville, Ohio. (As we know it today, 1942, *Millwood Township.*) It is the tract of land on which Jeptha S. Webster's house stands, now occupied by Norval E. Day. It is located seven-eights of a mile west of the present Methodist Church in Quaker City, where the road is closest to the railroad.

He made some improvements on his own land and helped his father with his home and mill. At the end of two years he went back to Pennsylvania and worked at the carpenter business for about two years to get some money to complete the title to his land here. He came back to Ohio and found the land he had cleared and planted in orchard was grown up in brush. The rabbits had de-barked the young trees so badly that he gave up the orchard site and cleared more ground in the bottom, south of the present home site and planted another orchard. Some of these trees grew very large and bore as much as forty bushel of apples per tree. (W.V. Webster, a grandson, saw some of these trees standing when he was a boy some ten years old.)

The first house of Thomas Webster Sr. was a two story hewn log structure about twenty by twenty feet built by him probably in 1813, and located three hundred feet west of the present house on the Jeptha Webster farm. It was down in the hollow by a good spring of water. Another hewn log house was built over the spring. It was about eight by ten feet and the logs were approximately twenty inches wide. These large logs were obtained from trees cleared on his ground.

The second house of Thomas Webster Sr. was an oak frame dwelling built about 1825. The sills were hewn out and sized to six by eight inches. The studding were split and trimmed to two by four inches. The plastering lath were split from oak about one-half by one and one-half inches by four feet long. The house must have been one and one-half story high. A part of this second house was dismantled and the remainder was moved and used for a chicken house.

The third and present house was located on the site of the second house. It was built in 1839 and 1840 and was a substantial structure framed together in modern style. The weatherboarding was of black walnut one and one-half inches thick and six inches wide, split out of logs and dressed by drawer knife and planes. All of this work was done by hand.

The house, facing the south, was about thirty by forty-five feet, two stories high, with an added room and porch extending to the west. There was a large cellar under all of the main building walled with large dressed sandstone quarried on the place. A door on the first floor near the middle of the south side of the two story part had six stone steps leading to it. On the north side, a door opposite the one of the south side had one stone step.

Two bedrooms were in the east end of the house, each about fifteen feet square. A hall about seven feet wide extended along the north side between one of the bedrooms and the west room, with a similar hall above. The stairway to connect these halls was along the north wall. The parlor was the large room downstairs south of the hall; it had a fireplace in the west hall.

The room to the west which could be entered from the hall was two steps lower than the rest of the house, and had a large fireplace on the east side backing against the parlor fireplace. The porch south of this room was ten feet wide. From it large stone steps led to the cellar. There were four bedrooms on the second floor. The windows each had two sash and each contained six panes of glass about ten by twelve inches.

One of the interesting pieces of furniture was a combination table and bench which was in the west room. This table top was hinged near one side and when not needed as a dining room table could be tilted back. A board seat ran the length between the table legs and was used to sit on while the table top made the back of the bench. This was home-made and there was a similar table in the John Bundy home east of Barnesville.

Thomas Webster Sr. and his boys built a large stock barn which is still standing on the Jeptha Webster place. In the top of that barn -- when Willis V. Webster was a boy -- there was about two ton of flax that was never used. He got some of it (about a handful), cleaned it up, and used it for smoothbore gun wads. It worked alright. About seventy-five feet north of the barn a double corn crib was built. The cribs were on each side with a driveway between. There was a wooden scoop for shoveling corn, which had been made by the Websters.

The Websters had tools of all kinds: Jack planes, joiners, smoothing planes, pannel planes, and several kinds of beading planes; a heavy broad ax, square, beveling square, ax, hand saws, whip saws, keyhole saws, crosscut saws, brace and bits, augers of all sizes up to two inches, about three sizes of frows, as well as tools for splitting stone and dressing them.

Thomas Webster Sr. in the year 1844 -- in company with his two oldest sons Joseph G. and Jeptha S. Webster -- started a general store in a two story hewn log house near the west end of their new home. The store house must have been the first dwelling house, which was taken down and rebuilt for the store. They continued in the mercantile business here about four years, until they moved the store to town. They continued in partnership until 1852 when they dissolved, with Joseph assuming the entire business.

Farther east (about one-fourth mile) on the north side of the clay pike was a hewn two story log house. It may have been built for a dwelling, but was used for a subscription school for several winters. (A subscription school is one in which the parents paid for their children's education, there being no public system of education at the time.) The Webster and Linn children went to school there. Some of the Websters taught there. They had greased paper instead of glass for windows and had wooden pins fitted in holes bored in the wall on which boards lay for desks -- and slabs with holes, in which legs fit, for seats. The little children sat on slab benches and kept their books by them on the bench. The older scholars used the desks along the wall. Goose quill pens, kept in order by the teacher, were used for writing.

About one-eighth of a mile farther east at the north side of the clay pike, just over the line on Michael King's entry, was another two story hewn log house built with a cellar under it and used as a dwelling. Several different families had lived in it. The school house and this one were about twenty feet square. Willis V. Webster (a grandson of Thomas Webster Sr.) helped to take these houses down and Thomas Webster Jr. had a hog pen made from the timbers. It is standing today (1942) at Walter A. Webster's home.

Written by: Thomas Webster, Columbus, Ohio. This information was secured from Willis V. Webster by his son, Thomas Webster, Great-Grandson of Thomas Webster Sr.

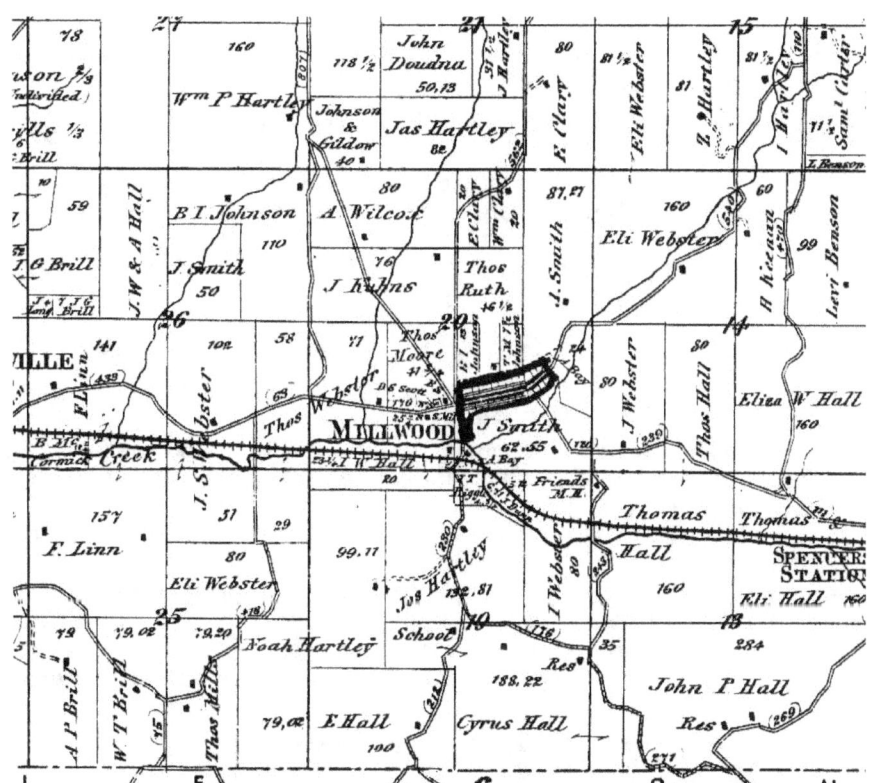

STRAWBERRY PLANTS For Sale!

BY THE DOZEN OR THOUSAND.

HAVE YOU A GARDEN? If you have you should GROW YOUR OWN BERRIES.

In 1893 two short rows across our home garden produced 100 quarts of very large Strawberries. This last season our receipts from 1000 plants, planted on one-twelfth of an acre, amounted to $65.00.

We Make a Specialty of Garden Collections

of Berry Plants and have spared no expense in securing the best new varieties. If you want Early Berries, Late Berries, Big Berries and lots of them, get our $2 collection, which consists of the best strawberries for home use in existence. Do not depend on buying your supply of Berries from market growers, when you can have an abundance of the best, fresh from your own garden.

OUR $2 GARDEN COLLECTION.

25 Timbrell, 25 Greenville, 12 Parker Earle, 25 Sharpless, 50 Cumberland, 25 Mitchel's Early, 25 Haverland and 25 Gaudy's Prize.

Timbrell, Greenville and Parker Earle are superb new varieties, and the plants of these alone would cost more, if purchased of any reliable nurseryman, than our price for the entire collection.

You only have to buy strawberry plants once. After you start a bed you always have your own plants. Start right. Get the best.

We have special plant beds on rich new ground, and have a fine lot of Timbrell, Enhance, Greenville, Parker Earle, Muskingum, Buback, Warfield, Haverland, Sharpless, Cumberland, Crescent and Gaudy's Prize plants. We can also furnish Gregg and Palmer Raspberry plants. Get our prices before purchasing elsewhere.

Call on or addrss,

Webster Bros.

One-Fourth Mile West of   QUAKER CITY, OHIO.

DR. EPHRAIM WILLIAMS

Soon after Dr. Ephraim Williams began to practice as a physician in Barnesville, Ohio, one of the older doctors had a patient with a bad case of typhoid fever. In due time the disease yielded but left the patient weak in mind as well as body. The doctor also was unable to get her up and some of the other doctors in the area were called for help, but the result was the same.

At length it came to Dr. Williams' turn and as he had knowledge of similar conditions, he considered -- as he rode along -- how he would proceed. After examining the patient carefully, he told her she was in a bad way. He told her that he did not have the medicine with him that he wanted her to take, and asked her husband to come to his office for it the next day.

In the meantime, he made some bread pills with enough innocent bitter to disguise them. The doctor had already gained her confidence so she would try anything he suggested and each visit he would mention some different thing to try, such as sitting up a short time, then the next time longer, then take a few steps and more the next time, and so forth.

When he thought the proper time had come, he suggested she ride out some, and set a certain day for her to come to his office. Thus he succeeded in getting her nearly back to normal and thereby made himself a valuable reputation that gave him a wide practice.

The secret of his success was not made known at that time, but it was said he laughed over it when telling his relatives the story when he was an old man.

Written by: Robert H. Smith

RICHARD WILLIAMS
1770 - 1852

Richard Williams was the only son of Robert and Elizabeth Dearman Williams. (She was Robert Williams' first wife. After her death, he married Anna Shoebridge.) Richard was a half-brother to Uncle John S. Williams.

When Richard Williams was a young boy, on one occasion he was at a gathering of young folks. In the afternoon they decided to take a walk (as that was about the only way to go anyplace in those days), and as there were not enough young men present for the young women, Uncle Richard made the remark that he would take the three Sarah's and it so happened -- in later years -- that he did take the three Sarah's, and married each after the preceding one died."

He first married Sara Dew by whom he had one son, Robert, who died very young.

On 11th Month 6th 1796, he married in Friends meetinghouse in Core Sound, North Carolina, his second wife, Sara Stanton (daughter of Benjamin and Abigail Macy Stanton), by whom he had ten children. He was a sea captain for many years and at the age of 32, he abandoned his seafaring life.

His step mother, Anna Shoebridge Williams, had three other children. *(Elizabeth, Samuel and John.)* When Elizabeth was 22 -- later to become our great-grandmother Garretson -- Uncle Samuel was 21, and Uncle John S. Williams was 10 years old -- Anna Williams and these three children came from North Carolina to Belmont County, Ohio. They came with the families of Joseph Dew, Lavina Hall, Jonas Small, and nine other families; and settled at Concord, Ohio, where they moved into their cabin on Christmas day 1800.

Two years later -- on Seventh Day, 7th month 31st 1802 -- Richard came to their cabin and with the help of his neighbors, soon set up a cabin of his own near the meetinghouse, for himself and family and opened a school. He had left his family at or near Wheeling, until his cabin was built. His half-brother John says, "I had never been sent to school. He put me in three syllables in Dilworth's Spelling book. I think the first lesson commenced with the word abandon. I abandoned that lesson and that book, for I swallowed the whole of it very soon. The teachers could keep me back in recitations, but not in knowing."

(Children of Richard and Sara Stanton Williams: Elizabeth 1799, Abigail 1802, Dearman 1804, Deborah 1806, Asa 1808, Mary 1811, Benjamin 1814, Lydia 1816, David 1818, Edward 1821)

One of the children of Richard and Sara Stanton Williams -- Elizabeth -- was born 9th Month 9th 1799 in North Carolina. She married 5th Month 30th 1822, Micajah Dillingham of Delaware County, Ohio, at Friends meeting at Kendal Stark Co., Ohio. She was past 80 years of age at the time of her death, which took place near Damascus, Ohio.

Abigail was born 9th Month 19th 1802. She married 12th Month 26th, 1825 to John Fawcett, Salem, Ohio, and died 11th Month 10th 1835 at Salem, Ohio, at the age of 33.

Dearman was born 11th Month 12th 1804. He married 11th Month 27th 1830 to Mary Farmer of Sandy Spring, Ohio, and died 11th Month 27th 1867 in Humboldt Co. Iowa.

Deborah was born 11th Month 30th 1806. She married 5th Month 27th 1829 to Daniel Osborn, of Delaware Co. Ohio, and died 5th Month 2nd 1834.

Asa was born 12th Month 27th 1808. He married 5th Month 21st 1834 to Elizabeth Cadwalder of Salem, Ohio, and died 1st Month 23rd 1861.

Mary was born 4th Month 7th 1811. She married Joseph Emmons of Agusta Meeting of Friends Ohio. They had no children. She died 3rd Month 15th 1838.

Benjamin was born 4th Month 3rd 1814, and died 10th Month 10th 1855 near East Rochester, unmarried.

Lydia was born 5th Month 2nd 1816. She married 5th Month 1st 1851 to Joseph Stanley of Damascus, Ohio, and died about 1897 or 1898 at the house of her daughter in Brookhaven, Miss.

David was born 9th Month 25th 1818. He married 8th Month 9th 1853 to Hannah S. Mickle of Washington, Pa. They had no children. He died 7th Month 1st 1877 near Marshalltown, Iowa.

Edward was born 2nd Month 5th 1821. He married Hannah Bruff of Damascus, Ohio (born 8th Month 27th 1823; died 10th Month 11th 1882). Edward died 9th Month 2nd 1894 at Damascus, Ohio.

Richard Williams, their father, was born 11th Month 28th 1770 in Cartaret County, North Carolina. He died 3rd Month 10th 1852 in Damascus, Ohio, at the home of his son Edward, at the age of 81 years, three months and 11 days.

Written by: Elma Doudna Bailey, Daughter of Joseph W. Doudna, and fourth generation of the Kidnapped boy.

Robert W. Hampton of Whittier, Iowa originally gave the details contained in this sketch of his Uncle Richard Williams.

WOLF DEN STORY

One of John Doudna's neighbors, having had trouble with wolves killing his sheep, set some guns for them. He and Zadock Boswell, who lived adjoining, placed the guns, star fashion, their muzzles pointing inward to a trap as a common center. From the trap, strings extended to the triggers of the guns, so that when the bait was disturbed, the triggers were pulled and the guns were discharged.

It was harvest time and he was up late putting up hay. When he had gone to the house and was about to go to bed, he heard the guns go off. He immediately went to Boswell's and the two of them went to see the results. It was entirely satisfactory, as a large wolf lay dead at the trap.

At another time, he and his son were hunting a hog when they found a den of wolves. He left his son to watch while he went for help. When they returned, he decided to crawl into the den. He tied a rope to his leg so those on the outside could pull him out if necessary. He took his gun and crawled several feet under the rock, thinking he might "shine" the old one's eyes as they called it and shoot her. But he could not see her and the litter of whelps could get so far back into the crevices of the rocks that he could not reach them.

He was not to be undone in that way, so he went to work and made a large stick trap which he set on the side toward the den. Then he walled up the mouth of the den at the side of the trap so that the adults could not get out while the young ones could.

In the morning, four or five of the young ones were in the trap, but the old ones were nowhere to be found. He then posted his friends about the den at different places and made one of the whelps howl. This brought the old ones in sight of the men, and a well directed shot by one of the men, who was posted in a hollow log, killed her. The next night another young one was caught in the trap. Thus the den was broken up.

Written by: Kenneth Lloyd Doudna, a great-great-Grandson of John Doudna.

FEW FACTS CONCERNING THE EDMUND FOWLER FAMILY AND HOME

Edmund Fowler, who was born in Columbiana County, Ohio, in 1834, was the son of Caleb and Sarah Smith Fowler. The Caleb Fowler family came to Washington County and lived some two miles northwest of Bartlett. As a lad, Edmund walked with his father through the woods to the Plymouth Meeting. *(Plymouth Monthly Meeting was located in northwestern Washington County not far from Morgan County.)*

After Edmund had grown to manhood and was in Iowa, he met Mary Pearson Miles, whom he married there December 16th 1858. She too was a native of Ohio, as she was born in Miami County in 1830. Sometime, probably in the early 1860s they came to Washington County, Ohio, bought a few acres of unimproved land, and established their home three-fourths of a mile north of Bartlett and within easy reach of Plymouth Meeting.

Both to the east and the west of the land runs a public road. The portion of land chosen for a building site was a plum thicket several rods back from the west road. Only a few steps south of the house site was a little stream of water that furnished water for chickens, cows and horses.

Since Edmund was a carpenter by trade, he built the house and outbuildings, of which there were several. The house was a story and a half frame structure with sleeping quarters upstairs and at the west end of the downstairs. In the center was a spacious living room, extending the width of the house. At the east end was a kitchen, and possibly a pantry. Beyond was the well-kept garden. Among the out-buildings were a barn, cellar house, and an evaporator house. These were all plainly, but neatly built. Here, with Edmund and Mary Fowler, lived their three children: Irene, who married Joshua Smith; Orland, who married Hannah Dean; and Sarah, who married Albert Warrington and after his death, Albert Bedell.

When failing health compelled Edmund to relinquish his trade as carpenter, he returned to other occupations, keeping a small apiary, farming in a small way, running a fruit evaporator, some legal business and so on.

The Fowlers made this their home until after the Meeting to which Edmund as a lad walked with his father through the woods, became so small that it was laid down and meetings were held in their home.

As a child, the writer visited in this home where Edmund, Mary, and their daughter Sarah lived in their orderly way in this quiet, peaceful place, where kindly human nature had produced an atmosphere of blending harmony. Subsequently, the Fowlers moved to Columbiana County and the home became the property of others.

Recently, the present owner has moved to another property and at times, Sabbath School and worship services have been held here by a religious group without regular meeting house of their own.

Written by: Elizabeth Burgess. Some of the facts have been given by Sarah Fowler Bedell and Alden Hobsen.

INDEX OF NAMES

Arnold, Hannah (Mrs. Lemuel Patterson), 126

Ashton, Dorothy Stratton, 103–104

Bailey, Allen, 7–8, 38, 123, 126

Bailey, Alva Caleb, 14–17, 35

Bailey, Anna Mary, 31

Bailey, Anna (Mrs. Clarence Patten), 1, 9, 17, 84, 129

Bailey, Asenath Doudna (Mrs. Irving), 13, 59, 90

Bailey, Benjamin, 123

Bailey, Clara (Mrs. Fred Bundy), 13, 15, 17

Bailey, Edmund, 11

Bailey, Edna (Mrs. Louis Taber), 134

Bailey, Edwin Macy, 13–17

Bailey, Elam, 56

Bailey, Elizabeth, 8, 123

Bailey, Elizabeth Stanton (Mrs. L. P.), 9, 13–17, 27

Bailey, Elma Doudna, 22, 59, 82, 127, 196

Bailey, Eva Patterson (Mrs. Allen), 126

Bailey, Exum, 123

Bailey, Florence (Mrs. Ernest Patterson), 126

Bailey, Ida (Mrs. Harvey Binns), 123

Bailey, Jane (Mrs. Benjamin Patterson Sr.), 126

Bailey, Jane (Mrs. Robert Plummer Jr.), 136

Bailey, Jehu, 85

Bailey, Jesse, 1, 7–8, 13, 96

Bailey, Jesse Sr., 7, 129, 159

Bailey, Jesse Stanton, 14–17

Bailey, Joel, 11, 126

Bailey, John, 7–8

Bailey, Joseph, 149

Bailey, Lem, 35

Bailey, Lindley Patterson, 7–8, 13–17, 35, 123, 129, 143

Bailey, Lloyd, 35

Bailey, Lucy Crew (Mrs. Benjamin), 123

Bailey, Lydia Holloway, 11

Bailey, Margaret Doudna, 11, 144

Bailey, Martha Edgerton (Mrs. Steven II), 123

Bailey, Mary, 7

Bailey, Mary (Mrs. Micajah), 136

Bailey, Micajah, 136

Bailey, Oscar Joseph, 13–16, 90

Bailey, Phariba (Mrs. Eli Patterson), 7, 126

Bailey, Rachel, 7

Bailey, Rachel (Mrs. Lewis Naylor), 123

Bailey, Rosella (Mrs. Jonathan Binns), 123

Bailey, Ross, 3, 7

Bailey, Ruthanna Patterson (Mrs. Joel), 11, 126

Bailey, Sara M., 143–144

Bailey, Sarah, 7

Bailey, Sarah J., 16

Bailey, Silas, 7–8

Bailey, Stephen, 123

Bailey, Stephen II, 123

Bailey, Tabitha (Mrs. Eli Patterson), 126

Bailey, Talitha Patterson (Mrs. Stephen), 123

Ball, David, 101

Ball, Gaynor Burgess, 101

Ball, Nathan, 101

Barker, George F., 4

Barlow, Amos, 125

Bedell, Albert, 199

Bedell, Sarah Fowler (Mrs. Albert), 199–200

Binford, Angelina (Mrs. Jared Patterson), 123

Binford, Micajah, 123

Binford, Sarah Patterson (Mrs. Micajah), 123

Binns, Belinda Hobson, 103

Binns, Harvey, 123

Binns, Ida Bailey (Mrs. Harvey), 123

Binns, Jonathan, 123

Binns, Rosella Bailey (Mrs. Jonathan), 123

Bishop, Aaron, 15

Blane, James G., 15

Blower, Jeptha, 29

Boswell, Ruth, 75

Boswell, Zadock, 197

Bowman, Thomas, 103

Branson, Themes, 177

Brantingham, Alfred, 58

Briggs, Sarah, 161

Brooks, Giles, 24

Broomall, Amy (Mrs. Joshua Patterson), 126

Bruff, Hannah (Mrs. Edward Williams), 196

Bundle, Joe, 143

Bundy, Achsah? (Mrs. Jonathan), 21

Bundy, Ann, 165

Bundy, Anna Stanton (Mrs. Nathan), 27, 164

Bundy, Asenath Doudna (Mrs. William Bundy), 37–38

Bundy, Bernita, 38
Bundy, Caleb L., 27–28
Bundy, Chalkley, 29, 30–32, 49–52, 175
Bundy, Chalkley II, 31
Bundy, Charity (Mrs. James Stanton), 163, 165, 167
Bundy, Clara Elma, 27
Bundy, Clark, 38
Bundy, Deborah Hanson (Mrs. Caleb Bundy, also Mrs. Chalkley Bundy), 30, 31, 175
Bundy, Dempsey, 23, 25
Bundy, Dillwyn C. (D.C.), 25, 33, 38, 89
Bundy, Elizabeth, 33, 165
Bundy, Elizabeth (Mrs. Frame), 159
Bundy, Elizabeth Steer (Mrs. Dillwyn C.), 89
Bundy, Emma, 31
Bundy, Ezekiel, 23–24, 27, 33, 165
Bundy, Joel L., 31
Bundy, John, 16, 30, 35, 58, 98, 159, 175
Bundy, Jonathan, 19–21
Bundy, Joseph S., 27–28
Bundy, Lindley, 31
Bundy, Lindy, 13
Bundy, Lucinda (Mrs. Hanson), 31, 52
Bundy, Marie, 39
Bundy, Mary C. (Mrs. Smith), 30, 80, 143, 154, 174
Bundy, Mary Elizabeth, 30, 31
Bundy, Mary M. (Mrs. John Colpitts), 27–28
Bundy, Mary (Mrs. Dempsey), 23
Bundy, Mary (Mrs. Ezekiel), 27
Bundy, Mary P. (Mrs. Eli Stanton), 3, 159–160
Bundy, Nathan W., 27, 29, 31
Bundy, Prudence Wood (Mrs. William Bundy) 37, 165
Bundy, Rachel Crew (Mrs. Clark), 38
Bundy, Rebecca E. Doudna, 31, 49–50
Bundy, Ruanna Frame, 13
Bundy, Ruth Patten (Mrs. John), 159
Bundy, Sarah C. Holloway (Mrs. Cooper), 73
Bundy, Sarah Doudna (Mrs. Chalkley), 29, 30–32, 52
Bundy, Sarah Overman (Mrs. William), 23–24, 37, 165
Bundy, William, 23–24, 30, 37, 98
Bundy, William (Black Bill), 24–25, 37–38
Bundy, William II, 25
Bundy Nathan W., 31
Burgess, Elizabeth, 101, 200

Burgess, Gaynor (Mrs. Ball), 101
Burkhart, Vernon, 123
Burr, Edith Hobson, 101
Burson, Joseph, 122
Burt, Betty, 104
Burt, Edith Hobson (Mrs. Harold), 104
Butcher, Ella, 15

Cadwalder, Elizabeth (Mrs. Asa Williams), 196
Campbell, Inez, 177
Carter, Edith R. (Mrs. Dillwyn W. Doudna), 59
Carter, Marietta (Mrs. John A. Doudna), 59
Chalfant, Ann Webster (Mrs. Jesse), 111
Chalfant, Jesse, 111
Chambers, Deborah (Mrs. John Webster Sr.), 187
Cole, Charleyn, 151
Colpitts, Clifford B., 27–28
Colpitts, Mary Bundy (Mrs. John), 27–28
Connard, Georgia (Mrs. Barclay Patterson), 126
Conrow, Mary J. Hobson, 103
Cook, Alva, 59
Cooper, Sara, 179
Cooper, Sarah C. Bundy Holloway, 73
Cope, Anna (Mrs. Hall), 177
Cope, Rachel E., 70
Cox, Joseph, 23
Cox, Sarah (Mrs. James Edgerton, Sr.), 69–70
Coyler, John, 23
Crew, Lucy (Mrs. Benjamin Bailey), 123
Crew, Mary, 82
Crew, Rachel (Mrs. Clark Bundy), 38
Crew, Rebecca (Mrs. Isaac Patterson), 126
Crews, Aquilla, 56–57

Davis, Francis, 41, 56, 58, 79, 177
Davis, Mary (Mrs. Francis), 41, 177
Davis, Tabitha Stanton, 4
Dawson, Chalkley, 27
Dawson, Joel, 43, 134
Day, Norval E., 183, 189
Dean, Hannah (Mrs. Orland Fowler), 199
Dearing, Debora Webster, 113
Dearing, Yvonne Ardel, 159
Dearman, Elizabeth (Mrs. Robert Williams), 55, 195

DeMotte, John B., 4, 6
Dennis, Increase (Mrs. Hezekiah Thomas), 72, 179
Dew, Joseph, 195
Dew, Sarah (Mrs. Richard Williams), 195
Dewees, Rebecca, 70
Dickinson, Anna, 140
Dillingham, Elizabeth Williams (Mrs. Micajah), 195
Dillingham, Micajah, 195
Doudna, Achsah, 21
Doudna, Alfred, 124
Doudna, Ann Eliza Wilson (Mrs. Joseph F.), 44
Doudna, Anna, 46, 55
Doudna, Anna (Mrs. Peter Sears), 147, 149
Doudna, Asenath, 21
Doudna, Asenath Elma (Mrs. Irving E. Bailey), 59
Doudna, Asenath Garretson (Mrs. John III), 61
Doudna, Asenath Hall (Mrs. John III), 53, 55–56
Doudna, Asenath (Mrs. William "Black Bill" Bundy), 37–38
Doudna, Belinda Hobson (Mrs. Joseph F.), 43
Doudna, Beulah M., 53
Doudna, Charity (Mrs. Joseph Edgerton), 69
Doudna, Clishe, 165
Doudna, Dillwyn W., 59
Doudna, Edith Carter (Mrs. Dillwyn W.), 59
Doudna, Edwin F., 43
Doudna, Elisha, 46, 58
Doudna, Elizabeth, 45, 46
Doudna, Elma (Mrs. Bailey), 82
Doudna, Ethel (Mrs. Joseph Wylie), 126
Doudna, Eunice, 51
Doudna, Ezekiel, 49
Doudna, Henry, 27, 45, 144, 146, 147, 149, 164, 174
Doudna, Henry II, 46, 47
Doudna, Hosea, 43, 48, 75, 95, 149
Doudna, Isaac, 46, 58
Doudna, James, 46
Doudna, Jesse B., 47
Doudna, Jesse I, 55, 56, 58
Doudna, Jesse I., 61–62, 126
Doudna, Joel, 31, 49, 51, 167
Doudna, John, 30, 51, 124, 125, 144–145, 149, 197
Doudna, John A., 53, 56, 59, 61
Doudna, John I (the "kidnapped boy"), 45–48, 55
Doudna, John II, 46–47, 53, 55, 61

Doudna, John III, 53, 55–56, 61
Doudna, John IV, 58
Doudna, Joseph, 134
Doudna, Joseph F., 43–44, 165
Doudna, Joseph H., 46, 59
Doudna, Joseph W., 46–48, 53, 55–59, 61, 63, 81, 149, 196
Doudna, Josiah W., 43
Doudna, Kenneth Lloyd, 59, 197
Doudna, Knowis, 46, 47
Doudna, Knowis Jr., 47
Doudna, Lizzie C. (Mrs. Alva B. Hartley), 59
Doudna, Louisa Patterson (Mrs. Jesse I), 126
Doudna, Margaret "Peggy" (Mrs. Bailey), 46, 144
Doudna, Marietta Carter (Mrs. John A.), 59
Doudna, Martha, 164
Doudna, Mary, 53
Doudna, Mary Farmer (Mrs. Hosea), 43
Doudna, Mary H. (Mrs. Hoyle), 43
Doudna, Mary J., 59, 146
Doudna, Mary (Mrs. Isaac Doudna), 46
Doudna, Mary (Mrs. Isaac Hall), 58
Doudna, Miriam Hall (Mrs. John II), 55, 61
Doudna, Rebecca (Mrs. Bundy), 31, 49
Doudna, Rosetta Bundy (Mrs. Frank A. Louhoff), 59
Doudna, Rosetta Hall (Mrs. Joseph W.), 46, 53, 58–59
Doudna, Ruth S. (Mrs. Hibbs), 43
Doudna, Sara, 53, 55, 61
Doudna, Sara A., 59
Doudna, Sarah Knowis (Mrs. John I), 46, 55
Doudna, Sarah (Mrs. Chalkley Bundy), 29, 30–32, 52
Doudna, Wallace, 126
Doudna, Walter, 51
Doudna, William "Billy," 46, 171
Doudna, Zilpha (Mrs. John H. Edgerton Sr.), 46–47
Doudna, Nora Hartley (Mrs. Joseph H.), 59
Dyson, Elijah, 185–186

Edgerton, Anna Hall (Mrs. James II), 65–67, 69, 93
Edgerton, Charity Doudna (Mrs. Joseph), 69
Edgerton, Christiana Peele Hall (Mrs. Joseph), 65, 69
Edgerton, David, 67, 176
Edgerton, James, 13, 44, 58, 59, 182
Edgerton, James II, 66, 69
Edgerton, James Jr., 115–116

Edgerton, James Sr., 69–70, 115
Edgerton, Jesse, 70
Edgerton, John H. Jr., 47–48
Edgerton, John H. Sr., 46–47
Edgerton, Joseph, 65–67, 69–70, 115–117
Edgerton, Martha (Mrs. Steven Bailey II), 123
Edgerton, Mary Hall (Mrs. Richard), 66, 69
Edgerton, Mildred Rachel (Mrs. Wilmer Hall, II), 125
Edgerton, Richard, 66, 69
Edgerton, Sarah Cox (Mrs. James Sr.), 69–70
Edgerton, Sarah Walton (Mrs. Samuel), 67, 181–182
Edgerton, Walter, 70
Edgerton, Zilpha Doudna (Mrs. John H. Sr.), 46–47
Emmons, Joseph, 196
Emmons, Mary Williams (Mrs. Joseph), 196
Emmons, McCagey, 104
Engle, Caleb, 136, 138
Engle, Rachel (Mrs. Caleb), 136–138

Farmer, Mary (Mrs. Dearman Williams), 196
Farmer, Mary (Mrs. Hosea Doudna), 43
Farmer, Taylor, 59
Fawcett, Abigail (Mrs. John), 195
Fawcett, John, 195
Fawcett, Mary 'Matie' Stanton, 162
Fields, Isaiah, 35
Flanner, Abbie, 140
Flanner, Catherine, 85
Fogle, 177
Fowler, Caleb, 199
Fowler, Edmund, 101, 199
Fowler, Esther, 70
Fowler, Hannah Dean (Mrs. Orland), 199
Fowler, Irene (Mrs. Joshua Smith), 199
Fowler, Mary Pearson Miles (Mrs. Edmund), 199
Fowler, Orland, 199
Fowler, Sarah (Mrs. Albert Warrington, also Mrs. Albert Bedell), 199
Fowler, Sarah Smith (Mrs. Caleb), 199
Frame, Aaron, 51, 58, 71–73
Frame, Achsah Smith (Mrs. Aaron), 71–72
Frame, Amasa, 4, 141
Frame, Elizabeth Bundy, 159
Frame, Florence, 72, 179

Frame, James, 58, 175
Frame, Lavinia Wright (Mrs. Aaron), 73
Frame, Lura, 179
Frame, Ruanna (Mrs. Lindy Bundy), 13
Frame, Ruanna Thomas (Mrs. William), 71
Frame, Talitha Thompson (Mrs. Aaron), 71
Frame, Thompson, 71, 82, 141, 174
Frame, William, 71–73, 90
French, Mary Bundy (Mrs. William French), 24
French, Otho, 83–84, 172
French, William, 24

Galloway, Ella Coventry, 48, 61
Garretson, Asa, 56–57, 58
Garretson, Asenath (Mrs. John Doudna III), 61
Garretson, Elizabeth Williams (Mrs. Joseph), 55, 127
Garretson, Joseph, 55, 81
Garretson, Joseph, Sr., 76
Garretson, Mary, 55
Garretson, William, 55
Garrett, James, 186
Garrettson, Asenath (Mrs. John Doudna III), 55–56
Gibbons, Edward V., 85
Gibbons, Joseph, 85
Gibbons, Lavina, 85
Gibbons, Penina Williams (Mrs. Joseph), 85
Gill, J.J., 140
Gore, Anna (Mrs. Thomas Webster Sr.), 184, 189
Green, Hanna (Mrs. Tatum), 87
Green, John, 90
Green, Joseph, 87, 165
Green, Lydia (Mrs. Patterson), 87
Green, Mary (Mrs. James Steer), 87, 89–90
Green, Rachel Hoyle (Mrs. William), 87, 90, 165
Green, Rebecca (Mrs. Hall), 87
Green, Sarah (Mrs. Parker), 87
Green, William, 87, 89–90, 105, 167, 171, 173
Green John, 87
Gregg, Albina (Mrs. John Webster, the pioneer), 185–186
Gregg, Joshua, 39
Grier, Ezekiel, 95
Griffith-French, Elizabeth (Mrs. Wm. Henry Patterson), 126
Grimshaw, Tabitha (Mrs. Benjamin Hoyle), 105–106

Hall, Ann White (Mrs. Isaac), 55, 93

Hall, Anna Cope, 177

Hall, Anna Livezey (Mrs. John), 47, 48, 123–124, 125–126

Hall, Anna 65–67, 69, 93 Hall, Blanche D., 95

Hall, Christiana Peele (Mrs. Joseph Hall), 65, 69

Hall, Cyrus, 93, 121, 183, 185

Hall, Deborah Parry (Mrs. Nathan), 95

Hall, Edward, 121, 184, 185

Hall, Eliza, 93

Hall, Elizabeth (Mrs. Silas Hartley), 123, 125

Hall, Ellen Strahl (Mrs. Cyrus), 121

Hall, Elma, 95–96

Hall, Elsie H., 95

Hall, Elvira, 94

Hall, Everett, 95

Hall, Helen (Mrs. Harold Holloway Sr.), 97, 167

Hall, Homas, 93

Hall, Isaac, 55, 93, 121

Hall, Isaac W., 93

Hall, Jesse, 93

Hall, John, 123, 186–187

Hall, John A., 93–94

Hall, John G., 125–126

Hall, John P., 93

Hall, Joseph, 66, 69

Hall, Joseph W., 58

Hall, Lavina, 195

Hall, Margaret V., 95, 97

Hall, Mary Doudna (Mrs. Isaac), 46, 58

Hall, Mary (Mrs. Richard Edgerton), 66

Hall, Mildred Rachel Edgerton (Mrs. Wilmer II), 125

Hall, Miriam (Mrs. John Doudna II), 55, 61

Hall, Moses, 93

Hall, Nate A., 93

Hall, Nathan, 95

Hall, Phebe Webster (Mrs. John), 93

Hall, Rebecca Green, 87

Hall, Rosetta (Mrs. Joseph W. Doudna), 53, 56, 58

Hall, Sara Webster (Mrs. Joseph W.), 58

Hall, Sarah Stanton (Mrs. Wilford), 98, 143, 159–162

Hall, Stella, 177

Hall, Thomas Parry ('Tommie'), 95–98, 179

Hall, Wilford T., 38, 44, 95, 97–98

Hall, Wilmer Sr., 125

Halleck, Fits-Green, 140

Halls, John G., 62

Haloway, L. L., 165

Hammond, Charles, 186–187

Hampton, Robert W., 196

Hanson, Deborah (Mrs. Caleb Bundy, also Mrs. Chalkley Bundy), 99, 175

Hanson, Elijah, 99, 154

Hanson, Eliza, 99

Hanson, Eliza (Mrs. Elijah), 154–155

Hanson, Lucinda Bundy, 52

Hanson, Susanna Scribner, 99

Hardesty, Anna (Mrs. Benjamin Patterson II), 126

Harper, Alexander, 187

Hartley, Alva B., 59

Hartley, Elizabeth Hall (Mrs. Silas), 123, 125

Hartley, Elizabeth J., 126

Hartley, Henry, 187

Hartley, John, 162

Hartley, Lizzie Doudna (Mrs. Alva B.), 59

Hartley, Mary Webster (Mrs. Henry), 187

Hartley, Nora E. (Mrs. Joseph H. Doudna), 59

Hartley, Silas, 123, 125

Henderson, L.T., 186–187

Herrick, Samuel, 187

Hibbs, Ruth S. Doudna, 43

Hobson, Alden, 101, 104, 200

Hobson, Belinda (Mrs. Joseph F. Doudna), 43–44

Hobson, Belinda (Mrs.Binns), 103

Hobson, Benjamin J., 103–104

Hobson, Dorothy (Mrs. Stratton/Ashton), 103–104

Hobson, Edith (Mrs. Harold Burt), 101, 104

Hobson, Eliza Worthington (Mrs. Thomas), 103

Hobson, John A., 103–104

Hobson, Mary J. (Mrs. Conrow), 103

Hobson, Mary Stanley (Mrs. Thomas), 103

Hobson, Sarah A. (Mrs. Masters), 103

Hobson, Thomas, 103–104

Hobson, Unity Johnson (Mrs. Thomas), 103

Hodgin, Eli, 172

Hodgin, Robert, 29

Hodgin, Sara, 172

Hodgin, William, 49

Hoge, Anna M., 87, 141

Hoge, Anna M. (Mrs. Joseph), 167–168
Hoge, Anna Steer (Mrs. Joseph), 89–91
Hoge, Joseph, 89, 167–168
Holloway, Anna Marie, 6
Holloway, Dorothy L., 143, 163, 169
Holloway, Emma, 80
Holloway, Harold L., 163, 169
Holloway, Harold L. Jr., 162
Holloway, Harold L., Jr., 97
Holloway, Harold L. Sr., 162
Holloway, Harold Sr., 97
Holloway, Helen Hall, 162
Holloway, Helen Hall (Mrs. Harold Sr.), 97–98, 167
Holloway, Lydia (Mrs. Joel Bailey), 11
Holloway, Martha M., 80
Holloway, Paul, 6
Homes, Jane (Mrs. Samuel Webster), 187
Hoyle, Benjamin, 87, 105–107, 164, 167, 173
Hoyle, Benjamin Jr., 106
Hoyle, Hannah (Mrs. Smith), 106–107
Hoyle, John, 105, 106
Hoyle, Laura J., 106
Hoyle, Mary H. Doudna, 43
Hoyle, Mary Millhouse (Mrs. Benjamin), 106–107, 164
Hoyle, Rachel (Mrs. William Green), 87
Hoyle, Sarah, 106
Hoyle, Tabitha Grimshaw (Mrs. Benjamin), 105–106
Hoyle, William, 106

Jefferson, Thomas, 53, 55, 106
Johnson, Joe, 124
Johnson, Unity (Mrs. Thomas Hobson), 103
Judkins, Anderson, 109
Judkins, Carolus, 109
Judkins, Charity, 109
Judkins, Elizabeth, 109
Judkins, James, 109
Judkins, Jesse, 1, 109
Judkins, Joel, 109
Judkins, Thomas, 109

Kennard, Joseph, 3
Kennard, Mary, 176
King, Joseph, 125

King, Michael, 183–184, 191
Kinney, James, 39
Knowis, John, 144–145
Knowis, Sarah (Mrs. John Doudna I), 46
Kugler, Charles, 3–4, 6

Ladd, Benjamin, 140
Ladd, Elizabeth (Mrs. William Patterson, Jr.), 123–124
Lee, Alden, 37
Leeds, Eliza Foster, 11
Leeds, Henry, 11
Leek, Martha "Aunt Martha," 137
Lewis, Esther (Mrs. Benjamin Lundy), 140
Lewis, Henry Clay, 126
Lewis, Hiram, 125
Lewis, Sarah Patterson (Mrs. Henry Clay), 125–126
Livezey, Albert, 119, 123, 125
Livezey, Anna (Mrs. John Hall), 123–124, 125–126
Livezey, Charles, 119, 123, 125–126
Livezey, Elizabeth Patterson (Mrs. Jesse), 119, 123, 125
Livezey, Jesse K., 119, 123, 125
Livezey, John P., 123
Livezey, Joseph Exum, 123
Livezey, Oliver, 123, 125
Livezey, Walter, 119
Livezey, William, 119
Llewellyn, Anna C., 80
Logan, John D., 15
Louhoff, Frank A., 59
Louhoff, Rosetta Doudna (Mrs. Frank A.), 59
Lowery, Jane (Mrs. Benjamin Patterson Sr.), 126
Lundy, Benjamin, 140
Lundy, Esther Lewis (Mrs. Benjamin), 140
Luzerne, Eva (Mrs. Allen Bailey), 126

Macy, Abigail (Mrs. Benjamin Stanton), 195
Madison, James, 23, 106
Marmon, Hannah (Mrs. Joseph Patterson), 124, 126–127
Marshall, Elizabeth (Mrs. John Webster Sr.), 187
Marshall, Thomas, 23, 25
Masters, Sarah A. Hobson, 103
Matthews, George, 29
Matthews, Joe, 29

Matthews, Lin, 29
Maxwell, Sarah, 115
McDonald, Beulah Patten (Mrs. Robert D.), i, 5, 28
McDonald, Beulah Pattern, 5, 104
McDonald, Robert D., 5
McGrew, Anna, 177
McIlvane, Carl, 15
McKnight, Mag, 15
McNichols, George, 24
Metcalf, Jesse, 98
Meyers, Charles, 125
Mickle, Hannah S. (Mrs. David Williams), 196
Miles, Mary Pearson (Mrs. Edmund Fowler), 199
Milhouse, Anna, 144
Millhouse, Elizabeth, 164
Millhouse, Lydia, 174
Millhouse, Mary (Mrs. Benjamin Hoyle), 106–107
Millhouse, Robert, 164
Morlan, Charles, 137
Morlan, Ellen, 137
Naylor, Lewis, 123, 173
Naylor, Rachel Bailey (Mrs. Lewis), 123
Newman, Stoke, 29

Osborn, Daniel, 196
Osborn, Deborah Williams (Mrs. Daniel), 196
Outland, Carry (Mrs. William Henry Patterson), 126
Overman, Sarah (Mrs. William Bundy), 23, 37

Parker, Benja, 20
Parker, Sarah Green, 87
Parker, Thomas C., 39, 165
Parry, Deborah (Mrs. Nathan Hall), 95
Patten, Anna Bailey, 1, 9, 17, 84, 129
Patten, Beulah (Mrs. Robert D. McDonald), i, 5, 28
Patten, Isaac, 154
Patten, John, 154
Patten, Ruth (Mrs. John Bundy), 159
Patten, William, 154
Patterson, Amy Broomall (Mrs. Joseph), 126
Patterson, Angelina Binford (Mrs. Jared), 123
Patterson, Anna Doudna (Mrs. Exum, later Mrs. Joseph King), 123–125
Patterson, Anna Hardesty (Mrs. Benjamin II), 126

Patterson, Asenath (Mrs. Jesse Bailey), 7–8
Patterson, Barclay, 126
Patterson, Benjamin II, 126
Patterson, Benjamin Sr., 126
Patterson, Carry Outland (Mrs. William Henry), 126
Patterson, Clary (Mrs. Henry Stanton), 163–164, 165, 167
Patterson, David, 126
Patterson, Edward, 126
Patterson, Eli, 126
Patterson, Elizabeth, 7
Patterson, Elizabeth Griffith-French (Mrs. Wm. Henry), 126
Patterson, Elizabeth Ladd (Mrs. William Jr.), 123–124
Patterson, Elizabeth (Mrs. Jesse Livezey), 119, 123, 125
Patterson, Ernest, 126
Patterson, Eunice Starbuck (Mrs. David), 126
Patterson, Eva Luzerne (Mrs. Allen Bailey), 126
Patterson, Exum, 123–124
Patterson, Florence Bailey (Mrs. Ernest), 126
Patterson, Frederic, 126
Patterson, Georgia Connard (Mrs. Barclay), 126
Patterson, Hannah Arnold (Mrs. Lemuel), 126
Patterson, Hannah Marmon (Mrs. Joseph), 124, 126, 127
Patterson, Isaac, 126
Patterson, Jane Bailey (Mrs. Benjamin Sr.), 126
Patterson, Jane Lowery (Mrs. Benjamin Sr.), 126
Patterson, Jared, 123
Patterson, Jeremiah, 123
Patterson, John, 123
Patterson, Joseph, 81, 124, 126, 127
Patterson, Joshua, 126
Patterson, Keziah (Mrs. Willliam Sr.), 123–124
Patterson, Lemuel, 57, 126
Patterson, Lib, 8
Patterson, Louisa (Mrs. Jesse I. Doudna), 126
Patterson, Mary, 123
Patterson, Phariba Bailey (Mrs. Eli), 7, 126
Patterson, Phebe, 123
Patterson, Rachel, 7
Patterson, Rachel E., 70
Patterson, Rachel (Mrs. John Plummer), 123
Patterson, Rachel Starbuck, 123
Patterson, R.E., 144
Patterson, Rebecca Crew, 126
Patterson, Ruthanna (Mrs Joel Bailey), 11, 126

Patterson, Sara (Mrs. John Shoebridge Williams), 126
Patterson, Sarah, 123
Patterson, Sarah (Mrs. Henry Clay Lewis), 125–126
Patterson, Sarah (Mrs. Micajah Binford), 123
Patterson, Sarah Steward (Mrs. David), 126
Patterson, Silas, 7, 123
Patterson, Tabith Bailey (Mrs. Eli), 126
Patterson, Talitha (Mrs. Stephen Bailey), 123
Patterson, Tilman, 144
Patterson, William Henry, 58, 126
Patterson, William Jr., 123–124
Patterson, William Sr., 123–124
Pearson, Mary (Mrs. Edmund Fowler), 199
Perry, Eliza J. (Mrs. John Webster Jr.), 187
Peters, Bob, 129
Peters, Robert, 109
Peterson, Jim, 33
Peterson, Lizzie, 29
Peterson, Mark, 73
Pickett, Anna, 133
Pickett, Edward, 131
Pickett, Elizabeth, 133
Pickett, Hanna Steer (Mrs. Thomas I), 133
Pickett, Howard Richard, 131
Pickett, Isaac, 133
Pickett, John, 133
Pickett, Louisa D. (Mrs. Steer), 133–134
Pickett, Mary (Mrs. Taber), 133–134
Pickett, Pearley, 143
Pickett, Perley, 133, 141, 174
Pickett, Rebecca Schofield (Mrs. Perley), 141
Pickett, Rebecca Worthington (Mrts. William), 133–134
Pickett, Sara M., 133–134
Pickett, Thomas I, 133
Pickett, Thomas II, 133–134
Pickett, Warren Edward, 131, 175
Pickett, William, 131, 133–134, 175
Plummer, Abraham, 135
Plummer, Elizabeth (Mrs. Jeremiah Patterson), 123, 135
Plummer, Hannah (Mrs. John Webster Sr.), 93, 111, 183, 185, 189
Plummer, Jane Bailey (Mrs. Robert Jr.), 136
Plummer, John, 123, 135
Plummer, Mary C., 136
Plummer, Rachel (Mrs. Robert Sr., Mrs. Caleb Engle), 135–138

Plummer, Robert Jr., 39, 87, 136–138
Plummer, Robert Sr., 83, 135–138
Plummer Rachel Patterson (Mrs. John), 123
Price, Lee Price, Lee, 73

Queen, James W., 4

Raley, Asa, 134
Ratcliff, Mildred, 105
Richardson, Hannah Vail (Mrs. Samuel), 95
Richardson, Lydia (Mrs. Thomas Webster Jr.), 184
Richardson, Rebecca Webster (Mrs. Thomas Hall), 95–96
Richardson, Samuel Webster, 95
Roberts, Beulah, 96
Romans, Susan Webster (Mrs. T. J.), 187
Romons, Thomas J., 165
Round, James M., 145

Schofield, Abigail Steer (Mrs. Jonathan T.), 141
Schofield, Issachar, 71–72
Schofield, Jonathan, 71, 72, 76
Schofield, Jonathan T., 141
Schofield, Rebecca (Mrs. Perley Pickett), 141
Schofield, Thomas, 25
Scholfield, Andrew, 164
Scholfield, Cidney, 164
Scholfield, Edith (Mrs. Issachar), 164
Scholfield, Iona T., 165
Scholfield, Issachar, 164
Scholfield, Jonathan T., 174
Scholfield, Jonathun, 164
Scholfield, J.T., 174
Scholfield, Martha, 164
Scholfield, Rachel (Mrs. James Stanton), 163, 167
Scholfield, William G., 164
Scribner, Susanna, 99
Scroggins, Samuel, 186, 187
Sears, Anna, 97, 165
Sears, Anna Doudna (Mrs. Peter), 144–145, 147, 149
Sears, Benjamin, 149
Sears, Benjamin S., 151
Sears, Edwin W., 151
Sears, Esther (Mrs. Benjamin), 11, 149
Sears, Hulda, 165

Sears, John, 165
Sears, Mary B., 151
Sears, Peter, 97, 151, 174
Sears, Peter Sr., 147
Sears, Phariba (Mrs. Peter), 151
Sears, Phebe, 165
Sears, Sarah D., 151
Sears, William H., 6, 11, 46, 141, 149–151, 174
Shannon, George, 113
Shannon, Jane (Mrs. George), 113
Shannon, Wilson, 113
Sharon, William, 140
Shepherd, D. O., 39, 109
Shepherd, Jorden, 144
Shoebridge, Anna (Mrs. Robert Williams), 55, 195
Sinclair, Phebe (Mrs. Thomas Smith), 157
Skinner, Walter, 87
Small, Jonas, 195
Smith, Achsah (Mrs. Aaron Frame), 71–72
Smith, Alice Doudna, 44
Smith, Barclay, 106, 125, 157
Smith, Elizabeth (Mrs. Charles Livezey), 119, 123, 125, 174
Smith, Elizabeth (Mrs. Samuel), 72
Smith, Elizabeth Williams (Mrs. Robert H.), 157, 164, 165
Smith, Ephraim, 157
Smith, Hannah Hoyle (Mrs. Smith), 106–107
Smith, Harvey, 76
Smith, Irene Fowler (Mrs. Joshua), 199
Smith, Joel, 157–158
Smith, Jonah, 157
Smith, Joshua, 199
Smith, Louise (Mrs. William H. Stanton), 4, 6
Smith, Mary C. Bundy, 99, 143, 154
Smith, Phebe Sinclair (Mrs. Thomas), 157
Smith, Rebecca, 157, 165
Smith, Robert H., 87, 129, 157–158, 164, 193
Smith, Robert Sr., 33, 158
Smith, Samuel, 72
Smith, Sarah (Mrs. Caleb Fowler), 199
Smith, Sinclair, 106, 157, 174
Smith, Thomas, 157
Smith, William, 157
Stanley, Joseph, 196
Stanley, Lydia Williams (Mrs. Joseph), 196

Stanley, Mary (Mrs. Thomas Hobson), 103
Stanton, Abigail Macy (Mrs. Benjamin), 195
Stanton, Anna (Mrs. Nathan Bundy), 27, 164
Stanton, Benjamin, 106, 140, 195
Stanton, Charity Bundy (Mrs. James), 163, 165, 167
Stanton, Clary Patterson (Mrs. Henry), 163–164, 165, 167
Stanton, Cory, 164
Stanton, Daniel, 165
Stanton, David, 163, 165, 167
Stanton, Deborah H. B., 143
Stanton, Edith, 163, 167
Stanton, Edmund, 164
Stanton, Edwin M., 140
Stanton, Eli, 3, 27, 159–160, 161, 162, 167
Stanton, Elizabeth (Mrs. Lindley P. Bailey), 13, 17, 27
Stanton, Emma C. (Mrs. Willis Webster), 159–160, 184
Stanton, Henry, 163–165, 167
Stanton, James, 109, 163–165, 167–168
Stanton, Jane (Mrs. William), 134
Stanton, Joseph, 13, 27, 164, 165, 167
Stanton, Joseph E., 41
Stanton, Lindley, 163, 167
Stanton, Louise Smith, 4, 6
Stanton, Lydda, 163
Stanton, Mary Bundy (Mrs. Eli), 159–160
Stanton, Mary Hodgin (Mrs. Joseph), 13, 27
Stanton, Mary 'Matie' (Mrs. Fawcett), 162, 165
Stanton, Mary P. Bundy, 3
Stanton, Rachel Scholfield (Mrs. James), 163, 167
Stanton, Sara (Mrs. Richard Williams), 55, 195
Stanton, Sarah 'Sadie' (Mrs. Wilford Hall), 98, 143, 159–162
Stanton, William Henry, 1, 3–6, 41, 129, 134, 159, 176–177
Starbuck, Elizabeth, 165
Starbuck, Eunice (Mrs. David Patterson), 126
Starbuck, John, 167
Starbuck, Rachel (Mrs. Silas Patterson), 123
Starky, Bill, 49
Steer, Abigail (Mrs. Jonathan T. Schofield), 141
Steer, Anna M. (Mrs. Joseph Hoge), 89–91
Steer, Charles, 89–90, 176
Steer, Elizabeth (Mrs. Dillwyn Bundy), 89
Steer, Ella, 89
Steer, Hanna (Mrs. Thomas Pickett I), 133
Steer, James, 89–90, 171, 174, 175

Steer, Joseph G., 89, 172
Steer, Lindley B., 174
Steer, Louisa, 89
Steer, Louisa D. (Mrs. William G.), 175, 177
Steer, Louisa Pickett, 134
Steer, Mary Green (Mrs. James), 89–90
Steer, Rachel G., 89, 176
Steer, Vacy, 175
Steer, William G., 87, 89–91, 131, 134, 141, 165, 171–173, 175, 177
Steer, Wilson, 80
Stewart, Sarah (Mrs. David Patterson), 126
Strahl, Ellen (Mrs. Cyrus Hall), 121
Stubbs, Elizabeth, 144
Stubbs, Isaac, 35, 144
Stubbs, Joseph, 35
Stuckey, Helen Louis (Mrs. Thomas Webster III), 184

Taber, Edna Bailey (Mrs. Louis J.), 134
Taber, Louis J., 80, 134, 173
Taber, Mary Pickett, 134
Tatum, George, 30, 167
Tatum, Hanna Green, 87
Taylor, Jonathan, 106, 139
Test, Samuel, 176
Thomas, Abisha, 179
Thomas, Anne Gore (Mrs. Thomas Sr.), 184
Thomas, Asahel, 95
Thomas, Ashel "Asa," 179
Thomas, Camm, 179
Thomas, Carson, 81
Thomas, Catherine, 179
Thomas, Cidney, 179
Thomas, Eliza R., 179
Thomas, Elizabeth (Mrs. Camm), 179
Thomas, Henry Camm, 179
Thomas, Hezekiah, 179
Thomas, Increase Dennis (Mrs. Hezekiah), 72, 179
Thomas, Mason, 35, 57
Thomas, Phebe Dennis, 179
Thomas, Philip Mason, 179
Thomas, Priscilla, 179
Thomas, Rebecca, 179
Thomas, Ruanna (Mrs. William Frame), 71

Thomas, Ruth, 179
Thomas, William, 179
Thomasson, Unice, 70
Thompson, Talitha (Mrs. Aaron Frame), 71

Updegraff, Jonathan T., 140

Vail, Abigail, 70
Vail, Hannah D. (Mrs. Samuel Richardson), 95
Vail, Isaac N., 174
Van Law, Sally, 30
Vernon, James, 136

Waldo, C.A., 5
Walton, Anna, 67, 80
Walton, James, 70, 129, 177, 182
Walton, Samuel, 67, 181–182
Walton, Sarah Edgerton (Mrs. Samuel Walton), 67, 181–182
Walton, Sarah Pickett, 80
Walton, Sina, 177
Ward, Sarah (Mrs. Abraham Plummer), 135
Warrington, Albert, 199
Warrington, Sarah Fowler (Mrs. Albert), 199
Webster, Abner, 185
Webster, Albina, 185
Webster, Albina Gregg (Mrs. John Sr.), 185
Webster, Ann (Mrs. Jesse Chalfant), 111
Webster, Charles P., 185
Webster, Debora, 113
Webster, Deborah Chambers (Mrs. John Sr.), 187
Webster, Eliza J. (Mrs. John Jr.), 187
Webster, Elizabeth Marshall (Mrs. John Sr.), 187
Webster, Emma Stanton (Mrs. Willis), 159, 184
Webster, Frederick Stuckey, 184
Webster, H. S., 154
Webster, Hannah Plummer (Mrs. John Sr.), 93, 111, 183, 185, 189
Webster, Helen Louis Stuckey (Mrs. Thomas III), 184
Webster, Jane Homes (Mrs. Samuel), 187
Webster, Jeptha S., 189, 190
Webster, John Jr., 187
Webster, John Sr., 43, 183, 185–187, 189
Webster, Joseph G., 190
Webster, Lydia Richardson (Mrs. Thomas Webster Jr.), 184
Webster, Mary L., 187

Webster, Mary (Mrs. Henry Hartley), 187
Webster, Phebe (Mrs. John Hall), 93
Webster, Samuel, 187
Webster, Sara (Mrs. Joseph W. Hall), 58
Webster, Susan (Mrs. T. J. Romans), 187
Webster, Thomas III, 184
Webster, Thomas Jr., 184, 191
Webster, Thomas Sr., 183–184, 187, 189–190
Webster, W. V., 76
Webster, Walter A., 191
Webster, Warner, 187
Webster, William, 183
Webster, Willis V., 184
Webster, Willis W., 155, 189–191
Wehr, John, 95
Wever, C.W., 127
Wharton, Bird, 15
Wharton, Susan, 15
White, Ann (Mrs. Isaac Hall), 55, 93
Wichel, Mary, 66
Williams, Abigail (Mrs. John Fawcett), 195
Williams, Anna Shoebridge (Mrs. Robert), 55, 195
Williams, Asa, 196
Williams, Benjamin, 196
Williams, David, 196
Williams, Dearman, 196
Williams, Deborah (Mrs. Daniel Osborn), 196
Williams, Edward, 196
Williams, Elias, 23
Williams, Elizabeth Cadwalder (Mrs. Asa), 196
Williams, Elizabeth Dearman (Mrs. Robert), 55, 195
Williams, Elizabeth (Mrs. Joseph Garretson), 55
Williams, Elizabeth (Mrs. Micajah Dillingham), 195
Williams, Elizabeth (Mrs. Robert Smith), 157, 164
Williams, Ephraim, 165, 193
Williams, Hannah Bruff (Mrs. David), 196
Williams, Hannah Mickle (Mrs. David), 196
Williams, John S., 81
Williams, John Shoebridge, 127, 195
Williams, John Stanton, 195
Williams, Joseph, 85
Williams, Lydia (Mrs. Joseph Stanley), 196
Williams, Mary Farmer (Mrs. Dearman), 196
Williams, Mary (Mrs. Joseph Emmons), 196
Williams, Penina (Mrs. Joseph Gibbons), 85
Williams, Prudence, 97
Williams, Prudence (Mrs. Thomas), 151
Williams, Richard, 55, 195, 196
Williams, Robert, 55, 195
Williams, Samuel, 37, 195
Williams, Sara Patterson (Mrs. John Shoebridge), 127
Williams, Sara Stanton (Mrs. Richard), 55, 195
Williams, Sarah Dew (Mrs. Richard), 195
Williams, Thomas, 151
Willliams, Sarah, 164
Wilson, Ann Eliza (Mrs. Joseph F. Doudna), 44
Wilson, Elizabeth, 56
Wilson, Israel, 167
Wilson, Samuel, 186
Wilson, Thomas, 165
Winder, James J., 165
Wood, Prudence (Mrs. William "Black Bill"), 37
Worthington, Eliza (Mrs. Thomas Hobson), 103
Worthington, Rebecca (Mrs. William Pickett), 133–134
Wright, Lavina (Mrs. Aaron Frame), 73
Wylie, Ethel Doudna (Mrs. Joseph), 87, 126
Wylie, Joseph, 87, 126

www.ingramcontent.com/pod-product-compliance
Lightning Source LLC
Chambersburg PA
CBHW081215230426
43666CB00015B/2740